POWER STRUGGLE
OVER AFGHANISTAN

AN INSIDE LOOK AT WHAT WENT WRONG—AND WHAT WE CAN DO TO REPAIR THE DAMAGE

KAI EIDE

Skyhorse Publishing

English translation © 2012 Kai Eide
Original title: Høyt spill om Afghanistan
© 2010 CAPPELEN DAMM AS

Skyhorse Publishing books may be purchased in bulk at special discounts for
sales promotion, corporate gifts, fund-raising, or educational purposes. Special
editions can also be created to specifications. For details, contact the Special
Sales Department, Skyhorse Publishing, 307 West 36th Street,
11th Floor, New York, N.Y. 10018 or info@skyhorsepublishing.com.

Skyhorse® and Skyhorse Publishing® are registered trademarks of
Skyhorse Publishing, Inc.®, a Delaware corporation.

www.skyhorsepublishing.com

10 9 8 7 6 5 4 3 2 1

Library of Congress Cataloging-in-Publication Data

Eide, Kai, 1949–
    [Høyt spill om Afghanistan. English]
    Power struggle over Afghanistan: an inside look at what went wrong—and
what we can do to repair the damage / Kai Eide.
       p. cm.
    Includes bibliographical references and index.
    ISBN 978-1-61608-464-6 (alk. paper)
    1. Nation building—Afghanistan. 2. Peace-building—Afghanistan.
    3. Postwar reconstruction—Afghanistan. 4. National security—Afghanistan.
    5. Afghanistan—Politics and government—2001-6. Afghan War, 2001–
    I. Title.
    DS371.4.E4313 2011
    958.104'71—dc23
    2011030237

Printed in the United States of America

CONTENTS

Introduction...v

CHAPTER ONE   Karzai's Surprise Move 1

CHAPTER TWO   Afghanistan's Thirty Years of War 7

CHAPTER THREE   A City Under Siege 13

CHAPTER FOUR   Can the UN Deliver? 20

CHAPTER FIVE   Struggle in the UN Family....................30

CHAPTER SIX   Where Did All the Money Go? 41

CHAPTER SEVEN   Do We Have a Strategy?........................54

CHAPTER EIGHT   Civilian Deaths: First Conflict
                           with the Military.................................59

CHAPTER NINE   Karzai Becomes Confrontational...........67

CHAPTER TEN   More Mistakes and More Casualties......70

CHAPTER ELEVEN   Growth of the Insurgency 77

CHAPTER TWELVE   Afghanistan's Women............................83

CHAPTER THIRTEEN Kabul Under Attack............................92

CHAPTER FOURTEEN Karzai's Tactical Surprise 99

CHAPTER FIFTEEN   Five More Years with Karzai?................107

CHAPTER SIXTEEN   New Ministers and New Expectations..112

CHAPTER SEVENTEEN	Obama's Dream Team Stumbles	120
CHAPTER EIGHTEEN	Clinton's Surprise Announcement and the Hague Conference	132
CHAPTER NINETEEN	Finally, a Real Strategy?	141
CHAPTER TWENTY	Old Warlords Enter the Scene	148
CHAPTER TWENTY-ONE	Countdown to Elections—and the First Clash with Galbraith	159
CHAPTER TWENTY-TWO	Election Day and More Foreign Interference	168
CHAPTER TWENTY-THREE	The Secret Guest	177
CHAPTER TWENTY-FOUR	A Dangerous Plan	188
CHAPTER TWENTY-FIVE	A Race to Rescue the Elections	193
CHAPTER TWENTY-SIX	Galbraith Is Fired and Takes Revenge	197
CHAPTER TWENTY-SEVEN	Senator Kerry Intervenes	202
CHAPTER TWENTY-EIGHT	Mr. President, I Have Decided to Resign	205
CHAPTER TWENTY-NINE	Attack on the UN!	212
CHAPTER THIRTY	Election Endgame: Karzai's Troubled Victory	220
CHAPTER THIRTY-ONE	The Military Buildup	225
CHAPTER THIRTY-TWO	Offensives in the South	232
CHAPTER THIRTY-THREE	An Agenda for Afghan Ownership	237
CHAPTER THIRTY-FOUR	The Inauguration and a New Government	241
CHAPTER THIRTY-FIVE	The Battle for Election Reform	249
CHAPTER THIRTY-SIX	Another Conference—but Where?	253
CHAPTER THIRTY-SEVEN	A Complicated Partnership	257
CHAPTER THIRTY-EIGHT	The Fragmented Region	266
CHAPTER THIRTY-NINE	Negotiate with the Taliban?	278
CHAPTER FORTY	Who Is Karzai?	296
CHAPTER FORTY-ONE	Reflections	306
CHAPTER FORTY-TWO	Departure	310
	Acknowledgments	313

INTRODUCTION

Early in the afternoon on March 6, 2010, the small UN jet accelerated down the runway at Kabul airport and quickly gained altitude.
It was my very last flight out of the Afghan capital as UN envoy.
The morning had been hectic, with a speech to mark International
Women's Day two days early, as my final appearance before leaving
Afghanistan. Two years had passed since my arrival in Kabul. At
that time the most urgent task had been to bring some order to a
chaotic international engagement in Afghanistan. I had arrived with
hopes of being able to make a difference and help shape a strategy
that could finally work. Now I was tired and bitter: tired from two
dramatic years of a constantly worsening security situation, political
disagreements, and personal rivalries, as well as the media attention
that followed it all; bitter from the strong feeling that I had not
achieved what I had come to achieve.

The previous day I had said farewell to President Karzai during
a small ceremony in his palace. Our relationship had been close and
friendly for almost two years. The farewell ceremony had been a
rather formal event. He had given me an important Afghan decoration for my work, but there had been little time for reflections on the

two years that had passed. Karzai was disappointed in me because he believed I had not stood up strongly enough against the United States and other foreigners who had interfered so blatantly in the presidential elections. And I was disappointed in him because he had become more dependent on the warlords and powerbrokers that had destroyed Afghanistan in the past and should not be allowed to contaminate its future.

But the most important reason for my bitterness was my ever-growing disagreement with Washington's strategy in Afghanistan. It had become increasingly dominated by military strategies, forces, and offensives. Urgent civilian and political requirements were treated as appendices to the military tasks. The UN had never been really involved or consulted by Washington on critical strategy-related questions, nor had even the closest NATO partners. More importantly, Afghan authorities had mostly been spectators to the formation of a strategy aimed at solving the conflict in their own country. During a visit to Washington shortly after the Obama administration had taken over, one of the senior ministers of Karzai's government sent me a text message. "Neocolonialism," it read. That was all. In my opinion, the U.S. strategy was doomed to fail.

As the Learjet circled over Kabul, gaining altitude before flying over the mountains that surround the city, I looked down on the capital for the last time. Kabul had become a fortified city with a constant proliferation of concrete walls, sand bags, barbed wire, road-blocks, security checks, bomb-sniffing dogs, and speed bumps. The city I left in March 2010 was very different from the one in which I had walked freely around during my first visit in September 2003. As a result of the worsening security situation, the ability of the UN and other civilian organizations to operate across the country had become severely limited.

I have long been fascinated by Afghanistan's beauty and by its people, and I have missed them both every day since I left the country. During my many flights, I used to look out of the window to see how much snow had fallen on the mountain ranges and to see the color of the ground beneath me. Would the crops be sufficient this season? Would there be more food shortages, or would there be floods? Would we reach vulnerable areas with emergency aid in time?

On a helicopter trip over Bamiyan province, in the central part of the country, I could see a man and a woman with their donkey, high up on a mountain ridge. We flew almost close enough to see their faces, and still the distance between us felt indescribable. Voter registration for the presidential and provincial elections was taking place and my days were filled with challenges related to the election process. The two people below me had far more important concerns than how they would get their registration documents. We lived so close to each other, but we existed in two very different worlds.

In so many meetings with foreign dignitaries, I had to come back to some basic facts to illustrate the challenges we were facing. Afghanistan is a country with weak and sometimes nonexistent institutions. Its infrastructure is so poor that 3,000 donkeys were hired to bring election material to remote parts of the country during the 2009 elections. The illiteracy rate is still around 70 percent, and in remote villages it can be hard to find anybody who can read or write. Afghanistan lacks the middle class that is required for sustainable development to take place quickly. A significant part of the country is engulfed in an armed conflict. All of this combined makes rapid progress impossible. Yet, we have been eager to set deadlines that would permit us to withdraw our international engagement and declare success. As a result of our inability to understand the country and therefore to formulate workable strategies, support for our engagement in Afghanistan has declined. We are trapped between an impatient public and a growing insurgency in a country where quick fixes do not exist.

We have become impatient and so have the Afghans. Dr. Sima Samar, the leader of the Afghan Independent Human Rights Commission (AIHRC), wrote to me in late 2010 that the Afghan people are losing hope. A year later, they have little hope left. So many sacrifices have been made in terms of lives and suffering; yet, a solution to the conflict seems to have slipped even further away.

My two years as UN envoy were—at that time, at least—the two most dramatic years since the fall of the Taliban in 2001. When the Norwegian version of this book was published in fall 2010, I argued that if the existing negative trends could not be reversed during the next year or so, they would become unmanageable and it could be too late. As I now finish the English version, one year has passed and the negative trends seem to have continued. Certainly, the additional 60,000 international troops—an astonishing number—that arrived in Afghanistan since President Obama was inaugurated have stemmed the growth of the insurgency in some parts of the country. But the Taliban has not been defeated, not even significantly degraded. Afghanistan is going through a period of profound uncertainty. The tension between Karzai and key partners in the international community has increased. The conflict between the government and the National Assembly has led to a political standstill, where the entire political system seems to be imploding. The friction between Afghanistan's ethnic groups has intensified. And efforts to bring the Taliban into political talks have not brought tangible results, but experienced a damaging blow when the Chairman of the High Peace Council, Burhanuddin Rabbani, was killed in September 2011.

I still hope that it is not too late to turn the trends and to find a solution to the conflict that brings peace and protects the progress and reforms that have been made over the last decade. But to find this solution would require very significant changes in the way we approach Afghanistan and the conflict. We must recognize that—even after ten years—short-term deadlines will not lead us closer to, but further away from, a solution to the conflict. And we must place political initiatives above military offensives. There is still—in spite of the setbacks—no acceptable alternative to a policy of dialogue and reconciliation with the insurgency. At the Bonn conference in December 2001, all the Afghan participants managed—after twenty years of conflict—to come together and agree on a new interim administration, with the assistance of Afghanistan's neighbors. Ten years later, a policy of national unity and a strong involvement of the country's neighbors are urgently needed. It may be unappealing to many—inside and outside Afghanistan. Perhaps it is too late and no longer even realistic. But the only alternative could well be a civil war of the kind we experienced in the early 1990s, which led to the birth of the Taliban movement.

This book is a personal account of my two years as the United Nations Special Representative (SRSG) to Afghanistan. It is by no means comprehensive, and I do not claim to offer anything more than my own views, reflections, and conclusions, drawn from my day-to-day experiences and personal involvement. It covers my own period in the country and was first published in November 2010. For the English edition I have made minor additions in order to bring it more up to date with developments since I left Afghanistan. I have chosen to be as open as I can; too open, some may say. The book contains accounts of conversations that were not intended for the public domain. Where I have chosen to include them, it is because information has already been leaked, and others have already given their account of meetings, events, and the relationships between the most important participants. I hope that my contribution will help build a more complete understanding of what happened during this period.

CHAPTER ONE

KARZAI'S SURPRISE MOVE

On January 15, 2008, I was sitting next to the Norwegian foreign minister, Jonas Gahr Støre, and across from President Karzai at his palace in Kabul. I was then political director in the Norwegian foreign ministry. Over lunch, the discussion centered on the dramatic attack on the Serena Hotel in Kabul the night before. We were all shocked by what we had experienced. Carsten Thomassen, a prominent Norwegian journalist, had been killed, and a close colleague from our foreign ministry had been severely injured. There were many other casualties. For President Karzai, it had also been a new and shocking experience. This was not a lonely suicide attacker as we had seen so many times before, but a complex attack in the heart of the capital carried out by a group of well-armed insurgents from the so-called Haqqani network dressed as police officers.

Early in the afternoon we had received the first warning of a possible attack against the area where the hotel was located. The most dangerous moment, I thought, would be the next morning, when we left the hotel for our first meetings. Suicide bombers normally got their vests strapped around their bodies very early in the morning and did not wait long before detonating their deadly load. But there had been many such warnings during previous visits, and I didn't think more about it. A little later, I was in the hotel lobby with Mr. Thomassen, the Norwegian journalist. He wanted to meet the former Taliban foreign minister, Mullah Wakil Ahmad Muttawakil, and sought my advice. Helene Sand Andresen, from the Norwegian embassy in Kabul, dragged me away and insisted that I had to leave with her immediately to prepare the next day's meeting with the president. We were late, so we rushed out of the hotel entrance to our car and drove out the gate, heading toward the presidential compound. Seconds after we left the hotel, we heard an explosion, and then another. Soon, text messages came from the Norwegian foreign minister and from my friend Dr. Zalmai Rassoul, the Afghan national security advisor: "Are you safe?" We could hear that the attack was still ongoing. The gates to the presidential compound, where Rassoul's office was located, had been blocked in case other attacks should follow. By some miracle, we had escaped from the hotel twenty seconds before the attack started. The rest of the Norwegian group was either caught in the lobby—with fatal consequences—or trapped in the basement with their lives in danger as the terrorists hunted for foreigners.

After a while, the discussion with Karzai turned from the traumatic attack to current political issues. The Norwegian foreign minister asked the president about the process of finding a new UN envoy for Afghanistan. The previous envoy, Tom Koenigs, from Germany, was stepping down after two years in Kabul and the UN secretary-general was searching for a successor to head the UN Assistance Mission in Afghanistan (UNAMA). Nodding in my direction, President Karzai replied, "I want him." All were taken by surprise. Karzai asked me about Paddy Ashdown, who had been the frontrunner for the job in media and diplomatic speculations for weeks. Did I know Ashdown? What did I think of him? Karzai's questions revealed his own skepticism. I answered his questions politely. Of course, I knew Ashdown quite well and praised his experience and great energy as the international community's "high representative" in Bosnia and Herzegovina from 2002 to 2006, when I was Norwegian ambassador to NATO. Foreign Minister Støre looked at me, wondering how he should react to Karzai's surprise move. Did I know anything about this? Should he support me? We had never talked about any such candidature. And none of us knew how to respond.

I had followed the process of identifying a new UN envoy for some time. I had visited Washington in October of 2007. My interlocutor was Under Secretary R. Nicholas Burns in the State Department. We had been close friends as ambassadors to NATO a few years earlier. Burns asked me privately what I thought about Ashdown as the new UN envoy to Afghanistan. As a person, I liked him and nobody could question his qualifications. But I was not sure that his nationality and his style would fit well in the Afghan context. In Sarajevo he had been the "king," with the authority to dismiss politicians and civil servants, and to propose and censure laws. Nothing of importance could happen without his approval. He had made full use of his authority, more than any of his predecessors and successors. I feared that the Afghans would not be happy about his abrasive style. Even Bosnia and Herzegovina were still struggling; Serbs, Croats, and Bosniacs were pulling in different directions more than twelve years after the Dayton agreement. The country remained in a dangerous political stalemate. Some even feared that the Dayton agreement could collapse. Ashdown's tough style had not produced the results many had expected and hoped.

Furthermore, Ashdown was British. The Afghans would instinctively be critical toward him in light of the long and complex British involvement in Afghanistan. Twice in the nineteenth century, the British invaded Afghanistan, fearing Russian expansion toward the south and in the direction of India—the crown jewel of the British Empire. The first Anglo-Afghan war started in 1839. Three years later, the British forces were brutally massacred—only one single soldier survived and managed to reach the British outpost in Jalalabad, now in the very easternmost part of Afghanistan. In 1878, the British tried again but met the same fierce opposition. The third

Anglo-Afghan war ended with Afghanistan being recognized as a sovereign state in 1919. These are events and wars that the Afghans still talk about proudly.

In Washington, Burns told me that he would try to call Ashdown the very same day. The process had begun, and Ashdown's candidature seemed to meet support from the major countries. The signals from Kabul also pointed in his direction.

The debate was not just about who would take over, but what kind of mandate the new envoy would have. The need for better coordination of international activities was obvious to everyone. The UN would have to play a more prominent role. Some Western countries discussed a proposal to merge several roles and give the new envoy three "hats," representing the UN, NATO, and the EU at the same time. This would give the position more clout in dealing both with the Afghans and the international community. But it soon became clear that the proposal for a "triple hatting," as it was called, did not have sufficient support, and it was put aside. In my opinion, that was the right decision. Those who favored the proposal believed that it would provide clear lines of command and greater authority. It was the ultimate answer to any problems of coordination. My view was that, on the contrary, it would create confusion. His or her interlocutors would never know if the envoy was speaking on behalf of the global community, a military alliance with a limited membership, or a political union from one particular continent. It would bring the envoy into constant conflict with different employers. I also feared that this merged solution would blur the lines between military and civilian roles and unnecessarily turn civilians into targets for the insurgency. Finally, the UN's role as a potential intermediary between the Afghan government and the insurgency would be even more difficult. The UN would be seen as too closely linked to the international military forces, and the insurgents would simply not distinguish between them.

The Afghans were clearly not enthusiastic about the possibility of having Ashdown come in as a new "superenvoy" or "viceroy." They wanted more authority transferred to Afghan institutions, not less, a sentiment in accordance with recent international statements. The word "Afghanize" had become an important part of the political jargon: to give the Afghans a greater say in defining and implementing a common strategy and shaping their own future. Nevertheless, the rumors told us that Karzai had given his approval to the appointment of Ashdown.

For a while I did not think more about Karzai's surprise initiative during the lunch in Kabul. The big surprise came in late January: the media suddenly reported that the president had rejected Ashdown. Karzai had reportedly been angered by media stories in which Ashdown was portrayed precisely as the viceroy Karzai did not want. This was seen as a 180-degree turn by the Afghan president, but in reality there had been serious doubts in his mind for quite some time. The media probably provided the pretext that he needed. Karzai had behaved in a way that I would later come to experience often, one in which unpleasant decisions were postponed as long as possible—sometimes even longer.

The selection process had to start all over again. Four candidates were mentioned: Slovak Foreign Minister Jan Kubis, former Canadian Deputy Prime Minister John Manley, former Turkish National Assembly President Hikmet Cetin, and me. Following an interview in mid-February with UN Secretary-General Ban Ki-moon, I was offered the job. Ban Ki-moon had secured the support of the permanent members of the UN Security Council. My candidature had been discussed in the Afghan government. Hikmet Cetin was known to the Afghans and was popular among many of them, but most of the government had given me their support. My main supporter was probably Haneef Atmar, the minister of education, whom I had known for almost five years, as well as Rangin Dadfar Spanta, the foreign minister, and Zalmai Rassoul, the national security advisor. Together, we had spent many hours discussing issues ranging from the building of schools to reconciliation with the Taliban.

For me, it was not an easy decision. Until August of 2006, I had been Norway's ambassador to NATO. I had returned from abroad after ten years of separation from my family. I had just remarried and was looking forward to starting a normal family life as soon as my assignment in Brussels ended. Another absence would certainly be a heavy burden and put a new marriage on hold for another two years. I also knew what the international media would say: Kai Eide, the second choice, was appointed because Karzai did not want a bulldozer like Ashdown. Some diplomats had jokingly spoken about the need for an "800-pound gorilla" to meet the urgent coordination challenges of Afghanistan. My role would be that of a more traditional UN envoy.

At the UN headquarters in New York, I received contradictory advice. Jean-Marie Guehenno, the head of the Department of Peace-Keeping Operations (DPKO), argued strongly in favor of accepting the offer. Hedi Annabi, his deputy, who tragically lost his life during the earthquake in Haiti in 2010, warned me against going to Afghanistan. He was convinced that developments in the country would go in the wrong direction and that the UN could end up with much of the blame. But it was a unique professional challenge to play a role in one of the most pressing and complex conflicts of our time. The offer was an expression of confidence from Ban Ki-moon as well as from Karzai. I remembered that when the former Norwegian foreign minister, Thorvald Stoltenberg, was asked to become UN mediator in the Balkans in 1993, he thought, "If I turn this down, then I will regret it for the rest of my life." I had been offered the most important opportunity in my professional life. Hopefully, I could make a difference. It was an offer that was simply impossible to decline.

CHAPTER TWO

AFGHANISTAN'S THIRTY YEARS OF WAR

My own interest in Afghanistan dated back to the mid-1970s. I read everything I could find about the ongoing power struggles in Kabul. The country was entering a long and dark chapter of its history. The last Afghan king, Zahir Shah, had been removed in 1973 by his cousin Daoud Khan, who declared Afghanistan a republic and took control as the country's president. The king had ruled for forty years and was visiting Rome when the coup took place. Five years later, Daoud was in turn removed in a Communist takeover. Nur Mohammad Taraki took power amid a bitter rivalry between the two factions of the Communist Party. The following year he was murdered, but his rival, Hafizullah Amin, did not manage to stay in power for more than a few months before he met the same fate. Both had been ruthless to the population. On Christmas Day, 1979, Soviet forces invaded the country and installed Babrak Karmal as president. Afghanistan suddenly attracted the attention of the entire world.

At the time of the Soviet invasion I was a junior diplomat at the Norwegian embassy in Prague in Communist Czechoslovakia. Of course, its leaders supported the Soviet invasion. The temperature in East-West relations rose dangerously. The following year, the

United States and other countries boycotted the Olympic Games in Moscow. The invasion was a serious setback for the emerging dialogue between East and West and the early attempts to bring the Cold War to an end.

Following bitter opposition by Afghan resistance groups known as mujahideen, the Soviet presence ended in a painful humiliation of the Communist superpower. On February 15, 1989, the last Soviet soldier, General Boris Gromov, crossed the "Friendship Bridge" over the Amu Darya River that separates Afghanistan from what was then the Soviet Republic of Uzbekistan. The Afghan Communist regime remained in power for another three years under Mohammad Najibullah, until 1992 when the last Communist ruler was ousted. Finally the mujahideen were able to enter the capital and take power. Professor Burhanuddin Rabbani, an ethnic Tajik and one of the most powerful and conservative mujahideen leaders, soon became president.

But the drama had not come to an end. Having beaten their Communist enemy, the dominant mujahideen factions started to fight each other, shelling parts of Kabul into rubble. Destroyed buildings from this period can still be seen in the capital. The chaos that followed led to the foundation of the Taliban movement during a meeting in Kandahar in 1994. One of the participants at that meeting, Mullah Abdul Salam Zaeef, later spent years at Guantanamo and now lives in Kabul. He became a generous interlocutor during my stay in Afghanistan. The Taliban seized control over most of the country, with the exception of a small part in the north. Its rule is well documented—public executions, flogging, and other brutal forms of punishment; massive suppression of women; bans on radio, TV, movies, and music; and the destruction of the huge Buddha statues in the Bamiyan province in March 2001. Al Qaeda was able to consolidate its presence in the country, and Osama Bin Laden could plan his terrorist attacks against Western targets undisturbed from inside Afghanistan.

When the attacks against the World Trade Center and the Pentagon took place on September 11, 2001, I was in my office in Vienna at the Norwegian Delegation to the Organization for Security and Cooperation in Europe (OSCE). Seeing the planes crashing into the towers in Manhattan, we knew that at that very moment the world had changed dramatically. Now it was only a question of when the inevitable U.S. retaliation would be launched. Less than a month later, on October 5, the U.S. intervention in Afghanistan began. The Taliban regime quickly collapsed, but its leader, Mullah Mohammad Omar, as well as Osama Bin Laden, escaped across the border to Pakistan.

A few months later, from my new assignment as Norwegian ambassador to NATO, I followed the buildup of the international presence in Afghanistan: the establishment of the International Security Assistance Force (ISAF), its takeover by NATO in late 2003, and the slow deployment of NATO-led forces across the entire country. I witnessed the gradual return and growth of the Taliban, first in the south and the east and then in other parts of Afghanistan. During the summer of 2006, I returned to the Norwegian Ministry of Foreign Affairs as political director, with Afghanistan as my most important responsibility. I tried to visit the country every third month. When the announcement of my appointment came in March of 2008, I knew many of the key Afghan politicians and international partners in Kabul.

The position of Special Representative of the UN Secretary-General (SRSG) has two components: in addition to being the political head of the UNAMA, the SRSG is the leader of the entire UN family, including more than twenty specialized humanitarian and development UN agencies. When I arrived in New York for the first meetings with my new employers, the UN Security Council had just adopted a new, more precise mandate for UNAMA, spelling out the main tasks more clearly than before. At the center of the mandate were tasks that had become more and more pressing: there was an urgent need to bring order to the delivery of development assistance; the civilian and military organizations did not work well together; the quality and reach of Afghan government institutions were poor; the country was vulnerable to food shortages, floods, and other natural disasters, and the need for improved coordination of humanitarian assistance was therefore great. Finally, there was a serious lack of cooperation among the countries in the region around Afghanistan, with Pakistan providing safe havens to the Taliban and other insurgency groups. In all these areas, the UN Security Council wanted to see the UN in a more aggressive leading role. In addition, UNAMA was tasked to provide assistance to the upcoming presidential and provincial elections and to support the government in efforts of reconciliation with the Taliban.

The mandate was not only demanding; I would soon find out that it was also controversial, not least within the UN family. It required closer UN cooperation with the Afghan government and the international military forces, but a number of UN agencies saw such cooperation as a threat to the independence of the UN. It could blur the lines between civilian and military activities, make the UN staff more vulnerable, and harm its efforts to provide humanitarian assistance to areas where the Taliban was present. It could certainly have a negative impact on attempts to play a role in reconciliation, since the Taliban would see the UN as being too close to the enemy, the international military forces. These views were widely shared among nongovernmental organizations (NGOs) in Afghanistan. Very soon, the discussions over how to implement the mandate became a controversial theme both within the UN family and between the UN and other international actors on the ground, in particular the international military forces.

During my visit to New York in March of 2008, a new "group of friends" was formed. It was an informal gathering of a few key UN ambassadors under Canadian leadership. The purpose was to give me and the ambassadors a forum for more open political discussions (since the meetings of the UN Security Council were open to the media) and to mobilize support when bureaucratic hurdles in the UN system in New York made it difficult to implement our mandate in Kabul. At the first meeting, one of the ambassadors asked me how quickly I expected to see visible progress in the international coordination in Afghanistan. I should, of course, have asked for time in Kabul before giving any answer. Instead, I was careless and said that I hoped to see positive changes over the next few months. I was accompanied by Tom Gregg, a young Australian advisor from UNAMA. He had already spent several years in the UN Mission, in field offices as well as at headquarters in Kabul. As soon as we left the Canadian delegation, he took my arm and said, "Please don't give them any indications about how quickly you can produce results. It will all be much more demanding than you think."

It was a stern warning from a staff member I had only met the day before. As we walked down to the UN building in Manhattan and sat down in the Delegates' Lounge, Tom went over the situation in UNAMA in greater detail than anybody had cared to do before. One-third of all positions in UNAMA were vacant, he said. There was no clear political direction in the mission. The first priority would be to rebuild the UN mission and make sure that we had the kind of staff required to implement the mandate. That would be an uphill battle, he warned. Recruitment was notoriously slow and fewer people were willing to come to Kabul. But only then would we be able to address the political challenges seriously and influence others to improve their performance.

Tom Gregg was blunt, but I quickly understood that he was right. Soon I was also given a copy of a report written by Ambassador Michael von der Schulenburg, a senior German-UN employee who had recently returned from a visit to a number of UN offices in Afghanistan where he had been asked to assess their performance.

The report was depressing reading, and its conclusions corresponded with what Tom had just told me.

A new SRSG can choose a limited number of staff for his or her own office, and Tom Gregg had almost recruited himself. He certainly did not shy away from correcting me when necessary, which I took as a sign of strength and integrity. He remained one of my most valuable staff members until he left Afghanistan at the end of 2008. The other member of my office that I selected was Hanne Melfald from the Norwegian Ministry of Foreign Affairs. I had met Hanne a year earlier in the ministry, before she started her assignment as political advisor to the Norwegian military in the northern Faryab province. I met her again when she had just returned from Afghanistan and I had just been appointed as UN envoy. She understood difficult political problems, was energetic, had experience from UN agencies and now from Afghanistan. She seemed to have Tom's stubbornness and readiness to give me unpleasant advice. I expected a polite "No, thank you" when I asked her to come back to Afghanistan with me almost before she had managed to unpack. To my surprise, she accepted.

During my final conversation with Ban Ki-moon before leaving New York, he had one message to me: "Build a close relationship with President Karzai as soon as you can." Lakhdar Brahimi, the first UN envoy after the fall of the Taliban, had been particularly close to the president. It was a time when Afghanistan had no government institutions and the reconstruction was in its initial stages. For a period a troika consisting of Karzai, Brahimi, and the U.S. ambassador, Zalmai Khalilzad (himself of Afghan origin), seemed to discuss and decide on most matters. When Brahimi left, the UN's contact with the president had become less and less frequent. It was almost impossible for anyone to follow in Brahimi's footsteps. We had a long way ahead of us if we were going to turn UNAMA into an instrument of coordination within the international community and become a key interlocutor for the Afghan government.

CHAPTER THREE

A CITY UNDER SIEGE

My last few days in Oslo were silent days filled with expectations, but even more with the sense that I was abandoning my family again. I received the last assessments from the UN security team in Kabul about preparations for my arrival. They were not encouraging: the plane taking me to Kabul from Dubai could be attacked with rockets during landing and while taxiing to the terminal; snipers could attack on the way from the plane to the car; and there could be explosives placed on the road to my new residence. The risk assessment of every movement was marked "critical." I knew that there had been media attention and controversies around my appointment. And the security situation in the capital was more fragile after the attack on the Serena Hotel. But the UN security report seemed a bit exaggerated; obviously the team in Kabul wanted to be on the safe side in their assessments. Eventually the arrival plans and the risk assessments were changed. On March 28, I flew in from Dubai in a UN propeller plane so small that I had serious problems getting into it in Dubai and out of it in Kabul. It was a turbulent flight, a warning of the political turbulence that was to come.

I had my first meeting with the media at the airport and emphasized that I had come to serve the Afghan people and that it was important to me to respect Afghanistan's religion, culture, and history. These were not empty words. The UN had been in

Afghanistan since the late 1940s, and it would remain in the country until the Afghan *people* no longer needed its assistance. The UN had not come to the country as a result of the attacks on the United States on September 11, 2001, nor would it withdraw the day that "the war against terror" was over. It was important for me to emphasize that the UN was different from the many other international organizations that had come to Afghanistan in the aftermath of Al Qaeda's attacks. Of course, the UN Mission depended on the support of the UN Security Council and the consent of the Afghan government. But the UN also had to distinguish itself as different and independent when that was required. The reference to the religion, culture, and history of the Afghan people stemmed from the deep frustration I felt whenever I saw international representatives go far beyond their roles as guests in Afghanistan. Nothing angered Afghans more than this. It is hard to find any people so skeptical of foreign intervention and so sensitive about their own pride.

After my brief press conference at the airport, the motorcade took me through Kabul to my future residence, passing workshops made of metal sheets and containers and then small houses as we drove the few kilometers toward the center and Massoud square. We passed the heavily fortified U.S. embassy and found ourselves in Wazir Akbar Khan, the protected part of the city where so many embassies and international representations are located. The driver and my Romanian bodyguards (or close protection team, as they are called) were silent and focused. It was a silence I would soon become used to, driving to the airport on days when tension was particularly high. The last stretch before we arrived at my new home was filled with control points, speed bumps, bomb-sniffing dogs, and police. After a fifteen-minute drive from the airport, we turned left onto Street 15 and disappeared quickly through the gates of my residence, known as Palace 7. The gates were closed, and I found myself in the house that was to be my home for the next two years.

Originally the grounds had belonged to the royal family and the huge building was planned by the last king for one of the princes. The Taliban had taken it over during its rule. The Afghan government had then given the building to Brahimi when he arrived in 2002, and since then it had been the residence of the UN envoy. One room in the basement had, according to the stories, been a Taliban torture chamber. Now it was part of the living quarters of my close protection team, twelve of them, all living with me under the same roof. The recent history of the house was somber, but the location was perfect—only a few minutes away from my office, the presidential palace, and key ministries, with the British and Canadian embassies as my next-door neighbors.

It was a goodbye to any private life for quite a while, even if a beautiful, walled garden provided a certain breathing space. The palace had a large, cold lobby and meeting rooms of different sizes on the ground floor. Upstairs was my own apartment as well as bedrooms for visitors and security, along with an improvised fitness area. The enormous walls and floors were almost empty. When a Norwegian journalist described the house at the time, he wrote that the only item that made Palace 7 look like a home was a photo of my wife. Gradually it improved, with Afghan carpets and other items for decoration. Thanks to the Romanians, the garden became the home of a peacock and a hen, along with two cats and a turtle. The master of the house, Ka ka Sher—"Uncle Lion"—had been employed by the UN since the 1980s, throughout Soviet occupation, civil war, and the Taliban regime. This sixty-year-old man from the Panshir was treated with great respect, even by Afghan ministers who came to visit. Over two years, we shared good and difficult days. And he understood my moods better than most. Every evening the ritual was the same: he made a final tour of the house before getting on his bicycle and saying, "See you tomorrow! *Insha'Allah*." If it is God's will—they were words that had a special meaning in a city where anything could happen at any time.

President Karzai received me quickly for my courtesy call. Having passed all the roadblocks, my cars entered the compound of the old Arg Palace, where the Afghan kings had lived. Visitors have to walk the last little stretch, passing the mosque to the left and a parade ground to the right before entering the building of the presidential offices. In the staircase is a huge calligraphy in which "Allah" is inscribed ninety-nine different ways in gold on a black background. During my two years in Afghanistan, I always slowed down to admire it as I walked up the stairs.

The president came toward me in his traditional green chappan. "God has his ways, Mr. Eide. God has his ways," he said, smiling. Both of us were thinking of that lunch discussion with the Norwegian foreign minister, two and a half months earlier. President Karzai spoke quickly and in a way that projected energy and interest. He asked about my family, the trip, and my first impressions. It was more than a superficial routine. His hospitality and curiosity are important parts of him and his Afghan character.

Next, the politics—we went back again to the dramatic Serena attack in January and what it revealed. It would have been impossible if the Pakistanis had not continued to equip and provide safe haven for Taliban and Haqqani fighters operating inside Afghanistan. Karzai was angry and his views reflected the harsh public exchanges between him and President Musharraf at the time. The president also had other pressing concerns. He said there were fears of serious food shortages during the coming months. The harvest could be bad due to serious drought, and world food prices had risen sharply. Finally, he raised another familiar topic: a political solution was the only way out of the conflict with the Taliban. He had to gather support for a policy of reconciliation. I assured him that I did not only see myself as the representative of the international community to the Afghan government, I would also do my best to understand and explain the Afghans and their authorities to my international partners. That was a message Karzai appreciated.

I told him about Ban Ki-moon's last words to me before I left New York and the president promised me the access I needed. It was a word he kept.

Then followed visits to ministers and advisors and a broad set of briefings from my Afghan interlocutors. The introductory round included, of course, the presidents of the two chambers of the National Assembly: Sibghatullah Mojadeddi of the Meshrano Jirga (The House of Elders or upper house) and Yunus Qanooni of the Wolesi Jirga (The House of Peoples or lower house). Eighty-year-old Mojadeddi, a Pashtun, had been Karzai's mentor during the mujahideen times and was a deeply respected and moderate politician. Qanooni, of Tajik ethnicity, was much younger and a prominent leader of the Northern Alliance. He had been minister of interior in the interim government after the Bonn conference in 2001 and a presidential candidate in 2004. Qanooni had been close to the legendary mujahideen commander, Ahmed Shah Massoud, who was killed by Al Qaeda two days prior to the September 11 attacks. During my visit with Qanooni, I made my first little blunder in my encounters with Afghan traditions. Qanooni said he would be happy to come to my residence for our next meeting. I answered that it would really be too much to expect him to come to my residence, which was located on the opposite side of Kabul. I did not want to take so much of his time, and it was certainly no problem for me to come to his office. When I sat down in the car a few minutes later, my Afghan interpreter corrected me: "Qanooni was showing you great respect by offering to come to your house. You should have accepted." It was the Nordic sense of efficiency colliding with the Afghan sense of respect and politeness. My interpreter had been right.

Among those I visited were people I already knew well: Foreign Minister Rangin Dadfar Spanta, a professor of political science, human rights advocate, and formerly a member of the Green Party in Germany; Defense Minister Abdul Rahim Wardak, a former mujahideen fighter and a huge bear of a man who I felt I could trust from the moment I met him; Haneef Atmar, the minister of education, with a razor-sharp brain, a radical political past, and years of experience as a staff member in a Norwegian NGO; and Zalmai Rassoul, the national security advisor, later foreign minister, a quiet man, educated as a medical doctor in France, for years a close assistant to the former king in Rome, and, I found, one of the wisest personalities in the Afghan leadership. All of these men shared the same concern: after seven years, the time had come to give Afghans more responsibility for the development of their own country. The Afghan government had to be seen as being in charge. Now foreign dominance created resentment among Afghans and damaged the legitimacy of the government as well as the support for the international community.

To conclude my introductory round, I invited all ambassadors and representatives from international organizations to a big reception at Palace 7. I remember it for one reason only: a high ranking representative from a very prominent country pulled me aside and asked, "Could a senior official from my country's intelligence agency be placed in your private office?"

I was used to electronic interception of phone conversations and meetings and expected that several intelligence services would follow me closely. During my time as the UN Special Representative in Bosnia and Herzegovina, a British NATO general had warned me that the commander of the NATO force received transcripts of my phone conversations. But asking me to place an acknowledged foreign intelligence official just outside the office door of a UN envoy was the most remarkable offer I had received so far.

Among the ambassadors in Kabul, some were particularly impressive. The Russian ambassador, Zamir Khabulov, and the EU representative, Francesc Vendrell, had played important roles already at the Bonn conference in December 2001. Vendrell, the UN envoy to Afghanistan from 1999 to 2002, had been one of its main architects. The British ambassador, Sherard Cowper-Coles, probably had the sharpest brain of all of them and was among the very first to argue that the conflict could only be solved by a political settlement. And the U.S. ambassador, William Wood, was Karzai's closest international interlocutor and became a true friend, which was a great advantage when we had to manage controversies between us.

Within UNAMA and the UN family, my arrival was regarded with relief and probably some nervousness: relief because the mission had been without permanent leadership for six weeks already, and the debate over Paddy Ashdown had created uncertainty; nervousness because of my unusual background, with eleven years at NATO headquarters in Brussels behind me. Many UN staff members were profoundly skeptical of the idea of a close relationship with a military alliance. I had already met my deputy, Chris Alexander, many times. He had been Canadian ambassador before coming to the UN and had an enormous network among Afghans and internationals. Chris always tried to maintain an upbeat tone, even in the most difficult periods.

CHAPTER FOUR

CAN THE UN DELIVER?

A few days after my arrival in Kabul, I had to return to Europe to attend the ISAF Summit in Bucharest, where more than forty heads of state and government participated. The UN was now at the center of attention as the Summit documents emphasized the urgent need to formulate a comprehensive concept that could include all the assistance provided to Afghanistan, civilian as well as military. "There can be no lasting security without development and no development without security" was the rather simplistic slogan of the concluding declaration. The declaration gave me and UNAMA strong support for the coordination mandate, including the need to bring civilian and military assistance together in one strategy. Heads of state and government looked forward to seeing the UN expand across the country. This was all positive. But there was something frightening in the fact that my name was the only one to be mentioned twice in the relatively short declaration.

"The speakers mentioned you more than my president," Spanta said half-jokingly during the discussion. I had a feeling that the Afghans did not like it. They wanted greater responsibility for themselves. They certainly did not want an international representative to come in and take center stage.

Only one speaker, Norwegian Prime Minister Jens Stoltenberg, tried to see the situation from my perspective. The challenge was not primarily to coordinate but to accept being coordinated, he said. The UN could only succeed if the participants changed their own behavior. If they did more of the same, then it would not work. I was grateful for all the political support provided around the table, but Stoltenberg's warning was particularly welcome. Of course, the UN had a mandate to coordinate, but political readiness from the donors was by far the most decisive factor.

At such meetings, leaders most often read from prepared written statements. However, one head of government impressed me particularly, German Chancellor Angela Merkel. Instead of reading from a prepared text, she looked directly at President Karzai and said, "We have come to your country, Mr. President. It is a country which is foreign to us. You must tell us what you want us to do and what you need." It was an invitation to a constructive dialogue and an approach that I rarely came across during my two years in Kabul.

The Summit declaration expressed a strong desire for a comprehensive approach to the conflict, an approach which could bring military and civilian efforts together as two components of one strategy. But the debate also revealed that, more than six years after the fall of the Taliban, the international community still lacked a clear political direction. It was obvious to all that the Taliban and its ability to return in strength had been underestimated. President Karzai declared that the Afghans would soon take over responsibility for the security of the capital, Kabul. Politically, it was a smart initiative that provided some hope for the future; but in reality, the security situation in and around the capital had also deteriorated and would become even more complex over the next few months.

Much of that spring was spent on a round of introductory visits to the capitals of the main contributors and political players. The reception was, with one exception, overwhelming and politically important. It is not often that a UN Special Representative can meet the president of the United States, the German chancellor, the British and Canadian prime ministers, and other leading politicians during introductory visits. The high level of attention reflected not only political support but also the increasing domestic pressure many governments faced as a result of their political, military, and economic investments in Afghanistan: they had to demonstrate results to their constituencies. However, what surprised me more than anything during these visits were all the questions: How did I see the situation? What did I think? What was my plan? I had just arrived and had only spent a few days on the ground. These governments had been in Afghanistan for years now. I had expected them to share their strategic thinking and experience with me, not the other way around. Certainly, some of the questioning stemmed from politeness and curiosity about the new UN envoy. But it also reflected a sense of confusion and unease that was spreading fast in the international community.

Politically, our meetings in Washington at the very end of April were the most important. I knew the national security advisor, Stephen Hadley, from meetings at NATO and elsewhere. I had observed Secretary of State Condoleezza Rice and Secretary of Defense Robert Gates at various NATO meetings, but they had—of course—never been my interlocutors. Rice invited me to dinner with the three of them the evening I arrived in Washington. It was a generous gesture. There was an atmosphere of openness and informality around the table that impressed me. Condoleezza Rice summed up the discussion by saying, "We should really make an effort to listen more to the Afghans. It is obvious that we don't understand the country well enough." I think we all agreed.

The next morning a meeting had been arranged with President George W. Bush. I had been in the Oval Office once before as a state secretary accompanying the Norwegian prime minister to a meeting with the current president's father, President George H. W. Bush, at the time of the unification of Germany, another important juncture in modern history. George W. Bush was friendly, but did not have his father's calm and collected character. He did not have any specific topic that he wanted to raise, which was to be expected; my meeting with him was a courtesy visit, a demonstration of his support rather than a meeting to discuss Afghanistan in any depth. I raised my deep concerns regarding the relationship between Afghanistan and Pakistan. The large Peace Jirga between the two countries in August of 2007, with hundreds of participants from each side of the border, had been an important event. But it had not led to regular meetings and interaction across the border the way it was intended. Instead of a constructive dialogue, the exchanges between Presidents Karzai and Musharraf had become bitter and angry, with public accusations from both sides. To fight the insurgency successfully would require a more constructive engagement from Pakistan. We seemed to be moving in exactly the opposite direction. President Bush nodded, turned to Condoleezza Rice and asked, "Condi, can we crank up another Jirga? "

The discussion turned to the forthcoming donor conference in Paris in June. I wanted the Afghans to get on the offensive and to reassure public opinion in donor countries that the Afghan government took our concerns seriously, particularly with regard to combating corruption. I mentioned Karzai's initiative at the Bucharest Summit a few weeks earlier, when he had declared that the Afghans would take responsibility for the security of Kabul. We needed a similar initiative at the Paris conference. I suggested to President Bush that Karzai should himself take a bold initiative to fight corruption. Bush could present this idea to him during one of his regular video conferences with Karzai. The president agreed and invited me to come up with a proposal for him. Then he changed the subject and asked, "What about the dope?" I must have looked confused. The broad Texas accent made one word slur into the next—the question was incomprehensible to me. It became even more embarrassing when he repeated the question and I still did not understand. Condoleezza Rice could see that I urgently needed her assistance. She leaned forward in the sofa and explained, "The president wants to know how you see the drug situation." After only a few days on the job, I did not have a satisfactory answer to give to him.

Before the meeting with the president ended, members of the media were invited into the room for brief comments. "He is a man of action," President Bush said of me, a comment that made its way to Norwegian TV later that evening. It wasn't long before I received a text message from my wife in Norway. It read: "Since when?" She still had my long hesitation on whether to take the job or not in mind.

I left Washington convinced that we had established a good relationship with the U.S. administration. In spite of disagreements on some issues, it was a relationship that lasted. Condoleezza Rice, Bob Gates, and Stephen Hadley were fully aware of the difficult situation I was facing. "Tell me what you need and what we can do for you" was Bob Gates's constant comment. All of them wanted the UN to do well and were ready to send me whatever personnel I needed. Of course my need for assistance was overwhelming, and I was already in the process of recruiting a prominent American to directly aid coordination and effectiveness. But too many Americans in the UN Mission could quickly create the impression among Afghans as well as internationals that the United States was now also dominating the UN. However, I did need political support to help me overcome the delays of the UN bureaucracy. And the Bush administration always gave me such support whenever I asked for it.

From Washington we continued our North American trip and met the entire Canadian leadership in Ottawa. I have always been impressed with Canadian contributions to international operations, both in the Balkans and in Afghanistan. However, although this visit was also friendly and supportive, disagreements emerged. The Canadian government had recently decided to spend 50 percent of all its civilian aid in Kandahar, the province where the Canadians had their military forces. In my opinion, they were going in the wrong direction. Several big troop contributors had now concentrated their economic assistance in provinces in Southern Afghanistan, where they had troops. The result was that provinces in the north and center of the country received less attention, even when they were in greater need of assistance. Furthermore, when donor countries tied their assistance to the provinces where they had troops, it also limited the Afghan government's ability to carry out nationwide planning. In the UN Security Council I called it a "donor-generated fragmentation" of the country. I feared that when the countries contributing troops started to withdraw their forces, they would also reduce their economic investment if their military and development engagements were too intertwined. When I returned to Kabul, I was told that the Canadian minister of development, Beverley Joan Oda, had been unhappy about my public remarks on this topic. It was a criticism she repeated gently when we later met in Kabul. But UNAMA had been given the task of coordination, so the donors would have to accept that we criticized a kind of spending we considered unhelpful.

The European tour included visits to London, Paris, and Berlin, in addition to a briefing to the NATO Council. The British had deployed their forces mainly in Helmand province in the south, one of the most challenging of the thirty-four provinces and a Taliban stronghold. They had taken the lead role in international counternarcotics efforts. And Helmand was by far the biggest poppy-producing province in the country. I was concerned to see that their focus was also increasingly on this one province and that even the British attention to the nationwide perspective was suffering.

The French had just started preparations for the big donor conference in June. The French government now wanted to play a more prominent role in Afghanistan. I knew the foreign minister, Berhard Kouchner, from his days as UN envoy in Kosovo. Kouchner had been in the country decades ago as one of the founders of Doctors Without Borders. He had been a true humanitarian all his adult life and seemed skeptical of a stronger

French military involvement, preferring a more significant contribution to the civilian development of Afghanistan. But President Nicolas Sarkozy was promising French military assistance instead, with no real increase in civilian-development aid. Kouchner was also a strong supporter of a reconciliation process and the need to engage in a dialogue with the insurgency.

In Berlin much of the discussion centered on the buildup of Afghan security forces. The Germans had taken the early international lead in police training, which was a critical element both for building respect for law and order and for fighting the insurgency. But the German efforts had been modest and overly bureaucratized, and they were criticized as ineffective by internationals as well as Afghans. Karzai had himself complained about the modest European role. Now Defense Minister Franz Josef Jung declared that the German police contingent would increase from thirty to forty-five officers—a 50 percent increase, but still a modest number. The EU eventually took over the responsibility from the Germans, but during my two years in Kabul never managed to live up to its commitment. Even in tiny Kosovo the OSCE had managed to build a modern police school and training program that turned out several hundreds of new police officers every year. Why had we not been able to do the same in Afghanistan? Of course the problems of a high illiteracy rate and drug abuse made the task much more difficult than in Kosovo. But the very modest investment in police training was an example of how the most critical challenges in Afghanistan had been neglected.

In the months and years that followed, I raised this question repeatedly with the EU foreign policy chief, Javier Solana. He was always an interesting interlocutor and curious about developments on the ground. But he was cautious with regard to engaging the EU more deeply in Afghanistan. I often felt that he considered the prospects of success to be slim and that he did not want the EU too involved in a conflict he thought was unsolvable.

The European trip included a visit to the NATO Council in Brussels. The secretary general, Jaap de Hoop Scheffer, had been a close friend for many years, and many of the ambassadors were my former colleagues. For the first time, I raised the question of reconciliation in a big, multinational gathering. I thought it would be important to tell the NATO ambassadors that, even if their focus was on the level of international troops and their rules of engagement, the decisive element would in the end be a dialogue with the Taliban. There was also another problem that worried me: the close relationship between some NATO members and former Afghan warlords. I complained that their governments continued to cultivate, protect, and even support a number of them, including Abdul Rashid Dostum of Uzbek ethnicity. The reason for raising the problem was an ongoing debate in Kabul over Dostum's possible arrest. Dostum and his people had attacked and brutally mistreated the ethnic Turkmen Mohammad Akhbar Bay, one of Dostum's former allies who had distanced himself from the notorious warlord. The attorney general had an indictment ready. I thought it would send a powerful signal if Dostum was arrested. However, the small group of international representatives that were involved was split. Some countries feared instability in the north of the country, where they had special interests or their own forces. It was an attitude that made every effort to marginalize warlords that had torn the country apart during the civil war impossible. We all talked about bringing the culture of impunity to an end. But as long as important NATO allies continued to protect such brutal leaders, how could we at the same time talk about ending impunity?

During a meeting with the U.S. ambassador to NATO, Victoria Nuland, I received a warning that surprised me in its directness. She made it clear that the United States would not tolerate any surprises, in particular with regard to the sensitive question of civilian casualties. She knew from my time at NATO that this was a source of growing concern in my country and in several others.

"No surprises," she said sternly. My experience was that the Americans themselves did not hesitate to surprise their allies or indeed the Afghans. The UN could not keep quiet when serious mistakes were committed and caused civilian casualties. Our human rights mandate was clear, and we had no intention of sweeping our concerns under the carpet.

The last destination on our introductory visits to Europe was Moscow. Russian Foreign Minister Sergei Lavrov is probably the most intelligent current foreign minister I know. I had met him several times, including during my assignment for former UN Secretary-General Kofi Annan in 2005 to prepare for Kosovo's future status. Our discussion focused on reconciliation with the Taliban. The Russians understandably had no troops in Afghanistan, and their civilian assistance was modest. They were deeply skeptical of any dialogue with the insurgency because of the problems the Russians themselves were facing with Islamist groups in the Caucasus. I mentioned that I had not seen any statement of Russian support for the UN Mission and hoped that he would use this opportunity to make one. But I suspected that the Russians thought I was too close to the United States and were uncertain about how I would tackle my role. As soon as I left Moscow, the Russian foreign ministry published a statement. It was a brief message noting tersely that I had been in Moscow and that the Russians reaffirmed their support for the UN. But the text ended with the ministry noting "the inadmissibility of attempts to erode the sanctions regime of the UN Security Council against persons and entities associated with Al Qaeda and the Taliban." It was a clear message: I obviously had some way to go before I had the confidence of Russian authorities and their support to a reconciliation policy.

The first rounds of introductory visits were over. We returned to Kabul with a feeling that the visits abroad had given us the support we needed. But the high expectations and the many warnings demonstrated how demanding our mission would be. My closest staff and I could feel the pressure building. We would have a grace period of some weeks, perhaps months, during which our international partners would wait and follow our activities closely. But that period of grace would soon come to an end.

CHAPTER FIVE

STRUGGLE IN THE UN FAMILY

The first meetings with my staff confirmed that Tom Gregg was right in the assessment he had given me in New York. There were well-qualified, highly motivated people in UNAMA as well as in the UN agencies. But there were few with solid experience in the areas in which expectations were high: aid coordination, institution building, and humanitarian affairs in particular. The UN Security Council had adopted an ambitious mandate. But no financial or personnel resources came with such a mandate. We had to recruit more well-qualified people, in a situation where deteriorating security made it increasingly dangerous for UN personnel and NGOs to move around the country.

When I first visited Afghanistan in 2003, the number of security incidents with the insurgency had been 508. This included everything from direct exchange of fire with international or Afghan military forces to suicide attacks and roadside bombs. During the next three years, the number of incidents increased more than tenfold to 5,106. In 2008, my first year as SRSG, it reached 8,893 incidents. There was also a significant geographic expansion of attacks by the Taliban and other insurgency networks. Such attacks spread from the traditional Taliban strongholds in provinces in the south and the east to provinces around the capital, Wardak, Logar, and Kapisa.

Some media reported as if the Taliban were standing at the gates of Kabul and had almost surrounded the capital, which was certainly an exaggeration. But the atmosphere in the capital was tense.

The attack against the Serena Hotel also represented a new trend with more complex and daring attacks against the capital. On April 27, 2008, during the celebration of the mujahideen victory over the Communist regime, terrorists attacked the military parade in Kabul. President Karzai and the entire Afghan leadership as well as foreign ambassadors were present. The investigations that followed showed that the security services had been infiltrated. I had declined the invitation to attend and was on my way to Europe when the attack happened. For the second time in three months, I had avoided an attack by pure coincidence. Ironically, I had spoken to Karzai about the parade a few days before it took place. I had mentioned the noise from the helicopters that had been conducting exercises above the capital day after day. Irritated, he asked one of his ministers if a parade was really appropriate. "It costs a lot of money, and the people are worried about whether they will have food to eat tomorrow," he said. But it was too late, and the parade went ahead.

A month and a half later, on July 7, a car full of explosives rammed into the gates of the Indian embassy in Kabul. More than sixty people were killed. It was the first big explosion I had experienced since the Serena attack. The windows of my office about a kilometer away trembled and dust covered the floor and the furniture. But we were at a safe enough distance.

The number of so-called asymmetric attacks increased dramatically: road bombs, suicide attacks, murders, and kidnappings that now also threatened aid workers and NGOs. Civilian organizations could to some extent protect themselves against direct and conventional fighting simply by staying away from areas where they took place. But it was impossible to predict where a road bomb might be placed or a kidnapping could happen. The increased vulnerability of aid workers was brutally illustrated when cars from the International Rescue Committee (IRC) were attacked in an ambush on August 13, 2008, on the road between Gardez and Kabul. Three female international staff members and one Afghan were murdered. It was a shock to all of us and a warning that NGOs were now on the target list of Taliban and other insurgency networks. There was a somber atmosphere among NGOs and civilian-aid organizations. But in meetings with many of them immediately after the attack, there was stubbornness more than fear and commitment to continue more than resignation. They would not allow insurgents to hinder them from serving the most vulnerable in the Afghan society. I often heard NGOs and aid workers being criticized by Afghan government officials, including President Karzai. International military and sometimes political leaders complained about their unwillingness to be "part of the mission"—a militarily dominated mission, that is. We had to encourage a more intelligent NGO attitude, they claimed. Such criticism was unfounded and unfair. Many of these unarmed NGOs traveled to places where most ISAF countries did not dare send their heavily armed soldiers in armored vehicles. Prominent military and civilians from NATO headquarters and some ISAF countries seemed to not understand that many NGOs had to base their work on acceptance by the population and often by elements of the insurgency.

Shortly after I arrived in Kabul, we seemed to be heading for a humanitarian crisis. The harvest was bad as a result of months of drought, and we could expect serious food shortages. President Karzai had warned me already during the first meeting we had that sharp increases in global food prices made the situation dramatically worse. A cold and harsh winter with heavy snowfall would cause the situation to deteriorate further. It would be difficult to reach remote parts of the country with food and other humanitarian assistance. With its lack of roads and difficult terrain, Afghanistan is extremely vulnerable. Villages and significant parts of the most inaccessible provinces can be effectively cut off for months during the winter. In Dai Kundi, a province in the central highlands of Afghanistan, there was not one single kilometer of asphalted road and not many kilometers of gravel road. But there were more than enough mountains and snow. Other provinces were not much better off. Agriculture had also been neglected for years, and irrigation systems were lacking or damaged, making the harvest dependent on rainfall. The worst-case scenario would be a combination of drought that would reduce the harvest, global price increases that would affect the availability of food imports, and heavy snowfall that would isolate villages and communities. That was precisely the situation that now seemed imminent.

In January 2008 the UN and the Afghan government issued a food appeal for $81 million to meet urgent requirements. Significant amounts of food, primarily wheat, had been purchased and distributed. Six months later, in July, another appeal had to be launched for an additional $404 million to avoid serious food shortages. That would cover the need for food and other urgent requirements through the winter season but also help farmers prepare for their next harvest. Five million Afghans were now affected by the drought and the rising food prices. While the average household spent 56 percent of its income on food in 2005, this had now risen to 73 percent.

In early April, a worried President Karzai had called ambassadors and Afghan ministers together in the palace to discuss the food shortages. The price of wheat flour had increased by 70 percent during the last months, after having almost doubled in 2007, he had said. People would not understand that the rising food prices were a result of global trends. The situation could cause a serious hunger problem, but it could also provoke social and political turmoil. Already, there had been protests in several parts of the country. Haneef Atmar, the minister of education, asked for food for the teachers. They were threatening strikes and unrest and represented the majority of government-employed civil servants. The deteriorating security also reduced access to unstable parts of the country. "We do not even know what the children now look like in the south," the head of one of the UN's humanitarian agencies complained when we discussed the ability of the UN to assist.

The UN had little capacity to handle a demanding humanitarian situation. It was obvious that strengthening our capacity to identify the requirements and coordinate the response now had to be a priority. The UN Security Council had given this task to UNAMA in its mandate. A plan for strengthening our overall humanitarian capacity was developed and presented to the UN headquarters in New York and to a number of humanitarian UN agencies. The plan would allow us to recruit more than ninety new staff members, international and Afghan, and deploy them in Kabul and across the country.

I was pleased that we had been able to respond so quickly. But I was unprepared for the reactions to the proposal, in particular from John Holmes, the British director of one of the UN agencies, the Office for Coordination of Humanitarian Assistance (OCHA). Nobody in the UN system had taken any significant initiative to strengthen the UN capacity to meet an emerging humanitarian crisis. OCHA did not have an office in Afghanistan and had never asked for one. Nevertheless, it became clear that Holmes did not want UNAMA to strengthen its humanitarian capacity. It had to be done through the opening of an entirely new OCHA office. After a heated discussion, the problem was raised to the level of the secretary-general, Ban Ki-moon. He gave me his full support and ruled against the opening of a separate OCHA office. Our plan was adopted and the case was closed. From now on, we could focus on vulnerable people on the ground in Afghanistan and not on turf-fighting in the

UN building in New York—or so I thought. A number of donor countries came forward immediately to provide financial resources to recruit personnel until a new budget for 2009 could absorb the costs. In a matter of a few weeks, we had the millions of dollars required. But in spite of Ban Ki-moon's clear decision, John Holmes continued the opposition. "You will never be able to recruit the staff you need before winter," he claimed. On the other hand, he was confident that he could get them in place in a matter of four to six weeks.

A group of NGOs turned to me, deeply concerned. Many of them would have preferred an OCHA office, and some even insisted. But most of them were concerned that the debate was causing us to lose valuable time. I was ready to review our experience as soon as the winter was over, but we had to meet the emerging crisis quickly. Nevertheless, Holmes persisted, and the disagreement continued to absorb time and attention. In September I informed the secretary-general that I had decided to give up. If others could do the job more quickly and robustly, then they should do it. I was embarrassed before the donors who had given me their generous contributions.

The establishment of the OCHA office went slowly. Afghan authorities expressed their frustration over the delays caused by the internal UN quarreling. In late June 2010, two years after this debate, Holmes received a letter from thirty-one NGOs complaining about the slow buildup of his humanitarian-assistance capacity. Basic coordination, planning, and information-management requirements exceed OCHA's capacity, they said. Holmes blamed lack of security and "slow bureaucratic procedures."

There were legitimate arguments on both sides in this discussion. A number of humanitarian NGOs emphasized that UNAMA was a political organization, with a mandate to work closely—too closely—with the Afghan government and the international military forces. Therefore, humanitarian assistance coordinated through

UNAMA would not be considered neutral and impartial, which would make it more vulnerable to attacks from the insurgency. In my view, this argument did not hold in practical life. Attacks against humanitarian workers and NGOs had been steadily increasing and had nothing to do with UNAMA's mandate or political role. The Taliban directed their attacks against humanitarian and aid organizations because they were seen as supporting the Afghan government, receiving money from countries that had troops in Afghanistan or trying to undermine Islam. Of course, UNAMA would not itself deliver assistance. That would be left to different UN agencies and to NGOs as well as the Afghan government. Our role would have been to assess the requirements and coordinate the assistance.

I understood well the distrust of humanitarian organizations toward the international military. Former U.S. Defense Secretary Donald Rumsfeld had argued for "strategic" delivery of humanitarian assistance. Food and other requirements could be given to those who supported ISAF and withheld from those who did not. His view represented a clear violation of an established humanitarian principle: that aid should be given to the most vulnerable parts of the population without regard to their political attitudes. I certainly had no intention of supporting Rumsfeld's approach.

By the late fall of 2008, the World Food Program (WFP) had prepositioned large quantities of food in twenty-three of thirty-four provinces. The Afghan government had also purchased significant quantities and started distribution. However, we knew that these quantities would only meet requirements until March of the following year. It would not be enough to get us through a long and cold winter. To make matters worse, some of the wheat that was purchased was of such low quality that it could not be used for human consumption. Other quantities never came to Afghanistan. The producing countries stopped their deliveries due to their own precarious food situation. We had insufficient food and insufficient ability to coordinate the assistance that could soon be required. Afghans as well as international organizations were deeply concerned.

Fortunately, the winter turned out to be milder than expected. And from November on, there was plenty of rainfall. The rain continued until April of 2009 and reached levels that had not been experienced in decades. As a result, grain production rose from 3.6 million tons in 2008 to 6.3 million tons in 2009. Prices went down. The humanitarian crisis had been avoided. Flying over various parts of the country that spring was sheer joy. The hillsides and plains beneath me were a beautiful green color in contrast to the brown that had dominated the horizon the previous year. But 2008's near crisis had demonstrated how poorly prepared we were to meet a disaster and how vulnerable Afghanistan was to changes in weather conditions and global price fluctuations.

The discussion over delivery of food support also revealed other weaknesses. Atmar had asked for food for the teachers, but specific groups of state employees could not be singled out for political reasons. Raising salaries seemed to be a better alternative in order to avoid unrest and keep the schools open. But to determine which salaries should be raised, we first had to determine the qualifications of the teachers. The review revealed that a significant number of teachers who received salaries could themselves neither read nor write. Afghanistan certainly had a long way to go.

The struggle to recruit personnel for humanitarian coordination had also illustrated how understaffed UNAMA was. One-third of all international positions were vacant. At first I thought that the deteriorating security conditions were to blame and that they frightened candidates away from applying. But I soon discovered that there was no lack of applicants and no lack of offers from governments that wanted to support us. Rather, a complex and time-consuming recruitment process had led to a situation where qualified candidates simply did not have the time to wait for a final answer. They had often found other engagements by the time the UN made an offer. It was painful to tell candidates and governments the truth; that even if I desperately needed new staff members, it could take up to a year before I had them in place in Kabul or elsewhere in the country.

We must have seemed like a pest to the administrative staff at UN headquarters in New York during this period. We bombarded them with cables and phone calls from Kabul almost every day, urging them to try all possible shortcuts. Certainly we were not the only UN mission with this kind of problem. It was a chronic problem that threatened a number of missions. By March of 2009, the vacancy rate had dropped from 30 percent to 12 percent. Three months earlier, a new budget for UNAMA had been adopted, doubling to $150 million, an increase that was probably unprecedented in the UN. It had taken a year, but the UN mission was finally in better shape.

There had been a serious lack of experts in donor coordination inside UNAMA. I needed a person with particular experience and weight to lead our coordination efforts and be an effective interlocutor to Afghan ministers and big donor agencies. Mark Ward, a friend from USAID, had already signaled his interest to me. He had spent time in Afghanistan and Pakistan and was now responsible for the entire region for USAID. He was ready to leave a prominent position in Washington to come to Kabul and to the UN Mission. Nobody could match his experience. And he had other important qualities. He knew the U.S. aid bureaucracies inside out. And he would not hesitate to criticize any donor, including the United States. When he finally arrived in Kabul, Mark Ward became my special advisor in donor-coordination and aid-effectiveness issues. His experience and energy quickly made him a source of enthusiasm inside the mission and the most prominent interlocutor of key ministers in the government. But it had taken eight months to recruit him. In the end Mark and I exchanged many emails with the headline "Almost giving up." But he did not, and I was grateful to him for his extraordinary patience.

In order to assist Mark Ward, I asked the UN headquarters to let me recruit some of the experts that member states had offered free of charge, at least as a short-term solution. The initial answer from New York was negative, but in late December of 2008, we were given permission to recruit unpaid personnel as a temporary solution. Some countries responded quickly and provided experts in agriculture and energy. It was a promising start. One donor country offered an expert in marine biology—to a country without a coast.

The internal discussion in the UN system about recruitment, aid coordination, and humanitarian assistance filled me with great frustration—and sometimes with despair. During a visit to New York in fall of 2008, I was sitting on the terrace at the top of the Beekman Tower Hotel. I looked over to the UN buildings a few hundred yards away and felt only resignation. Over there was my employer and a secretary-general who had given me his full support. But in the same buildings were also some of my most difficult opponents. There had been many well-intended reform committees. But the UN bureaucracy, with its impenetrable rules and regulations and its internal turf fighting, made it impossible to react quickly and to implement a demanding mandate.

Many of the Western embassies in Kabul understood my problems well and were sympathetic. One very prominent ambassador wrote the following to the foreign ministry of his own country: "At a time where [Eide] should be able to use his energy, leadership, and vision to bring Afghans and the international community together around the priorities from the Paris conference, he is worn out by battles with the UN bureaucracy. It is hard to pressure Karzai for reforms as long as Eide cannot put his own organization in order because of delaying tactics in New York." The U.S. ambassador wrote in a cable to the State Department in Washington that he thought I was close to resigning. There is such a need for the UN in so many places. But it can only become an effective instrument if some of the bureaucratic and political obstacles that today hamper its field activities can be removed.

CHAPTER SIX

WHERE DID ALL THE MONEY GO?

The public complaints about lack of aid coordination had increased from 2007 and were now coming from almost all directions. The international community complained and Afghan ministers complained. But few had looked at the problem in a systematic way, and none were prepared to accept criticism against their own aid policies. To behave in a more coherent way, we needed more than complaints and calls for a strong coordinator. We had to determine what had gone wrong and why.

In the early years after the fall of the Taliban, the economic resources provided by the international community were modest. Donors had their own priorities, determined by their own traditions, political preferences, and pressure groups, including strong NGOs. The need for coordination was not seen as an urgent requirement. In selected areas, the lead role was given to individual G-8 countries: the United States for the army, Germany for the police, the U.K. for counternarcotics, Italy for the justice system, and Japan for disarmament and reintegration of illegally armed groups. But there was no overriding coordination and the UN was reluctant to assume the role of aid coordinator. On the Afghan side of the table were ministers competing among themselves, unable and unwilling to decline generous offers from international donors.

Weak and uncoordinated ministers were confronting strong, but equally uncoordinated, donors.

The important Afghanistan Conference in London in January and February of 2006 had established a Joint Coordination and Monitoring Board (JCMB), with more than twenty international members and a significant group of Afghan ministers. The purpose of the JCMB was to improve the coordination of foreign aid. But the JCMB had become a talk shop without tangible results. Many of the ambassadors in Kabul were losing interest in the entire JCMB exercise and did not hide their frustration. Several of them had begun to suggest that it should be abolished entirely. Constantly meetings took place between embassies, ministries, and other partners. But the results were lacking.

To bring as many as possible of these activities under one umbrella, I proposed to consolidate the twenty-one existing working groups into three subcommittees under the JCMB. They would cover each of the main chapters of the Afghanistan Compact, the five-year plan adopted at the London Conference: security, governance, and economic and social development. It was a very simple reform inspired by an idea from Alastair McKechnie of the World Bank. The intention was to ensure that all issues that would require action were first prepared in one of the groups. The main JCMB could then avoid lengthy discussions and concentrate on political decisions. The proposal was accepted without much difficulty. At least we had a new structure in place.

But we had not addressed the really important parts of the problem: What were we going to coordinate? Nobody seemed to really know the amount of aid flowing into Afghanistan, and nobody knew where it was spent and for what purposes. How were we supposed to coordinate when such fundamental facts were missing? And how could we coordinate when there were no agreed priorities for the entire development effort and each donor was left to set its own? Several years had passed since the last national programs had been adopted within health, education, and rural development. They had been success stories, but we continued to repeat these same stories year after year to demonstrate that progress had been made since the Taliban fell. There was an atmosphere of stagnation. New initiatives and national programs were needed.

It was hard to find reliable information about international assistance and its impact. I listened to members of the Afghan government and discussed it with Mark Ward before and after he arrived in Kabul. A report from ACBAR, the coordination board for NGOs engaged in Afghan reconstruction, was published at the time I arrived and impressed me more than other documents I had read. It was written by Matt Waldmann, from the British organization Oxfam. The report had an appropriate title: "Falling Short." It painted a picture of an aid flow without direction and with little impact. The report was criticized for inaccuracy when it was released in March of 2008, probably with some justification, in part as a result of the lack of information from donors. But it illustrated the dimensions of challenges we were facing.

First of all, the report showed how hesitant the international community had been in providing assistance after the fall of the Taliban. At the time, Karzai had complained about the reluctance of Western donors. People had expectations for development and a better life, but little seemed to happen. Waldmann's report estimated that Afghanistan had received $57 per capita during the first two years, compared to $679 in Bosnia and Herzegovina and $233 in East Timor. A document prepared by the Afghan Ministry of Finance (the Donor Financial Review) in late 2009 confirmed this impression: during the first five years after the end of the Taliban regime, Afghanistan had received $292 compared to $1,528 in Iraq. Afghanistan had only received a portion of what had been given to other countries in conflict or postconflict situations. But the needs were certainly no less than in Bosnia or Iraq, countries that were in better shape than Afghanistan in almost every way. Obviously, there had not been any plan for Afghanistan in the years following the intervention, and Iraq had stolen attention away.

Second, how much of this assistance actually came to Afghanistan, and how much stayed in the donor countries? The report referred to comments by the director of the World Bank office in Kabul in 2006, who had stated that 35 percent of the aid was badly spent and that the waste was enormous. He had called it "plunder." The largest donor, the USAID, channeled almost half of its assistance through contracts with five big U.S. companies. For many of the projects, there could be up to five layers of international or Afghan subcontractors. Each would demand 10–20 percent profit, sometimes more. Altogether, it was estimated that 40 percent of the civilian assistance, which meant $6 billion since 2001, remained in the donor country. Over half of the assistance was tied to the purchase of goods and services from the donor country itself. It did not contribute to building Afghan competence or stimulating economic growth.

Third, how much of this assistance was allocated without serious consultations with Afghan authorities? According to information provided by the Afghan Ministry of Finance in early 2008, the government was unaware of how one-third of the civilian assistance—about $5 billion—had been spent. A significant number of donor countries did not provide information or provided only partial information about their spending. Afghan authorities had not been brought properly into the planning or the execution of projects.

Fourth, a significant part of the overall assistance went to so-called technical assistance—advisors and consultants to Afghan institutions. How much of this assistance was coordinated with the Afghan government? According to the OECD, less than 40 percent had been coordinated with government requirements. In a number of ministries, you could find consultants and advisors who, also according to the OECD, had been offered and allocated by donor countries according to their own wishes. A number of advisors had been recruited through private consultancy firms and had salaries of $250,000 or more. I knew of several such advisors placed inside the government, with salaries of more than $500,000 paid by international donors. Sitting next to them in the same ministries were Afghans with a salary of $1,500 to $2,000 per year.

Fifth, how was the aid distributed in various parts of the country? Figures were incomplete, but it seemed clear that the assistance focused strongly on provinces in the south and the east, where the conflict was most intense. If Helmand had been a state, it would have been the fifth-largest recipient of aid from the USAID. And Helmand only had a population of 800,000 people. In addition, significant amounts of British and other aid went to the same province. Kandahar, Uruzgan, and other conflict provinces received considerable amounts through the military Provincial Reconstruction Teams (PRTs), while very modest resources reached poorer provinces in the center and the north, such as Dai Kundi, Faryab, and Takhar. I had already complained about the heavy Canadian concentration on Kandahar. But there were several similar examples.

In an article published in the *Asia Times* on March 18, 2009, a reporter wrote ironically, "Do you want a billion dollars in development assistance? If you live in Afghanistan, there are two certain ways of attracting attention and assistance from the United States: Taliban attacks or a booming opium trade. For those who have neither, the future could look bleak." This was exactly how people in stable provinces saw the situation. They often asked me if violence was the only way to get the attention they deserved. Wouldn't it be better to reward them for stability and for reduction of the opium production?

But the most important question was: Did we have a set of real priorities that were agreed upon and shared by the government and the international community? In other words, did we have a development strategy? Obviously, for any coordination effort to be successful, we would have to move past a situation where every donor could set its own priorities and every Afghan minister could lobby donors for his own pet projects. More attention would have to be paid to long-term impact and sustainability. The amount of money spent was important, but it was not a good measure of impact or success.

An increasing portion of the financial resources was allocated through military structures, in particular the PRTs. They had by now been established in all provinces with two exceptions. Because they belonged to different members of the ISAF coalition, some PRTs had huge resources at their disposal for civilian projects and others had little or nothing, which made the problem of unequal distribution of assistance worse. The PRTs were also reluctant to consult Afghan authorities and to inform the government about their spending. When the PRTs were first established, they were meant to be temporary structures. Instead, they had become permanent and competing structures, slowing down the development of Afghan institutions instead of accelerating it. With increasing economic resources at their disposal, they contributed greatly to blurring the line between military and civilian activities and became an increasing problem for civilian-donor institutions.

In 2004, the U.S. military had $40 million at their disposal for civilian projects through the so-called Commander's Emergency Response Program (CERP). These resources were intended to help the military win the support—the "hearts and minds"—of the Afghan population. By 2010 the amount had reached $1 billion—spent by military personnel without professional experience or knowledge, without adequate advice from civilian-aid experts, and very often without consultation with the Afghans. The civilian assistance was becoming more and more militarized. It was the opposite of an exit strategy. It was an entrenchment policy. The military structures were becoming more and more permanent and the Afghans increasingly dependent on them.

In December 2009 Mark Ward and one of his staff reviewed the information we had available about civilian projects implemented by military PRTs. Altogether, 22,000 projects had been implemented, and they could determine the value of 18,000 of them. Over 80 percent cost less than $100,000 and were basically projects the Afghans would have been able to implement themselves had they been given the resources. Mark Ward characterized them as "low-hanging fruits" or "quick-impact, quick-collapse" projects, easy to implement in the short term, but vulnerable because they did not involve the Afghans enough to ensure that they could be maintained over time. A real development of the country would require greater resources directed to projects that could generate employment, provide income for the Afghan budget, and enhance Afghan knowledge in order to ensure maintenance and sustainability.

The Agha Khan Development Network (AKDN) was perhaps the most prominent example of how foreign donor could have a lasting impact on local Afghan communities. The AKDN did not select single projects for a village or a community, but tried to shape a local development strategy in close consultations with local inhabitants. It could include projects that would bring several communities together around shared interests, such as water procurement. They were based on total Afghan ownership, local accountability, and local pride. The Afghans cared about them because these projects were their own, in contrast to so many of the projects implemented by international military.

One of the myths of the international presence in Afghanistan is that the military is well coordinated under one command, while the civilian side is uncoordinated and chaotic. From my previous years of weekly meetings at NATO headquarters in Brussels, I knew that this was not the case. And my experience in Kabul confirmed that the military side was equally fragmented. Of course, ISAF had one commander. But until October 2008, he did not have command of the forces under Operation Enduring Freedom (OEF). Most U.S. Special Forces were not under his command. Some of them were not even under the OEF, but under a separate CIA command. The ISAF

commander could not instruct forces from various ISAF contributors according to what he saw as his requirements. Most ISAF
countries had restrictions with regard to where and how they could
operate. Some of them had serious limitations with regard to the use
of force. Some could not operate after dark. Others spent little time
outside their bases and had sporadic contact with the population.
They shared a commander, but apart from that they shared little.
Coordination on the military side was just as inadequate as it was
on the civilian side.

I agreed when prominent ISAF representatives urged us to
speed up our coordination of civilian work; however, if the military
had been prepared to coordinate its own activities with the Afghan
government and report its projects to them and to us, that in itself
would have been a major contribution to civilian coordination. The
irritation among Afghan leaders, President Karzai, and members of
his government over these "parallel structures" was growing. Karzai
saw them as rivals to the development of Afghan institutions, and
he was right.

The call for a comprehensive concept was the favorite theme
in early 2008, but little had been done to clarify what that really
meant. There was a strong desire among military officers to draw
the UN and other civilian actors into a strategy that was shaped by
military considerations, not least in the conflict provinces. During
strategy discussions, UNAMA and NGOs were sometimes invited
to give their presentations. But military considerations and requirements were at the basis for these discussions. UNAMA neither could
nor would convince UN agencies or NGOs to follow international
military into conflict zones and carry out development work under
its protection. That would have drawn civilian organizations into a
military logic they did not share.

To me, a comprehensive concept was something wider; it
meant a shared understanding of how our overall resources could be
employed with the greatest impact. Mark Ward and I wanted to real-

locate resources from conflict provinces in the south and east, where the impact of aid was low, to more stable provinces in other parts of the country, where the impact could be high. We already saw the conflict spreading to stable parts of the country. There was no reason to believe that this trend would not continue. I feared that provinces in the north and the central parts of the country could become "swing provinces," vulnerable to discontent. We needed a policy of immunization, where more stable provinces were vaccinated against instability and conflict. Economic development and better governance were important components of this vaccination policy.

A reallocation of economic resources was also important for another reason: The engines for economic growth were not in the unstable provinces in the south and east of Afghanistan. They were in some of the major cities and stable provinces in the north and center of the country. In these regions, there were significant resources that had so far been neglected but could change the entire country if harnessed. If we wanted economic growth based on Afghan resources and not on international aid, then the current distribution of assistance was counterproductive and represented a bad investment.

A visit to Bamiyan province in the central highlands confirmed this thinking. The province had great potential for tourism as well as industry. The largest iron ore deposits of Asia were to be found in this area and other stable parts of the country. There were several other valuable metal reserves and precious stones. Clearly, bringing these resources out of the mountains and to the market would require significant investments in infrastructure. But such investments would generate sustainable economic growth.

When the British used several thousand troops to move a turbine to the huge Kajaki Dam in Helmand in 2008, I wondered how long it would take to get the turbine operational in one of the most dangerous provinces in Afghanistan. Three years after the turbine was transported to the dam, it was still not operational.

It had been impossible to move cement and other necessary materials to the dam because of the constant threat from the Taliban. The Canadians identified the Dahla Dam in Kandahar as one of their flagship projects. But in late 2011 the dam was still not operational and the project had proven to be much more complicated than anticipated due to resistance from the Taliban. Clearly, the amounts of time and resources spent on such projects would have had a very different impact if they had been invested in infrastructure projects in stable parts of Afghanistan.

It was not difficult to discover other misuse of resources and poorly planned projects. During a visit to Kandahar province, I passed a cold-storage facility for agricultural products. It was a huge building. When I praised the project enthusiastically to our local staff member, he agreed: "It *could* have been very useful—if the dimensions had been right." For the moment, it was simply too big, and the Afghans could not afford the fuel to keep it cold. It was used as a storage facility, but not for agricultural products.

During a visit to Jalalabad, we were invited to a sewing course for young girls. I looked at one of the little girls and told her how good it was to be able to learn a profession she could use for the rest of her life. Her reply was clear: "I would much rather learn to read and write. When I am finished here, I cannot bring the sewing machine with me, and my family cannot afford to buy one." What was the point of an employment project for young girls who had no opportunity to make use of their new knowledge? Before leaving the province, we spent a couple of hours with the American PRT. The commander informed us that he had $140–50 million at his disposal for civilian projects. And he could easily have spent much more, he told us. When Hanne Melfald asked him if he reported his activities to the Afghan government, he seemed confused.

In Kabul, a new Chinese-built hospital was opened in 2009. Karzai invited me to join him for the opening. It was an impressive building with 350 hospital beds; however, it was built without any ventilation in a city full of pollution and with regular sandstorms. Two years after it was inaugurated, patients were still not treated at the hospital.

A U.S. power plant in the outskirts of Kabul was not only seriously delayed in its construction but also became almost $50 million more expensive than planned. In the end, the price was more than $300 million. It was so advanced, and the operational costs would be so expensive, that Afghans would not be able to run and maintain it. It was fueled with costly diesel, and produced power at a price that was seven times more expensive than the power line built in 2009 from Uzbekistan in the north to Kabul. As a result, this modern U.S.-built facility was mostly idle. U.S. investigators themselves questioned whether the project was economically justifiable.

ISAF and other international partners have for ten years imported enormous amounts of fuel and other products required to keep the international forces in Afghanistan. These imports, representing a very significant part of Afghanistan's total imports, comes via many hundred transportation companies using a large number of private security companies to get commodities safely into the country and to their final destination. As early as 2002, a so-called technical agreement was signed between the ISAF commander and the Afghan interim authorities. It included provisions concerning imports for ISAF and tax exemptions for such imports. The authority to determine what would be covered by this tax exemption was given to the ISAF commander. Over the years, this provision has been interpreted in a liberal way, to say the least. Employees of the smallest subcontractors have been exempted from paying taxes to the government. Millions of dollars have been lost in state income.

Perhaps this was a sensible arrangement in 2002, when ISAF was still modest in size and limited to the capital itself, and when there was only an interim authority on the Afghan side. Since then, ISAF has grown from a few thousand to 150,000 soldiers across Afghanistan. An Afghan government and Afghan institutions are in place, all of which need to finance their activities. During the summer of 2010, the Afghan government asked to renegotiate the existing agreement, or at least to redefine what should be covered by the tax exemption. So far it has not resulted in a new and more reasonable arrangement.

Since the importation of goods to ISAF and other internationals requires so many companies for transportation and for security, control arrangements break down and goods disappear illegally into the open Afghan market. Again, it weakens the government's ability to collect revenues, distorts the competition, and punishes companies that try to operate within the rules. And due to lack of accountability, money disappears into the hands of wealthy Afghans, who are often behind such companies, and is paid to local officials, criminal gangs, and to the Taliban in order to ensure safe passage. It is a system that has become so unwieldy that nobody is able to monitor the money trail.

The high salaries for international consultants (people that the Afghans never asked for), the profits that disappear back to the donor country to enrich contractors, the lost revenues, and the protection money that ends up illegally in so many hands—all of this is seen by Afghans as evidence of corruption on the part of the international community. Sometimes the criticism is unfair. Strict tender policies were intended to avoid corruption, but they also limit the choice of contractors, giving the chosen few the opportunity to earn huge amounts and driving up the cost of development projects.

Of course there were achievements during the first years after the Taliban was forced from power. Around 85 percent of the population now had access to some kind of health service. More than 5,000 health workers were trained and infant mortality was reduced significantly. Tens of thousands of children grew up who would have died during their first year if these improvements had not taken place. In 2010, seven million children were attending school; almost one-third of them were young women. Under Taliban rule the overall number was less than one million and girls were practically excluded. There were ten universities in the country compared to one during the Taliban regime. Thousands of miles of road were rehabilitated or constructed. The National Solidarity Program had launched 52,000 projects in 27,000 villages in order to provide water and roads and to build schools or clinics. However, these projects had one basic feature in common: they all had an Afghan ownership. They were nation-wide plans that brought the donor community together, projects built by Afghan hands and with money provided according to a joint plan. Afghans developed the capacity and knowledge required to ensure that projects could be sustained and would not collapse once the international community turned to the next conflict. These were examples we could all build on for the future.

CHAPTER SEVEN

DO WE HAVE A STRATEGY?

A large donor conference was scheduled to take place in Paris on June 12, 2008. The purpose was to endorse the newly finished Afghan National Development Strategy (ANDS) and to secure the funds required to implement it over the next five years. The ANDS was a product of two years of work and consultations among Afghans and with the international community. It covered all aspects of development. By being so comprehensive, it lacked focus and allowed donors to continue their policies unchanged based on their own priorities. Everything could be interpreted as being in line with the ANDS. There was, of course, a desperate need for almost everything in Afghanistan. But to stimulate sustainable development, we had to focus on a few areas that would have an impact across the board. The declaration from the Paris conference therefore had to support the ANDS but also establish priorities that could prompt donors and Afghans to think in a more strategic way. Schools, clinics, and roads were important, but to finance them in the future the Afghan state would require income.

Even if the Paris conference could be successful in terms of money pledged by the donors, we had to look beyond this horizon. One day the generosity of the donors would come to an end, and aid money would gradually disappear. New conflicts and challenges would take international attention away from Afghanistan. It could happen at almost any time. A long-term policy of generating Afghan income to replace donor resources was needed to enable Afghans to pay for the maintenance of donor projects and for the further development of their society. Agriculture and infrastructure were two areas of critical importance to future economic growth, but both had been neglected for years and did not have the right kind of leadership on the Afghan side. The same applied to the development of civilian institutions and better local government. These three areas had to be given greater attention.

The first drafts for the concluding declaration were written by key Afghan ministers, UNAMA staff, and some of the ambassadors in Kabul. The final product was presented to President Karzai. The declaration was to be issued under the authority of President Karzai, Secretary-General Ban Ki-moon, and President Nicolas Sarkozy, as the conference's host. I went through the text with the Afghan president and some of his closest ministers over the course of several lengthy meetings. Karzai was pleased with what he read and had few comments. But he had problems with two paragraphs: The first included a commitment to fight corruption more vigorously; the other emphasized the importance of giving civil society a greater role in the development of the Afghan society.

This was the first time I heard Karzai insisting on an argument that became very familiar to me over the next two years: that corruption was primarily a phenomenon caused by the international community, not by Afghans. There was no Afghan tradition for corruption, he claimed. I urged him to address the subject at the Paris conference to reassure the international public opinion that he recognized the problem and that he was personally prepared to act more forcefully. Criticism in the international community was growing rapidly. Donors needed to hear from the president himself that he would take his share of the burden in the fight against corruption. That would make it easier for them to ensure support for a long-term engagement in their own public. He would be applauded by donors and international media instead of being criticized, I told him. It was the same message I had asked President Bush to emphasize in his regular discussions with Karzai.

But Karzai stubbornly resisted, with his ministers sitting as silent supporters. A joint review of both international and Afghan practices could be acceptable to him, but not a one-sided commitment by the Afghan government. U.S. Ambassador William Wood also tried to convince Karzai to accept a more binding commitment. Together, we had hoped for assistance from President Bush in his video discussions with Karzai. But in the weeks leading up to the Paris conference, Bush did not raise the subject of corruption with Karzai. Bill Wood and I were fighting a hopeless fight. If Karzai had never heard about the corruption problem from Bush, why would he listen to Ambassador Wood and me?

Karzai was equally reluctant with regard to the role of the civil society. Attempts to convince him of its critical role for the development of Afghanistan were unsuccessful. He was skeptical about the civil society I was talking about, arguing that it was often corrupt and ineffective. He saw many of the new nongovernmental organization more as opponents than supporters and had criticized them publicly in the same terms. To him, civil society was mainly the traditional Afghan structures, the elders of the local communities and the religious leaders. Nobody talked more to them than he did.

Despite these disagreements, the Paris conference was a success in the end. Donors committed themselves to providing over $20 billion over the next five years, with the United States being by far the largest contributor, although upon reviewing the commitments, it became clear that only $14 billion came from new commitments. In terms of providing a clearer political agenda, I was also reasonably satisfied. The Afghan government committed itself to better accountability with regard to the spending of donor resources. Together with the Afghans, we succeeded in highlighting a small number of priorities that would be crucial for a sustainable development: greater emphasis on agriculture, infrastructure, and the strengthening of civilian institutions. The declaration also included some key principles for a more effective use of donor money. First of all, a commitment was given by donors that all assistance had to be subject to coordination, including the very significant resources spent through the military PRTs. Second, assistance had to reach all parts of the country, not just the insecure provinces. There was a commitment to avoid parallel international structures (such as the PRTs) that could compete with Afghan institutions. Donor countries had agreed to a set of priorities and to some guiding principles that could ensure greater aid effectiveness.

The difficult issue of corruption ended in a compromise very close to what President Karzai had wanted: an obligation to engage in a joint audit of spending between the Afghans and the international community. But there was no interest among international donors to engage in an exercise of this kind. Donors already had regulations in place to make sure that their resources were spent according to strict rules. The need for improvement was on the Afghan side, they claimed.

Unfortunately, during the following months, it became clear that the Paris Declaration had little impact on the donor community. Donor practices and policies continued as before. I felt that we had embarked on a Sisyphean exercise, where progress one day was followed by setbacks the next. But I hoped that, gradually, progress would be consolidated and that we had started a process that could lead to improvements in donor policies and aid effectiveness in the end.

At the time of the Paris conference, I had been in Afghanistan for two and a half months. My frustration with Karzai and his ministers over the corruption problem was increasing. But as time passed, my views also became more nuanced. Karzai was right in many respects where international practices and donor policies were concerned. Big donors did not have the control they claimed to have over their own resources. Over and over again, I was surprised to see how ineffectively resources were spent and how insufficient the mechanisms of accountability were. Over time, some of the donors themselves came to see this as well. The new U.S. Special Investigator General for Afghan Reconstruction (SIGAR) produced a number of reports revealing the shortcomings of some of the U.S. assistance programs. Other donors were unfortunately not as open and prepared to examine the effectiveness of their engagement.

CHAPTER EIGHT

CIVILIAN DEATHS: FIRST CONFLICT WITH THE MILITARY

"You are serving the Taliban," a prominent Western diplomat told me. "This is really not helpful." I received this message and others like it many times after the dramatic events that unfolded at the end of August 2008. At that time I had been invited by the Afghan government to a conference of provincial governors in Kandahar. Senior ministers from Kabul were present, as well as the ISAF commander, General David McKiernan. It was the first conference of its kind, an initiative by Jelani Popal, the head of a new Afghan government institution, the Independent Directorate for Local Government (IDLG). The intention was to bring government officials from Kabul and provincial authorities into a closer dialogue.

But August 22 will be remembered for something very different than the complaints of governors about lack of funds and police. Before our departure from Kabul to Kandahar that morning, we had heard reports of an attack by U.S. and Afghan forces against a village called Azizabad in the west of the country. The first reports indicated that a significant number of civilians might have been killed during the attack. Karzai's office mentioned figures as high as 100. ISAF had denied the reports and claimed that only insurgents had been killed. The operation had been aimed at a prominent Taliban commander.

Following a long period of surveillance, he had been tracked down and killed.

General David McKiernan, the ISAF commander, was sitting next to me at the conference table in Kandahar. We were both engaged in intense discussions with our respective staff members. The topic was the same: What had happened last night in Azizabad? From the UN offices in Kabul and Herat we received worrying information about civilian casualties. Hanne Melfald left the conference room to send a press release to our Kabul office expressing our deep concern. On her way, she was held back by an ISAF officer. He insisted that it had been a successful attack against a Taliban leader. The rumors that many unarmed civilians had been killed were false. Of course, his intervention only served to make my Norwegian adviser even more determined, and the press statement was transmitted to Kabul for immediate release.

During the next few days, our own UN experts were able to visit the village several times and see the damage. New information came in constantly from eyewitnesses and local authorities. It seemed solid and consistent. The lists of victims had been checked over and over again and were as reliable as they possibly could be under the circumstances. On August 26, we sent out another press release condemning the attack and estimating the number of civilian casualties at around ninety villagers.

U.S. representatives and ISAF responded quickly. Ambassador Bill Wood was angry, General McKiernan was bitter, and they both maintained their positions claiming that U.S. soldiers had been in the village after the attack and that they could verify that the number of civilians killed was a handful at most. There had even been a team of journalists from Fox News embedded with the U.S. units in the village and could confirm the United States's account. The UN experts simply did not believe that U.S. forces had been in the village after the attack; they would have been chased away by the angry crowd. We checked if Fox News had really been there. Again, we could only find a report filed by a Fox News team from an American base in the Herat area. There was no footage from the village itself.

Our American interlocutors insisted that the attack had been successful and that important insurgents had been killed. Why had we not consulted them before releasing our numbers? Why would their own soldiers, who had been on the ground when it happened, not tell them the truth? I understood their reactions. General McKiernan could not believe U.S. officers were hiding the facts from him. And we were not talking about two versions that varied slightly; there were two very different stories. I wondered at one stage if we were talking about two different attacks. The pressure on our own media staff was unpleasant. Foreign journalists, American in particular, questioned our figures and our version of the attack. Authorities in Washington as well as in Kabul were doing their best to undermine the credibility of our information. Meanwhile, the Afghan Independent Human Rights Commission (AIHRC) had carried out its own investigation and come to conclusions similar to ours. The Afghan government had already announced their findings, claiming a larger number of casualties than we had presented. But it was something special when the UN came out so clearly. It lent credibility to the story, making a stronger impression than if it had been presented by Afghan institutions and authorities alone.

The powerful opposition from the U.S. military and political authorities was intimidating. For a while I was concerned, even doubtful: Was it possible that we had been manipulated in some way? But our best human rights experts in Kabul and our Herat office had been engaged in this case. They had been well received in the village several times. And there were people in our team who knew Afghan society well. We had already received photographs from inside the building that served as a mosque. The number of bodies of young children was clear enough evidence that the U.S. version of events was incorrect. I showed some of the photos to my British colleague, Ambassador Sherard Cowper-Coles. He was deeply distressed and encouraged me to stand firm.

Soon, the first video footage from a mobile phone appeared, then from a camera. More footage followed. My staff and I sat down in front of the computer and looked at the videos over and over again. I screened them slowly, stopped to count dead bodies and note down the color of a blanket and the angle of a young girl's head. Had I counted her twice? In the end, I concluded that there was no way we could be wrong. And we stuck to the number that we had given a few days earlier: Around ninety civilians had been killed and among them were around sixty children. Perhaps there could have been a Taliban among them, or even two or three. But that would not change the story. It was obvious that the Azizabad attack was a gross mistake and represented a serious violation of existing regulations for the use of military force.

Americans as well as some Afghans continued to discredit the information we had. At NATO, the American delegation claimed that the videos were manipulated. A very prominent Afghan politician said that it was all an Iranian ploy and that the UN had been tricked. There had been Afghan soldiers in Azizabad with the Americans. Rumors said that they had gone into the village after the attack and even into the mosque. The Afghan military obviously also had reasons to discredit us and to contradict the figures that the Afghan government had announced.

I invited General McKiernan and Ambassador Wood separately to see the videos at my residence in Palace 7. Neither of them said much after having seen two of them. But it was obvious that they now had serious doubts about the version that was originally presented to them. I could understand their disappointment. To discover that their military officers provided such incorrect information must have been a shock. It was no longer possible to reject the story we had presented. But the pressure from Washington continued. We were asked to participate in a joint investigation with the international military and the Afghan army. At UN headquarters in New York, there seemed to be some support for this initiative. I disagreed. Both the other participants would have an interest in hiding facts. The UN could come under serious pressure to join a consensus that differed from the information we had. Judging from reports from decision-makers in Washington, I also wondered if the information we had provided in Kabul had reached them. It seemed that they did not know about the photos and the videos that we had obtained. I had no interest in continuing the debate over figures, a debate that could last for weeks. It had been important to investigate and to collect our evidence. Now it was time for the next phase: discussing measures to reduce the danger of similar attacks instead of continuing to quarrel over the Azizabad incident.

I decided to call the secretary of state, Condoleezza Rice. In the beginning, she criticized me for not having consulted the United States before making the figures public. Of course she had a point. But we had experience from another recent case: Following an attack on a wedding party in Nangarhar in eastern Afghanistan on July 6, the initial reports had indicated that forty civilians had been killed, including the bride. In that case, we did not issue our own findings in order to consult the Americans. But the consultations dragged out, making the UN appear weak and indecisive. That could not be allowed to happen again. In my view, once we were clear about our own findings, we had no choice: our mandate and our credibility compelled us to make the results of our investigation public. I informed Rice about the detailed work that had been undertaken, about the photos and videos we had at our disposal. I would never have reacted the way I did if there had been doubts. But I also told her that the time had come to bring the discussion to a more constructive phase and look at what could be done to prevent this from happening again. When the conversation was over, I thought it had been useful and that Rice understood my thinking, even if she did not explicitly accept my account of what had happened.

The same afternoon, I called the NATO secretary general, Jaap de Hoop Scheffer. This was an easier conversation. Again, I told him about the evidence we had collected and hoped that we could look toward the future instead of quarreling about what had happened. He knew that—with eleven years at NATO—I had no interest in damaging the alliance. Both of us were irritated about the fact that McKiernan had become my "opponent" in the Azizabad case. He was the ISAF commander. The attack had not been carried out by ISAF forces, but by U.S. and Afghan forces that were not under ISAF command. I had tried repeatedly to contact the U.S. officers who had been in command of the operation, but without success. Instead, McKiernan was the one who had responded to my criticism and come to my residence to see the videos. Now there was a risk that public criticism would unfairly damage ISAF.

U.S. media also started to rely more on our version. Carlotta Gall from *The New York Times*, probably the most experienced journalist in Kabul, made her own trip to Azizabad. A few days later, her article was finally printed. It supported our version of what had happened. She wrote that another dead child had been discovered in the rubble ten days after the attack. From then on our figures and our investigation were widely accepted and became the basis for the international as well as Afghan coverage of the incident.

The U.S. military opened a new investigation into the attack. I was assured that I would be kept informed about the outcome, but I never heard from the U.S. military again. Eventually, I read in the media that the investigation had been concluded and that, according to the United States, more than thirty civilians had lost their lives. It was never explained to me how the investigation ended up with this figure. We decided not to go into another round of discussions but only to refer to the outcome of our own investigation. The new

U.S. figure was a concession, even if the United States still had not accepted full responsibility for the tragedy in Azizabad. In the meantime, we had received information that the reliable "intelligence" that led to the attack had been provided by Afghans engaged in a local dispute. It was yet another example of how difficult it is to navigate in an Afghan reality where so much remains hidden from us.

Our experience with the U.S. military during this incident reflected a pattern we had seen before and would see again. At first, the United States or ISAF would deny that civilians had been killed in an incident. Later, they would reluctantly be forced to admit that they had been wrong and that there were civilian casualties. I was surprised that this almost automatic reflex was not replaced by a more credible approach, which would leave the international military a way out and not result in a loss of face every time it happened.

During the following weeks, there were expressions of gratitude from Afghans for the work we had done and the fact that we had stood firm on our findings. It was not often that our efforts led to such a number of reactions from politicians as well as from the Afghan public. The chairman of the upper house of the National Assembly, Sibgatullah Mojadeddi, told me that he had also warned Condoleezza Rice against the dangerous consequences of civilian casualties. Karzai was grateful that we had been firm and clear even if it meant confronting the United States. And international human rights advocates expressed surprise that we had challenged the international military so forcefully.

On September 29, I briefed the NATO Council in Brussels. I was still angered by the controversy with the military in Kabul. The NATO ambassadors found me less cooperative than they had hoped and expected. When they raised the need for a comprehensive approach to the conflict and for closer cooperation between the military and the UN, I must have offended some of them. The new U.S. ambassador, Kurt Volker, sent a cable to his superiors in Washington complaining that I did not want the UN and ISAF to be seen as part of one mission. Volker reported that I had given disappointing answers to the council, and he encouraged his political masters in Washington to bring me into line when I visited the U.S. capital shortly after. That did not happen. On the contrary, Stephen Hadley, the national security advisor, told me that he should have called me immediately when the Azizabad incident occurred. He should have understood that we would not have insisted the way we did if there had not been solid facts behind our criticism.

CHAPTER NINE

KARZAI BECOMES CONFRONTATIONAL

As a result of the Azizabad attack, Karzai demanded a new formal agreement regulating the presence of U.S. and other international forces on Afghan territory. Defense Minister Wardak sent a text to NATO in January 2009. A similar proposal had already been sent to Washington. I agreed with Karzai. The technical agreement between ISAF and the Afghan interim administration was from 2002 and, as I have mentioned, clearly out of date.

The text Defense Minister Wardak had sent to NATO was ambitious, too ambitious in some respects. But it was a starting point for discussions. I sent a letter of support to the NATO secretary-general and asked for a process of negotiations to be initiated. There was silence from NATO headquarters. At the end of January, Karzai's spokesman announced that if they did not answer within a month, then the Afghan government would let the people decide on the future of the international forces in their country. Soon Wardak's text was published in Afghan media. Karzai's public statements were probably not the smartest tactical moves he had made, but the continuing silence from Brussels was humiliating. My own support for him was—again—seen as "not helpful" from the U.S. embassy and the NATO office in Kabul.

I still believe that it was a mistake not to accommodate Karzai quickly. The lack of a serious response contributed to the impression that Afghanistan could be treated as a no-man's land instead of as a sovereign country. It reinforced the irritation in the presidential palace in Kabul every time there were civilian casualties. And it strengthened the impression in the Afghan public that even if the Afghan government had invited these forces to Afghanistan, it had little influence over their behavior.

On February 13, a limited agreement was signed between Defense Minister Wardak and General McKiernan. It gave the Afghans greater responsibility for planning and implementation of operations, including house searches and arrests. But it did not have any significant impact on the ground, and it was not the agreement the president had sought. For me, it was a question of demonstrating respect for the Afghan government. Our interests were not well served by giving the impression that we could ignore legitimate Afghan requests. We could all be frustrated at times by what we saw as unreasonable initiatives and outbursts from President Karzai. But if he and his government were not treated with respect, it would damage our own efforts further.

Karzai's irritation grew remarkably toward the end of 2008. I had not seen this side of his character since I arrived in late March. On the contrary, he had given the impression of wanting to avoid unnecessary confrontations. I had seen him express frustration in private with those whom he trusted. Now his increasingly confrontational approach and attacks on the international military forces shocked visiting ministers as well as ambassadors in Kabul. I understood his reactions and shared many of his concerns. The constant civilian casualties not only meant the loss of innocent lives, but also stimulated further recruitment to the Taliban. I feared that if we did not get the discussion about civilian casualties under control, but instead allowed the public confrontations to continue, the inevitable result would also be an even more skeptical public opinion in countries that had sent their sons and daughters to Afghanistan. Foreign delegations expected gratitude, not criticism. They came out of the presidential palace deeply upset.

In October 2008 the lines of command of the international forces were improved. McKiernan became the commander of ISAF as well as of U.S. forces in Afghanistan, with the exception of some of the Special Forces that continued to be under CIA command. We now had one commander to relate to and did not have to look for an OEF commander who was reluctant to discuss his operations. Toward the end of 2008, General McKiernan also issued tactical directives to ISAF forces and to the U.S. forces operating under OEF. He emphasized the importance of showing sensitivity to Afghan culture, traditions, and religion and of demonstrating caution and proportionality in the use of military force. He also underlined the importance of initiating investigations when claims of civilian casualties were made and to admit civilian losses as soon as possible if they had occurred. Both were important steps to reduce the danger of civilian casualties and the damage they caused in the relationship between the international forces and the Afghan government. But McKiernan did not receive the praise he deserved for his efforts. He was abruptly removed by the new administration in Washington in May 2009 and replaced by General Stanley McChrystal. I was sad to see McKiernan go in such a way. McChrystal's arrival brought the relationship between international forces and the Afghan population to the center of military thinking in Afghanistan. But it was McKiernan who had started this work.

CHAPTER TEN

MORE MISTAKES AND MORE CASUALTIES

McKiernan's new directives did not bring the confrontation over civilian casualties to an end. It would be unrealistic to expect that mistakes would not be made again and that civilian casualties could be avoided altogether. The attack on Azizabad was the most dramatic during my time in Kabul in terms of number of the casualties and the political tension it caused. But there were others that also made a strong impression on me.

Late one evening in April 2009, a car was attacked from the air by two British helicopters in Helmand province. The car was illuminated by the lights from the helicopters, shot at, and brought to a halt without any hostile act from its passengers. One of the passengers ran for cover behind a stone. He "took position behind a stone," I was told by the ISAF military who later briefed me about the incident. But he was not armed and did not prepare to counter-attack. The man was probably scared to death. One of the helicopters approached the car from behind, and the soldiers shot through the rear windows, "in order to be able to see those inside." By the end of the attack, the driver and all the passengers had been killed, with the exception of a little baby. Several hundred Afghans gathered at the funeral, shouting slogans against the international forces. Many prominent Afghan politicians were present. There was nothing that could possibly have justified the attack. When British Prime Minister Gordon Brown visited Kabul later the same month, I informed him about the attack and complained about the behavior of his soldiers.

A few days later, on May 9, 2009, U.S. planes attacked the village of Gerani in Farah province. Again there were suspicions of a significant number of civilian casualties. The high tension in the village made it impossible to enter and to carry out an investigation. It seemed clear that the Taliban had been in the village when the attack started. But the U.S. forces continued the attack by air until late in the evening. Had they used force in a way that was proportional to the threat? Should they have understood that there was a serious risk of loss of innocent lives? The local authorities and Karzai's office claimed that more than 100 civilian lives had been lost. The U.S. military disagreed. Several days later, we were able to interview the local population and the authorities. We concluded that around sixty-four women and children had been killed. The men that had lost their lives were not included, as there was no way of determining who among them had belonged to the Taliban. We prepared to issue a statement saying that the attacking forces should have understood that the risk of civilian casualties was high and that greater restraint should have been shown.

Before we issued the statement, I received a phone call from a U.S. military official, who had arrived to investigate the incident. A U.S. delegation had just returned from the area where the attack had taken place. General Raymond A. Thomas was in charge of the investigation. He had heard from the U.S. embassy that I was preparing to issue a statement and wanted to brief me immediately. The general and his team arrived in my office with several hours of video recordings taken from the plane that had launched the attacks. We spent the rest of the evening looking at the tapes and discussing what we saw. In the darkness, we could see white dots moving across the screen. They were Taliban fighters, General Thomas told us, fighters running for cover. We could follow them and see the attacks against buildings in the village. General Thomas concluded that the pilots had operated in full accordance with their rules of engagement and that no mistakes had been made. We were not convinced. The last attack late in the dark evening was particularly troublesome. How could the Americans know that there were no civilians in the building that was hit? To us it seemed likely that this was precisely where civilians would be hiding. But we had to be on solid ground. So far we lacked clear evidence, and I refrained from issuing our statement.

As had happened in the past with similar incidents, General Thomas promised to keep us informed about his further work, but it was the last we heard from him. Much later the media reported from Washington that the attacking forces that evening were reprimanded for having underestimated the risk of civilian casualties. Existing regulations had not been respected; for instance, the pilots had not kept their targets under constant observation and were therefore unable to verify if there were civilians in the building that was last attacked. We had been right in our assessment, and I felt bitter about not having publicized our findings. The reassuring attitude of General Thomas and the subsequent admission of mistakes, combined with the lack of information provided to us, made me even more skeptical of the U.S. military. There was so much spin, and sometimes deception, that the trust between us suffered a serious blow. I remembered the U.S. ambassador to NATO who had warned me against surprising the United States on the issue of civilian casualties. I would certainly have preferred a constructive dialogue. But my impression was that the denial reflex still dominated the thinking of the U.S. military when such situations occurred and made constructive dialogue impossible.

Later I learned about the investigation carried out by the International Red Cross (ICRC). They had concluded that 100 civilians had died. The ICRC was also confident that the little bright dots we saw moving across the screen that evening when General Thomas showed us the video were not Taliban fighters, but civilians trying desperately to escape.

On a later occasion, I again remained silent when I should have reacted sharply. On September 4, 2009, two fuel tankers had been attacked from the air in the northeastern province of Kunduz. The tankers had been hijacked by the Taliban but were stuck in a dried-out riverbed. The German military had asked for air support, and the attack had led to the loss of a large number of civilian lives. People seemed to have gone to the trucks during the night to collect gasoline from the tankers for their own use. I could not see that there was any legitimate justification for requesting air support. The Germans had not been involved in any armed confrontation, and no German soldier was in any immediate danger. The attack led to an intense debate in Germany and forced the chief of defense to resign from his position. Jung, who had been defense minister when the incident took place and in the meantime had moved to another position in the government, also had to resign. My reason for not reacting was related to the political situation in Germany at the time. The attack took place in the middle of an election campaign and I did not want to be drawn into it. But it was with a bad feeling that I kept silent.

Even if the air attacks caused the greatest number of casualties, they were far from the only cause of anger among ordinary Afghans. The use of dogs; the unannounced visits to women's quarters in hospitals and private homes; and the nightly raids and house searches, which often ended in the loss of innocent lives; were all seen by Afghans as violations of their culture and their norms.

During a visit to Kandahar, I was sitting with an elderly man from a village next to a military base. In the night flares were fired to enable the military to see any movement around the ISAF compound during darkness. One of the flares had landed on his son's back and caused serious burns. Twice the father had walked to the entrance of the camp and asked for a meeting to inform the base commanders about the incident. For two entire days he had been waiting in vain. It was a double humiliation: first, he had experienced the injuries to his son; then he had waited without being able to raise his legitimate complaint. Afghans do not easily forget such humiliation, and the wounds color their view of the foreign neighbors.

An old Pashtun from Uruzgan was arrested by international military in 2008, handcuffed, and forced to walk through difficult terrain. He was suspected of links to the insurgency. The man was transferred to Kabul, where the president heard about him and invited him to the palace. At the end of his story, the old man said, "I don't think I will live long enough to see this country become our own again." To Karzai, it was as if a knife had been sunk into his back. The old man was humiliated by what he had experienced, and the president was humiliated by what he had heard.

This and so many other stories remind me of what a Palestinian businessman told the Mitchell Commission during a visit to the Palestinian territory in 2001. Every day he had to pass through Israeli checkpoints with his children on the way to their school. Most often, the Israeli soldiers looked into his car and then allowed him to pass. But on regular occasions, they instructed him to step out of the car and lie face down while they examined him and the vehicle. The children were watching from their seats in the back of the car. To conclude his story, the businessman asked us, "Who am I to the children when they see me humiliated there on the ground?" Before we could respond, he gave the answer himself: "I am their hero. A father is his children's hero."

One morning during a period of intense debate over civilian casualties, I was on my way in my convoy from the UN office to the Ministry of Defense, which was a few hundred yards away on one of the safest roads in Kabul. My cars were stopped by U.S. soldiers, who forced us to a halt at the side of the road. One of my Romanian bodyguards stepped out of the car to explain that I was the head of the UN—as clearly indicated by the large UN sign on each side of the cars. Since the discussion seemed to continue without any progress, I also opened the door and stepped out on the road. The U.S. soldiers reacted promptly and pointed their automatic weapons at us. After a few intense minutes, the situation was solved when other U.S. military approached and saw the incident. The soldiers were part of the advance team of a recently arrived U.S. general. They wanted to keep the road clear and safe. The general was on his way to the same meeting that I was attending. When I entered the meeting room, my irritation was visible. I pointed at the U.S. generals sitting there, including McKiernan, and burst out, "This kind of behavior must come to an end. I have simply had enough!" McKiernan was obviously embarrassed but remained calm. On the other side of the table were Afghan ministers and advisors. They could barely hide their satisfaction. This time the outburst had come from me and not from them.

When I as UN envoy could experience such behavior at the hands of the international military, imagine the humiliations the Afghans endured—and they rarely received any apology. The talk about winning "hearts and minds" with village meetings, money, and projects was not worth much if this was how the Afghans experienced international forces in their daily lives. The reasons for these incidents varied. Possibly soldiers felt threatened and at risk. They may have reacted as the result of thoughtlessness, inadequate training, or a lack of understanding of Afghan culture and traditions. But these incidents were often a result of a lack of decent behavior, which would have provoked reactions in any society. Regardless, they created a crisis of confidence between the population and the inter-national military, a problem that General McChrystal understood well and that he placed at the top of his agenda when he arrived in Kabul.

Foreign representatives and media often characterize Karzai's reactions to such incidents as political tactic, a show for his constituency, in particular for the Pashtun population. But his reactions cannot be brushed aside as cynical or irrational behavior. Few things make Karzai feel as angry and humiliated as when he or Afghans are victims of a lack of respect. His reactions stem from the core of his personality and his intense pride. These are the incidents that made him threaten to join the Taliban, an unwise statement that shocked many politicians and media outlets in April of 2010. I have heard him make similar statements many times in private. What he is saying is that if you, as guests in my country, demonstrate such a lack of respect, then you also turn me into your enemy. Every mistake by the international military is also an attack against his credibility. He understands that it is impossible to eliminate fully the risk of civilian casualties. But if we had listened more carefully when his reactions first occurred, then many of the subsequent public confrontations could have been avoided.

UNAMA's work to address the civilian casualties led to criticism from several quarters. From parts of the international community, we were criticized for assisting the insurgency by drawing attention to mistakes of the international forces. Criticism from the Taliban intensified when we presented reports in 2010 which showed that the Taliban was increasingly responsible for the loss of civilian lives. Our regular statements were always widely reported. And I believe that they made a difference in the behavior of international and Afghan forces. Unfortunately, they were largely ignored by the insurgents and their leaders.

CHAPTER ELEVEN

GROWTH OF THE INSURGENCY

Our reactions were strongest when international forces had caused civilian casualties. It was in such cases that the debate really became heated and the confrontations were difficult to manage. The UN had to react; international forces had a UN mandate. And we had an interlocutor that we could easily reach. In contrast, when the Taliban or other insurgency networks committed similar acts, there were condemnations, but rarely anything more. On that side, there were no interlocutors to speak to. There was little hope of any change in the Taliban's behavior. Clearly attacks against civilians had increasingly become a key part of their strategy. There was a lack of balance in our reactions that made me feel uncomfortable.

I was embarrassed when Ambassador Frank Ricciardone, who had by then taken over as the deputy ambassador of the U.S. embassy, sent me an email in January 2010 in which he raised this lack of balance. We had just released the figures for civilian casualties in 2009. The headlines in the media were mostly that the number of such casualties had increased significantly. We should, of course, in our own presentations, have paid more attention to the fact that the number of casualties caused by the international and Afghan forces had gone down considerably.

By far the majority of the civilian casualties in 2009 had been caused by the insurgency—by the Taliban, the Haqqani network, and others. The figures for 2009 showed that this was the bloodiest year since the fall of the Taliban. Altogether, 2,412 civilians had lost their lives, an increase of 300 from 2008 and 900 compared to 2007. But casualties caused by the international and Afghan forces had gone down by 28 percent. That was a dramatic improvement. The insurgents had caused 67 percent of all these casualties; international and Afghan forces were responsible for 25 percent. The rest had been caused by others, including criminal groups. When the figures for 2010 were published in March 2011, the trends from 2009 continued: There was an overall increase in the number of civilian casualties to 2,770. But the international and Afghan forces were now responsible for only 16 percent of them. The insurgency had caused 75 percent.

In 2010, Mullah Omar had issued new guidance for the Taliban strategy. He had emphasized the need to avoid civilian loss of lives. But his statement was a piece of propaganda and did not lead to any changes. Its definition of civilian casualties was obviously different from ours. The Taliban considered representatives of civilian authorities and village leaders who had "cooperated" with the government or not cooperated with the Taliban—as well as their families—as legitimate targets. The emphasis on asymmetric warfare, with suicide attacks, road bombs, and car bombs increased. As a result, a large number of Afghans were killed simply because they happened to be in the wrong place at the wrong time.

There were an increasing number of attacks against schools and clinics. UNICEF reported that attacks related to schools increased to 613 during 2009. As a result of insecurity, 70 percent of the schools in Helmand and more than 80 percent in Zabul in the south of Afghanistan were at times closed, preventing girls in particular from receiving education. Aid workers and deliveries of humanitarian assistance were attacked and plundered by the Taliban as well as by criminal gangs. According to the Taliban, these aid workers were engaged in supporting an illegitimate government.

This was everyday life for many thousands of Afghans and for humanitarian NGOs in significant portions of Afghanistan. No figures and statistics could fully reflect the suffering inflicted by the Taliban on the population.

How was it then possible for the Taliban to recruit young people from the Afghan countryside to join the movement? And how is it still possible with 150,000 well-equipped international soldiers in the country, with an Afghan army that grows steadily, and with all the suffering caused by the Taliban?

There are many reasons, some of which we can identify and some of which are more difficult to understand. Many Afghans have lost confidence in the international forces. There is a crisis of confidence, as General McChrystal rightly stated in his strategic assessment of August 2009. People in the villages do not read or hear about the statistics produced by UNAMA or ISAF. They do not see McChrystal's strategic assessment and do not hear about tactical directives. And they cannot see any changes in the behavior of the forces the way we expect them to. A negative attitude to the international forces has taken hold and is extremely difficult to change. Afghans still experience or hear about incidents that confirm their impressions. Even if the numbers of casualties caused by international forces have gone down, the population now experiences other losses resulting from the military offensives in the south. They see their properties being destroyed, houses and other buildings flattened, agricultural land ruined, and even mosques leveled to the ground. The result is that significant parts of the population in these areas see the international community as invaders, not only in military terms, but also of their society in a wider sense, of their culture, religion, and traditions. It requires very little to maintain an impression once it has been created. While waiting on a street corner for a U.S. military convoy to pass in Kabul, one of our Afghan drivers said angrily, "The Americans have taken over our entire city!" It was quite incorrect, but this was how he—a person who worked every day with internationals—saw the situation in the capital.

The Afghans have heard about the vast resources that are provided by the international community to Afghanistan. But they do not see changes in their own lives that correspond to the expectations created by generous declarations from so many donors. There is a crisis of expectations that damages the reputation of international as well as Afghan authorities. Afghans firmly believe that vast resources go to corrupt international companies and to equally corrupt Afghans. And so a sense of bitterness spreads in the population.

Many Afghans see how their own authorities enrich themselves from donor money or from bribes. We complain about the culture of impunity; the Afghans feel it every day. Corruption and bribes demanded by police, justice officials, and local authorities hurt the poorest part of the population more than anybody else—those families who live on modest salaries and already find it difficult to survive. The 2010 estimates from "Integrity Watch Afghanistan" were revealing and frightening. Every year, the population pays $1 billion in bribes to these government officials, most of all to those who are set to enforce law and order. One in seven Afghans have had to pay such bribes, according to the report. Prominent positions within the police "service" in "interesting" areas can cost significant amounts of money, since such positions offer possibilities to collect money from illegal road blocks and other similar activities. Again, it is not only an Afghan phenomenon; I have witnessed the same in Bosnia, where skinny and badly paid police would randomly stop vehicles and demand cash before allowing them to continue. But the fact that it happens elsewhere does not make it more tolerable to the Afghan population.

I have spoken to many Afghans who describe in despair their experience with the justice system. If you do not have any money to offer, then your chances are slim. And if you happen to have financial resources, then you may very well be sent from one office to the next, with every official demanding his share, until your resources are gone.

Karzai sometimes claims that the big corruption is caused by the international community and that Afghan corruption is merely petty corruption. His claim is not true; here is a frightening relationship between international money and Afghan corruption, where Afghans amass wealth from donor resources. However, the "petty" corruption is almost equally serious in its effect on the population. If your monthly income is $60, a bribe of $20 does not seem so petty. It weakens the credibility and the legitimacy of the entire government structure and lowers the threshold for tolerating or even condoning attacks against the very same authorities.

These hostile attitudes against the international community and a government that is seen as lacking legitimacy have spread, often under the mantle of Islam, and are being preached every Friday from mosques across the country. Some of UNAMA's local Afghan employees often informed us that the mullahs were becoming more anti-Western and more critical of the government. A culture of anger has been allowed to spread, directed against the foreign presence and a government many feel is also foreign to them. The Pashtun population also meets these Afghan authorities in the shape of an army and a police force that are mainly recruited from and commanded by people from other ethnic groups. This reinforces their sense of alienation.

The Taliban is not "foreign" to the local communities in which it operates. Fighters are most often recruited from and operate within a few miles of their own villages. Families frequently send their sons to a madrassa in Pakistan for religious education and see them come back under Taliban influence. And it is not unusual for the head of a family to be intimidated into giving a son to the Taliban in exchange for security. The Taliban administers its own justice in an effective and brutal way. In areas outside government control, it is the only justice that exists. It is brutal and shocking to most Western representatives and also to many Afghans. But it provides a form of justice where the government enforces none. And it is a form of justice that Afghans have known for many generations; it is not exclusive to the Taliban period. There are ministers today in the Afghan government—some of whom are among the Taliban's fiercest opponents—who have administered the same kind of brutal justice in the past.

Many Afghans do not believe that the new institutions and the new government can provide a better life, only that they contribute to an atmosphere of corruption and lawlessness. And they feel that the international community has failed to bring them anything better. I have seen the same before, in the Balkans and elsewhere. It seems that the justice system is constantly neglected. We can build schools and health facilities. We can dig wells and build roads. We can even train and equip armies. But the justice system often seems to be at the bottom of the priority list, in no small part because finding the experts able to build a justice system in a very foreign environment is much harder, costlier, and more time consuming than any other task.

Of course, religious extremism plays a role in recruiting Taliban fighters. And there are young men who join for financial reasons in the absence of any other employment. But the main motives for recruitment today are, I believe, linked to the absence of a government people trust and the presence of international forces they fear. The combination of these two factors creates a fertile ground for recruitment. Grievances lead to recruitment and, once recruited, young Taliban fighters become victims of religious radicalization.

CHAPTER TWELVE

AFGHANISTAN'S WOMEN

The Constitution of Afghanistan is modern and guarantees men and women equal rights. It gives women 25 percent of the seats in the National Assembly, which exceeds most other countries by far. Afghanistan has signed a number of international human rights conventions. And the AIHRC is chaired by a woman. Around one-third of the seven million children attending school are girls, whereas under the Taliban they were basically excluded from education. An action plan for improving the condition of women in society has been adopted by the government. A law banning all sorts of violence against women has been signed by the president, but has still not been approved by the National Assembly. Despite these strides, women continue to be marginalized and subject to violence and discrimination in all parts of the country. The women of Afghanistan are hit hard by the combination of poverty, conflict, old traditions, and conservative interpretation of Islam.

Early during my time in Afghanistan, I was in an office in one of the provinces. The woman in front of me was struggling to tell me what had happened to her. Little by little, I heard a story of humiliation, brutality, and fear. I had heard similar stories before, but never directly from the victim. This woman had been engaged in the struggle for women's rights for years. She was one of few activists in the countryside, far from the capital, a person who every day put her life at risk. During the last months, she had received numerous threats. She had been afraid but continued her engagement. One night a group of men had entered her home, raped her, and abused her. The children had witnessed it all. Her husband was traveling elsewhere in Afghanistan but was returning soon.

Now she was full of fear. She did not fear the criminals, who had committed the crime against her. She feared her husband, her family and the others in her own town. Could she hide what had happened from him? What would be her future if it were discovered? She was afraid of being alienated from her children and her family, of having to leave them and possibly even being punished for adultery. She told her story little by little—a few words, then silence and tears. I had to hide my face in my hands. There was nothing I could do except listen.

In Bamiyan province, a family had discovered that their teenage daughter was pregnant. Her mother, assisted by one of the girl's brothers, cut her abdomen open with a knife and took the fetus out. Then she was stitched up again—and it all happened without any medical assistance or anesthesia, all because the family and the village could not be allowed to see that she was expecting a baby. The young girl almost died and was taken to a health clinic. Fortunately an American doctor saved her life. Afterwards she was taken care of by Sima Samar in one of her orphanages.

There was little that was unusual about these stories. Rape and violence against women is an everyday phenomenon in Afghanistan. Women and girls risk abuse in their homes and in their families, in their local communities, in offices, and in prisons and as a consequence of traditional ways of solving disputes between families. Sometimes the perpetrators have links to conservative and brutal warlords and power brokers, members of criminal gangs, and armed groups. Such people are above the law, and the perpetrators are almost never arrested or brought to court, nor are their crimes made known to the public. On the contrary it is the victims of violence and abuse that often become stigmatized and shamed for life.

Occasionally, a few brave people defy traditions and choose the long and difficult road of seeking justice. In Samangan province a young woman named Sara was raped by a gang of men in January 2006. Supported by her husband, she struggled to bring the perpetrators to justice. In the end they were sentenced to thirteen years of imprisonment. Less than two years later, in April 2008, they were freed, following a decree by the president himself. The couple protested. Early in May 2009, the husband was shot and killed by an unknown gunman.

Rape victims in Afghanistan know that the chances of pursuing their case successfully in the court system are incredibly low, while the risk of becoming stigmatized and shamed is high. It is no wonder that few dare to share what they have experienced or seek justice. Old practices are invoked by religious leaders to justify hideous crimes in the name of Islam. In reality these practices have nothing to do with religion. When UNAMA's human rights office analyzed these problems in 2009, several Sharia experts confirmed that mullahs very often had little knowledge of Islam. But they used religious arguments in support of centuries-old practices, reinforced by the brutality of decades of war and conflict.

In Herat, in the west of Afghanistan, a prominent mullah condemned a women's NGO as a center for blasphemy, encouraging people to burn down the office. In this environment nobody should be surprised that women working for NGOs or in government feel threatened and intimidated. Nevertheless, there are an increasing number of them who decide to accept the risk and participate in public life. Often we do not fully understand how courageous they are. When the UN Security Council visited Kabul in November 2008, a meeting with NGOs was included in the program. Among the NGO representatives were members of women's networks. They described their work and the challenges they were facing.

One prominent ambassador encouraged them to engage themselves beyond traditional women's issues. "You have to be brave," he said. There was complete silence in the room. These women were probably the bravest people the Security Council ambassadors would meet during their week-long visit.

On September 28, 2008, the most prominent policewomen in Kandahar, Malalai Kakar, was attacked and killed. On April 12 of the following year, Sitara Achakzai, a member of the provincial council of Kandahar and a well-known women's rights activist, met the same fate. Young women must be brave to enter the public space and let their voices be heard.

The marginalization of women is reinforced by the fact that women are the first victims of poverty. The maternal death rate in Afghanistan is higher than in almost any country in the world: Every twenty-seven minutes, a woman dies as a result of complications related to pregnancy and birth—that means 20,000 women every year. Average life expectancy for women is forty-four, which is twenty years below the global average. Afghanistan is one of very few countries in the world where the average life expectancy is lower for women than for men.

On Women's Day, March 8, 2009, I was with President Karzai in front of an assembly of several hundred women in the center of Kabul. In the first row sat Husn Bano Ghazanfar, the minister for women's affairs; Sima Samar, the leader of the AIHRC; and several representatives of women's networks. The wives of some of the ministers were also there. But the real surprise was the presence of President Karzai's wife, Zeenat Quraishi Karzai. It was the first and last time I saw her. She never appeared publicly with her husband and never traveled with him abroad. "Has the president become a revolutionary?" one of my friends in the government joked.

The president was the first to speak, condemning violence against women and encouraging them to participate in public life. He talked about girls in school and women in the National

Assembly, about the progress the country had made over the last few years. "In the next government, there will be more women," he said, "if I am reelected." The president spoke about women's right to vote and the power they had, as women represented 40 percent of registered voters at the time. Now they had to make full use of their right and their power, he said. It was Candidate Karzai more than President Karzai speaking to the women assembled in the audience. Some shouted their support to him as he was speaking and assured him that he would have their vote. One of them bravely criticized Karzai for not doing enough to fight violence against women.

He had encouraged women to participate in public life. I had prepared myself to challenge him on precisely this point in my own speech. There were women's networks with brave women who risked their health and their lives every day to promote their rights. There were qualified and well-educated women who could play important roles in governing and developing the country. But the leaders of the Afghan society, the president, the members of the government and of the National Assembly, the governors and local leaders—they were all silent. The president had encouraged women to go to the polling stations and use their right to vote. He had—for the very first time—brought his own wife to a meeting of this kind. Yet, what had he done in concrete terms during his presidency to give women space? Early in his presidential term there had been three women in the government, then two. Now only one was left and she was responsible for women's affairs, of course. Bamiyan province had a female provincial governor, Habiba Sarabi. One of the most competent of thirty-four provincial governors, she was the only woman among them. The president had told me that he would at least have three women in his next government. And there would be more female governors.

I had emphasized to him before that women needed more female role models in order to take that risky step into public life. But right now they needed—probably more than anything else—a genuine engagement from Afghanistan's male leaders. The few women who took part in public life were strong, but their voices often drowned in the conservative Afghan society. The most decisive contribution to enhancing their role would be a stronger engagement from the political and religious elites. But they had remained quiet. Not even from the most Western-oriented Afghan leaders—perhaps with a handful of exceptions—did I experience any real commitment to promoting the participation of women in public life. And I cannot remember hearing any of them speak up publicly.

To my surprise and disappointment, when the president had finished his speech, he left the hall. That had not happened at previous similar events. I was left at the rostrum without my main "target" in sight. Having delivered my message for more women in government, more female governors, and a stronger engagement from the leading men of the Afghan society, I looked at the president's wife. She was still there. I ended my speech by expressing disappointment that the president was no longer present, but asked her to convey my message to him. She nodded discreetly.

Women's rights and participation was a regular theme in my discussions with the president, most frequently when we reflected over possible changes in his government. But apart from that Women's Day, I only heard him raise the topic publicly once. It was at the opening of the National Assembly session in the middle of January 2009. With 25 percent of the audience being women, it was a theme that was difficult to avoid. A few days before the opening, Hanne Melfald and I had met with the president. I had specifically asked him to address abuse against women and the need to strengthen their role in society, and he did. In a few sentences, he emphasized the importance of ending violence against women as well as the practice of underage marriages. Then he looked at me where I was sitting as the only foreigner among the Afghan leaders in the front row. He raised his eyes, looked at the assembly, and improvised a few additional sentences beyond what was already in his manuscript. Did he remember our conversation or was it something that I imagined?

I often had discussions, both in the UN and with prominent Afghan women, about how far I should go in terms of engaging myself and the UN in such issues. Some of the most prominent and established women's leaders urged me to be cautious. We had to avoid making women's rights a debate between non-Muslim international representatives and conservative Afghan politicians. That could undermine the struggle Afghan women were waging and be seen as interference from foreign infidels. Other women activists had a different view and encouraged us to engage ourselves more forcefully. In younger women's networks, the opinion was often that it could not get much worse. If we did not engage ourselves on their side, then who would? They had to at least be able to count on the support of the international community. In such situations I wished even more that we had been able to recruit representatives of Muslim countries, both in UNAMA and in other parts of the international community, people who could discuss the rights of women on the basis of the same religion. But such candidates were hard to find.

Ten days after our celebration of Women's Day, on March 19, the president signed a new family law for the Shia minority—mainly Hazaras living in the central highlands in the middle of Afghanistan. The law had been in the works for years. There had been discussions in the government in 2007 and approval by both chambers of the National Assembly in February 2009. The approval in the National Assembly had been rushed, and no real debate had taken place. Female members claimed that they were not even aware that the law had been passed or what it contained. A political firestorm followed. There were demonstrations against the law in the streets of Kabul, met hastily by organized counter-demonstrations. As soon as the most controversial paragraphs had been translated into English, the international community started to react. The law represented a silent acceptance of child marriages; it gave fathers and the men of the family sole custody of children; it had provisions obliging women to comply with the sexual desires of their husbands; and it banned women from leaving the house without the husband's consent.

Prominent international leaders called Karzai to protest. I was having lunch with him one day in April when British Prime Minister Gordon Brown called to express his indignation. Karzai seemed surprised and unprepared for the strong international reactions. I also asked him to hold the law back and to amend the contentious paragraphs. He promised to keep me fully informed about any new steps. "The law is dead," said one of the president's closest advisors. I felt reassured. But I was wrong.

Karzai sent the law back to the Ministry of Justice. A number of amendments were presented by the AIHRC and by women's organizations. Finally a new version was presented to the president, and on July 19 he signed a decree turning it into law. Some of the controversial paragraphs were no longer to be found, such as the duty to comply with the husband's sexual desires and the ban against leaving the house without permission. But the new paragraphs were vague and open for interpretations that would not be much different from the previous version. In reality it seemed that the interpretation would depend on whether the judge had a conservative or liberal view. I had many conversations with Sima Samar about this law. She herself had been called to the president before he signed the final version, together with representatives of women's organizations. They had concluded that they would not stop the last revision from going forward. It was a far cry from what they had wanted and struggled for. But they also feared that another battle with conservative mullahs and politicians could make the law worse.

Why was there a need to regulate questions relating to the family status of the Shia minority in this way? The Sunni majority had such matters regulated through the Constitution, which is based on the Sunni Hanafi School. There were no similar provisions for the Shia minority. Over the last decades the Shias had become more politically mobilized. Their request for a separate family law had in fact been raised already in the 1980s. It had become an important symbolic matter for this religious minority.

Paradoxically, the very same day the president signed the revised version of the Shia law, he also put his signature under a law to eliminate violence against women. The law was based on international legal obligations Afghanistan had undertaken in the UN. It contained a ban against rape, against having more than one wife, and against marriage with underage children—which is to say that it contained provisions that were quite different from the Shia law. Which law would then take precedence in case of conflict between them? That was unclear. There were many strong reactions against the Shia law. However, it reflected the reality in Afghanistan as it was and continues to be in large parts of the country, the endless discrimination of women and their limited freedom of movement. Soon the international indignation died down, and the discrimination and abuse continued.

Fighting the marginalization of women is first of all a question of fundamental human rights. But it is also a question of how to build the Afghan society. I have never experienced any country being able to transform itself into a more modern and prosperous society when only half of its population is engaged. Afghanistan will need the involvement of the entire population to grow and develop, in economic and social terms and in terms of respect for law and order. Economic development and modernization will, I believe, be the most important engine in improving the conditions for women in the Afghan society, as it has been in so many other countries.

CHAPTER THIRTEEN

KABUL UNDER ATTACK

In the beginning of 2009, the security situation deteriorated even further. On January 17, a suicide bomber blew himself up in a car outside the German embassy. Seven civilians were killed and many more injured. Windows were smashed in a number of buildings nearby, including the offices of a UN agency. In Palace 7, a couple of windows were damaged and a door was blown in. But it could have been much worse; it was a Saturday, so many of the offices in the vicinity were empty, particularly those belonging to foreigners. It also seemed that the suicide bomber thought he was ramming his car into a fuel truck. Instead, the vehicle he drove into was a sewage truck. Had it been a fuel truck, the entire quarter would probably have vanished.

I had returned from New Year's celebration in Norway with a broken ankle and had to use crutches for two months. A Norwegian television team was visiting. When the explosion happened, I was in the bathroom, which had an entrance from my personal office. Instinctively, I threw myself against the corner of the room to hide from the window and avoid glass splinters. A few seconds later, my bodyguards entered and dragged me down the stairs and into the bunker in the basement, with my crutches hanging after me and the TV team as spectators. We waited there for some time wondering if there would be another explosion. A second explosion often followed quickly after the first, once people had gathered to help the victims of the first bomb. But this time there was no second explosion.

A few days later, we found ourselves in the bunker again. A fueltruck was parked in the street outside, and there were suspicions of explosives on board. Experts with dogs were brought to the scene. After a few hours, we were given the green light to go back to our offices. On the other side of the street, across from the entrance to the UN headquarters, was Camp Eggers, an American military base. I had been nervous about this camp for quite some time. All day, starting early in the morning, a long cue of trucks was waiting to enter the base; fuel trucks, sewage trucks, and vehicles carrying various kinds of deliveries. I had told the U.S. military how dangerous it was to have a large military base in the center of town. It put Afghans, UN personnel, and other civilians unnecessarily at risk. A short walk away, easily within range for a truck bomb, was a high school for Afghan children. I often had an unpleasant feeling when I entered the office in the morning. A serious explosion could eradicate the surrounding buildings completely. The U.S. military had reacted slowly to our concerns, insisting that the trucks had been carefully searched and escorted to the camp. Knowing how the Afghan security forces and all kinds of companies could be infiltrated, their reassurances did little to alleviate our concerns.

Now, however, the Americans also started to react. The attack outside the German embassy was just on the other side of the base. Traffic on the road outside our offices was restricted further; machine gun positions were built to stop a suicide bomber in a car from trying to force his way through the first roadblock. High concrete walls were built on two sides, forming a corridor where trucks had to wait before being allowed into the base. The road outside our main headquarters became a concrete avenue, with walls so high that it was impossible to see anything on either side of the street. The risk was significantly reduced. But a serious blast would still have a severe impact on our compound.

On February 11 came another explosion in the center of town, only a few hundred yards away. This time it was more than one bomb; it was a complex attack with suicide bombers using hand grenades, and automatic weapons. The shooting continued for hours. Several ministries were under attack and the number of casualties was high. The Haqqani network was probably responsible; this was the same group that had attacked the Serena Hotel a year earlier and probably also the Indian embassy. A few days later, we received a report that the same group was preparing an attack against a UN installation in the city. Security measures were again reviewed and tightened.

I was surprised by my own reactions when such attacks happened and how I seemed to cope with the situation. On one occasion, I was with Hanne Melfald in my office when we heard the thunder of an explosion and saw dust land on the furniture. I asked her to move the chair away from the window, then resumed our conversation, pausing as security and bodyguards interrupted us to report the damage.

The sound of rockets exploding in the vicinity of Palace 7 had become an almost regular experience. They were fired during the night, two or three, sometimes even seven. Since the targets were probably the Ministry of Defense and the presidential palace a few hundred yards away and the rockets were imprecise, there was always a chance that one of them would land in our own garden. Fortunately they never came that close. Normally I would wake up at the explosions and fall asleep a few minutes later. Sometimes I did not wake up at all, but would hear from the close protection officers the next morning that there had been explosions.

Every now and then, though, anxiety took hold of me. Some days in the office I would be overwhelmed by a sudden and unpleasant feeling that the window could be blown in the very next second and glass shattered across the room. On the road I would suddenly think that a car in front of us was parked in a suspicious way. And what was on board the fuel truck next to us in the dense traffic we could not avoid one morning? The atmosphere in the car was often one of total silence on the way down the Jalalabad road from Massoud square to a UN compound outside the city center. The escort cars would be on the right side and then on the left to protect against other vehicles or help get us through a roundabout quickly. As time passed I experienced this unpleasant feeling more and more frequently. The constant tension had an impact on me and probably on all my colleagues, international or Afghan. But among ourselves in Palace 7, we rarely spoke about it.

The security situation forced us to change our routines. We had tried to be unpredictable in our movements, traveling at different times and varying the routes we took from my residence to the office or other locations. My cars, however, were a problem. As with all UN cars, they were marked "UN" on each side in big letters. In addition, they had equipment that distinguished them from any other vehicle in Kabul. It was as though we were driving through the city with a big sign announcing who was inside. Eventually license plates were changed more frequently, and groups of decoy cars were sent to confuse anybody interested in us. Instead of cleaning the cars, the Romanian close-protection team let them become dirty and eventually replaced them with vehicles that would draw less attention. The Romanians warned me that if anything would happen, they might have to knock me unconscious to make their job easier. I wasn't sure if they were serious or joking, but fortunately, I never had the opportunity to find out.

Other routines had to change as well. I had enjoyed the short trips by car to a small supermarket in the area called Spinney's. It was great to be able to walk around inside for a few minutes, to buy cereal for breakfast, razor blades, or whatever small thing I could find. The young employees and customers would greet me with a friendly hello, and kids would try out a few English words they had learned. It was a taste of normal life, even with bodyguards around me. But toward the end of my stay in Kabul, these small breaks became less frequent. Later the supermarket next door was attacked; an entire Afghan family was wiped out. Foreigners were probably the targets of the attack, but it was innocent Afghan lives that were lost.

My closest office staff moved permanently into Palace 7 to enable us to continue working even if our security team had declared "white city," which meant no movement outside our homes. Such periods could last for hours or days. When the threat level was at its highest, even UN vehicles were not allowed to enter the vicinity of Palace 7 without prior notification and clearance (in case someone might try to steal a UN car to gain access).

Our UN staff in field offices often lived in a security environment that was more threatening than in Kabul. In Kandahar the UN staff was particularly limited in their movements. During most of my time in Afghanistan, they were mainly able to travel between their offices, their guesthouses, the offices of the local authorities, and the ISAF base. Toward the end of my stay their freedom of movement became even more restricted. I greatly admire the staff we had in such offices. They were unarmed in places where most ISAF countries did not dare send even well-armed personnel. The mental and physical strain of living and working in such conditions was great.

I had looked forward to my visit to Herat in the west, which I had heard was the most beautiful city in Afghanistan. But when I arrived at the airport in Herat, a helicopter was waiting to take us for a brief visit to the UNAMA compound and then to the governor's guesthouse. The day before my visit, rockets had landed dangerously close to the UN offices. It was one of a number of such attacks. Here too the security situation had become difficult. Several military helicopters escorted us to the meeting with the governor and other leaders and elders. Two hundred police and army soldiers guarded the area around the site, along with Italian military and officers from the Afghan intelligence service. I could only see Herat from the window of the helicopter as we passed over the city.

In Kunduz, in the northeast, the UN had just received a warning of an attack when I visited. We came directly from Baghlan, the neighboring province, where we had opened a new UN office. Hungarian military had escorted us from our new office to the helicopter landing pad. The cars were speeding along narrow roads. Peaceful Afghan women in burkas hurried to the side of the road to avoid being covered by dirt and water. Other cars were pushed to the roadside in order to give us unhindered passage. We did not win many hearts and minds among Afghans that day. I was embarrassed, surrounded by my UN cars in the middle of the military convoy. But here too a threat had been received and the Hungarians did not want to take any chances.

Afghanistan was fortunately not only threats and conflict. The most fascinating visits I made were my two trips to Bamiyan province, in the Hazara region in the center of Afghanistan. This is where the gigantic Buddha statues, 180 and 121 feet high, had been located. Hopefully, there is another "sleeping" Buddha hidden in the ground somewhere. If so, Bamiyan could again be a destination for thousands of Buddhist visitors. Bamiyan is also the location of the city of lamentation, so called because of the destruction wrought by Genghis Kahn in the thirteenth century. Only nine miles away are the remnants of the Red City, where the population lived for centuries, well protected in mountain caves. The city takes its name from the color of the rock.

Half an hour away by helicopter is the first national park of Afghanistan, Band-i Amir. The Bamiyan governor, Habiba Sarabi, and I were invited to go there in summer of 2009 with BBC's Lyse Doucet. The entire area is like a giant Grand Canyon, but even more beautiful, with six blue lakes at the bottom. It is also the site of a Muslim holy shrine, where the water is believed to have a healing effect. Lyse Doucet wanted to present another picture of Afghanistan and show that the country was more than war and conflict. That was certainly a project in which I was happy to take part.

The mountains of Bamiyan are spectacular. Approaching the airport in our helicopter, I could imagine one Olympic downhill ski slope after the other, envisioning how this area could be turned into an arena for international competitions and a center for winter tourism. Already a few tourists were coming here, mainly international visitors from Kabul. One hotel had opened, the Silk Road. It was run by Japanese owners and served the best sushi in Afghanistan. I was fascinated by this province and its resources. It had the potential to become a destination for so many: for tourists looking for historic sites and religious shrines, skiing adventures, and unbelievable natural wonders. But it also had the potential to become a center for industrial activities and nationwide economic growth, with all its minerals and other resources. I hope that those who govern will have the wisdom to seek the right balance between developing its natural resources and protecting its nature and history and accept that the resources of this area are the property of the Afghan people.

However, Bamiyan was the exception; the visits to field offices illustrated the difficult circumstances in which our staff worked, both in terms of security and living conditions. Even previously stable areas were experiencing increasing threat levels. But I also observed how different the UN was from all other international partners on the ground. While others made sporadic visits to the local population, mostly their leaders, the local population came regularly to us. That was a tremendous asset. By far the majority of our staff in the regional and provincial offices was Afghan. They were a bridge between the local population and international UN representatives. Unfortunately, the worsening security also made our outreach to the population more difficult and dangerous.

CHAPTER FOURTEEN

KARZAI'S TACTICAL SURPRISE

The first preparations for the presidential and provincial council elections had already begun when I arrived in Kabul in March of 2008. For the first time, the Afghan Independent Election Commission (IEC), whose members had been appointed by the president, would be responsible for the organization of the elections, in contrast to previous elections, when the UN had been in charge. The international community would now be in a supporting role, in addition to financing the elections. The UNDP had the main responsibility for providing support and assistance to the IEC through its Enhancing Legal and Electoral Capacity For Tomorrow (ELECT) project. A separate complaints commission had been established, the Electoral Complaints Commission (ECC), consisting of one representative appointed by the Supreme Court, one by the AIHRC, and three internationals elected by the UN Special Representative—myself. Any decision by the ECC would therefore require the consent of at least one international member. My own role was twofold: to oversee the work of the UN and to be the international community's main interlocutor with Afghan authorities.

A group of leading Afghan politicians and key international representatives had met during spring 2008 and agreed that the elections should take place in fall 2009. All our planning was based on this timeframe. However, we could not find any written evidence of the agreement. Soon, the agreement was questioned by the speaker of the lower house, Yunus Qanooni. He claimed that he had never agreed to this timing. He simply did not have the authority to make any such agreement on behalf of the National Assembly, in particular since the elections would then take place later than the Constitution permitted. According to the Constitution, the elections had to take place sometime between March 22 and April 22, 2009. Karzai's mandate would expire on May 22, 2009. Qanooni argued that if the elections took place after this date, then the president would have to resign until the elections were over. Beyond May 22 he would not be a legitimate president. We all knew that it would be impossible to stick to the dates stipulated in the Constitution. The time available would be too short. Election material would have to be designed and procured, voters and candidates would have to be registered, and the election campaign would have to take place. Security would have to be established, to the extent that it was possible, and ballot papers and other materials distributed across the country. Election staff in tens of thousands would have to be recruited and trained, and a voters' education program would have to be rolled out. If the deadlines of the Constitution were to be respected, this would mean that everything would have to be compressed into a very short period of time. Most of the election process would take place during wintertime, when significant parts of the country would be inaccessible. Even on the day of elections, there would be a risk that voters in part of the country would be unable to make it to the polls.

At first the president's position was that, according to the Constitution, he was elected for a period of five years. The first presidential elections had taken place in October of 2004 and Karzai had not been inaugurated until December. Accordingly, the president insisted, he would have full legitimacy as president well beyond the timeframe that had been agreed upon for the 2009 elections. But Qanooni was firm and showed no sign of changing his position.

Representatives of the international community referred to what had happened during the last presidential elections in 2004. There had been a political agreement among the Afghan leaders to hold the elections on a later date than stipulated in the Constitution. We appealed to them to come to a similar consensus now.

I urged Qanooni to help us get out of the impasse; however, he now had significant support from members of the National Assembly. Qanooni claimed that for years the president had neglected the National Assembly and its elected leaders. By doing so, Karzai had himself created an unnecessary opposition among them. There had been many attempts to engage the president in a dialogue, Qanooni said, but he had not listened. I agreed that the president should have sought a closer relationship to the National Assembly. But this was not reason enough to throw the country into a constitutional crisis and political instability. The next spring and summer we would be in the middle of a fighting season, which made it even more important to have functioning and legitimate institutions. However, my arguments had little effect and the discussion continued.

Together with my international colleagues, I examined all possible options to avoid a crisis. Could the president of the Supreme Court, Abdul Salam Azimi, make a declaration to the effect that the president would retain his legitimacy until elections took place? It seemed unlikely, since we knew that Azimi was reluctant to play a role in a political controversy, particularly because the Constitution was quite clear. Could the president remain in office as a head of a sort of interim administration, a caretaker government, with limited authority? This was basically a variation of what the opposition wanted—a weakened presidency for three hectic summer months. The president would never accept such a solution, nor would the concerns of the international community be met. Could another interim solution be found, with the speaker of the upper house, Mojadeddi, acting as president between the two dates? The idea of seeing the old and frail Mojadeddi governing the country, even for a brief period, frightened us, and the president would never let it happen. Would it be possible to declare a state of emergency, as the Constitution allowed? It seemed absurd to impose the serious restrictions of a state of emergency in order to have free and democratic elections.

The president threatened to convene a Loya Jirga, a traditional Afghan grand council, to solve the problem. That was an alternative none of us wanted, internationals or Afghans. A Jirga would be unpredictable and could put anything it wanted on its agenda, including matters none of us wanted to discuss now—the withdrawal of international forces or the introduction of stricter Sharia legislation. We were at an impasse.

On January 28, 2009, the IEC announced that the elections would take place on August 20. The choice of the date was based on the principles of universality, fairness, and transparency; it was a date that would allow us to prepare the elections in a decent manner and enable as many as possible to vote. However, it did not bring the disagreement to an end. The opposition insisted that between May 22 and August 20 the president would be without legitimacy. Now the first vice president, Ahmad Zia Massoud, also made it clear that he would not stand for reelection if the president did not step down when his term was over on May 22.

On February 3 I was called to meet with the president and a group of prominent Afghan politicians, including the leaders of the opposition. The discussion continued back and forth with familiar arguments. There was no progress. A few days later I was called to the president again. We had already reviewed the timetable several times together to see if there was any flexibility and if the elections could be advanced. I told him that there was simply no way they could be held before the summer. Karzai understood well. But he also gave me a warning about his thinking; he was planning a high-risk tactical game and wanted to inform me before he went on the offensive.

Richard Holbrooke had by then been appointed U.S. Special Representative for Afghanistan and Pakistan. He had been in Afghanistan for a few days, and we had already met. Washington was in the middle of an intense debate over sending additional troops to help secure the elections. But it would take time to deploy them. Holbrooke was with Karzai when I received a call one evening asking if I could join them at the presidential palace. When I arrived, Holbrooke was pressing Karzai for assurances. Would he stand by August 20 as the date for the elections? President Obama intended to announce a troop increase of 17,000, but he needed to be sure about the election date. Karzai felt uncomfortable but gave Holbrooke the assurances he was asking for.

A few days later, I left for the Norwegian mountains to celebrate my sixtieth birthday. The same day, February 28, the presidential palace in Kabul called to inform me the president had issued a decree instructing the IEC to conduct the elections in accordance with the Constitution, which meant that the date had to be well before his mandate expired on May 22. The decree created immediate confusion in the main international capitals. In Washington, there was more than confusion—there was anger. Karzai had just promised Holbrooke he would stick to August 20, and now, only a few days later, he was running away from his commitment. The Obama administration planned to issue a statement exhorting the president to stay firm on August 20. I was encouraged to do the same. Since I was aware of what was happening in Kabul, I asked my American interlocutors not to be too worried. I had regular contacts with the president's office. But Holbrooke understandably did not feel reassured, and a U.S. demarche was made urging the president to stick to the original date.

In Kabul, Karzai had turned the game around. Now he was the one to insist on respecting the Constitution. He had put the opposition on the defensive. The most prominent opposition leaders had all understood that the early elections they had asked for would be impossible. But they wanted to see the president enter the election campaign as a weakened president, without full legitimacy and authority, or—even better—as a candidate without the mantle of the presidency at all. His ability to use the government machine and to make promises to other leaders in exchange for support would then be damaged. The opposition understood that the only person to be served by an early election would in fact be the president himself. Opposition candidates would not have time to prepare and to carry out a real election campaign.

On March 4, after my return to Kabul, I was called into the president's office. Many of the country's political leaders were gathered, including the speaker of the upper house, Mojadeddi, and the deputy speaker of the lower house, Mirwais Yasini. The most prominent members of the government were also present, together with the president of the Supreme Court, Azimi, and the chairman of the IEC, Azizullah Ludin. The president made it clear that he would not sit one day without full legitimacy. In other words, the threat of early elections was still there. Ludin continued to argue for the date already set by the IEC. I argued that it was no longer a question of deciding if elections should take place in May or August. The question was if there would be any elections at all, which meant that August was the only realistic alternative. Azimi said that on previous occasions, a political understanding had been reached, even if it was not in strict accordance with the Constitution. Even Vice President Massoud now seemed to be more flexible. There were no belligerent statements and no insistence that the president would have to go if elections were postponed.

I had discussed the situation with the IEC chairman, Ludin, earlier in the day. He was prepared to send out a statement saying that the date of August 20 was still in effect. The meeting seemed to move in that direction. But just before it was about to conclude, a heated discussion erupted between Karzai and Ludin. I could not understand what they were saying to each other. But I could see the other participants starting to leave the room without any firm conclusion having been reached. I was confused and deeply worried. We could not continue planning without a firm date. A NATO ministerial meeting would also take place over the next few days, and I did not want the ministers to discuss Afghanistan and the elections with this chaos in Kabul. I ran out of the meeting room and down the stairs to collect as many of the participants as I could possibly bring back. The key members of the group assembled in the president's office. Ludin wanted to issue a statement immediately based on legal considerations to confirm August 20 as the election date. Azimi protested. In his view, there were no valid legal arguments for postponing elections to August 20 and Ludin did not have any authority to interpret the Constitution. If Ludin issued a statement on legal ground, then he would have to object publicly. The decision had to be made on the basis of practical considerations. In the end Ludin gave in and agreed.

A few hours later the IEC issued its statement. August 20 was fixed. International leaders and representatives welcomed the decision. Opposition leaders made ritualistic comments criticizing the decision, but they no longer seemed to object. A few days later Karzai also "accepted" the date. The entire process came to an end when Azimi, on March 29, issued a statement declaring that the president could continue with full authority until elections had taken place. We had avoided a constitutional as well as a political crisis; the date was fixed, and there was clarity with regard to the president's legitimacy during the three months between May and August. Finally we could proceed knowing how much time we had available for all the preparations.

The IEC had already conducted the voter registration. It had decided that it would be too complicated and demanding to register all voters at the same time under the current security conditions. The country was divided into four parts, and the registration took place in phases lasting until the end of February. Voters who still had their voting cards from the last elections would not have to register again. The registration process would be limited to those who no longer had their old cards and to new voters. Nobody knew how many had kept their old cards, but it was a general assumption that more people in the rural areas than in urban areas still had them. The number of registration points quickly proved to be inadequate. People had not been able to register in time because of the distance from their homes to the registration centers. Additional mobile offices had to be established, and the registration continued beyond the dates that had been set. However, irregularities were frequent. Some had registered twice or three times. People far younger than eighteen had registered to vote. In some provinces, the number of women registered was improbably high. In Kandahar and in Nangarhar, more voters had been registered than in the capital. It had to be wrong. But while there was a certain control of the process in the capital, such control was lacking in the other two provinces.

The IEC believed that most of these problems could be solved on the day of elections. On polling day the voters would have to dip a finger in indelible ink to prevent them from voting more than once. We knew that there would be irregularities and fraud and that we probably could not prevent it, but we had also, together with the IEC, put in place a number of mechanisms to detect fraud when it occurred.

CHAPTER FIFTEEN

FIVE MORE YEARS WITH KARZAI?

During most of the winter, we had been struggling with the disagreement over the election date and the problems related to registration. However, behind the scenes another discussion had surfaced. Karzai had become more aggressive over the last months. Could we live with this situation for another presidential term? Some key international representatives had serious doubts. Prominent Afghans, even those close to the president, also wondered how we could live with five more years of confrontations. The tension between the government and its main international supporters was constantly spiraling to new levels. Would it be better if Karzai decided to step down? The president had been described to me as a man who avoided confrontations if he could. He was a politician who preferred to solve matters the way he had learned from his father, the leader of an important Pashtun tribe, the Popalzais, through consultations and consensus building.

Until now my own meetings with the president had been calm and straightforward despite occasional disagreements. But since late fall 2008 his tone had changed and he had become confrontational. He could explode in meetings with his own advisors as well as with foreign representatives and visiting dignitaries. He seemed not to listen any more. When I met with him, he would sometimes come at me from all directions at the same time without letting me finish my arguments.

The British and the Americans were his main targets. The U.K. had the troops believed to be the best at fighting the kind of warfare we experienced in Afghanistan. So why had they not succeeded in Helmand? Why had the insurgents become stronger after the British arrived in that province, not weaker? The U.K. had also taken the lead in the fight against the narcotics production. But the poppy production had not fallen; on the contrary, it had increased sharply. And Helmand, where the British had their military, produced more opium than all other provinces together. What was really going on? The president seemed full of suspicion and was unhappy about the British performance. And he thought that if the British had to choose between Pakistani and Afghan interests, they would always listen more carefully to Pakistan than to Afghanistan. Pakistan was part of their old empire and was now a member of the Commonwealth. In Afghanistan the British had suffered bloody defeats that neither the British nor the Afghans had forgotten.

Sometimes his attacks against British or American representatives were made in public. In December 2008, we were marking Anti-corruption Day at the Amani High School, close to the presidential palace and even closer to the UN compound. There were several hundred Afghans in the audience. Karzai's speech was full of accusations against the international community. There was no admission of Afghan responsibility. And toward the end of his speech Karzai looked at the audience as if he was searching for somebody: "Is the American ambassador, Bill Wood, here?" he asked. He was not. "So, you see," Karzai continued, "Ambassador Wood complains about corruption every time I see him. But when we organize a meeting to fight corruption, then he does not take the time to join us." Some of the Afghans applauded. The few internationals present were silent and dismayed. The president knew well that Wood would not be there. He had already apologized to Karzai the day before and informed him that he had other urgent obligations outside Kabul that day.

Karzai's outbursts were also aimed at his own most loyal ministers and advisors. He would confront them with the most unfair accusations, often of being too pro-Western. They would sit and listen and not object—at least not in his presence. But once we left his office, they would express their concerns. Our meetings with the president were increasingly focused on damage limitation.

The fundamental questions became ever more pressing: Could we live with this situation for another five years? What would the costs be for Afghanistan? Did the international community have a solid interlocutor in the presidential palace? Could we bring him back on a less confrontational course? There had been confrontations between the president and the international community in the past. But it seemed clear that the discussions about civilian casualties caused by international military during summer and fall of 2008 had brought his irritation to a different level. Many of his closest ministers and advisors agreed with him in substance, but they were very concerned about his handling of the problem. There was a sense of crisis even among those who were close to him.

On February 5 I decided to raise the problem directly with him—or at least as directly as I could. He never took a day off. Even on Fridays, the Muslim holiday, he was in the office. I urged him to take a break, to get away for a week somewhere he would not be disturbed by the endless meetings every day. A few days away from Kabul in a calmer atmosphere could give him some rest. Predictably, he turned it down. He was not prepared to leave the country, even for a brief holiday. "A luxurious vacation outside Afghanistan would look very bad," he claimed.

His response led me to the more difficult part of the discussion. "Mr. President, you have been in the highest office of your country for six years," I said. "You have carried a heavy burden. Have you ever thought about how long you want to continue with this burden on your shoulders? You have started the building of a new and democratic Afghanistan. This can be your legacy to the country and the way you will be remembered in its history." I was worried about what his reaction would be. Would he explode and throw me out of the office? If he did, it would probably be my last meeting with him. But he did not react the way I had feared. Instead, he started to reflect on his past and on his future. He talked about his affection for his country and then about his son, Mirwais. Nothing was more important to him than to see his son be able to have his education here and live in a peaceful Afghanistan. He spoke slowly, thoughtfully, and I believe he was sincere. He did not want to cling to the presidency. To him, there were two alternatives: He could sit until the elections with full legitimacy and seek reelection, or he could leave office and see a successor take over. He talked about who could succeed him as president, people he had believed would be able to carry the same burden. But after a while, he had come to the conclusion that they could not, at least not yet. That afternoon, I felt that there was a profound sense of duty and commitment to his country in what he said and in the way he formulated his thoughts. I had never heard him like this before. A few days later, I met the president again with National Security Advisor Rassoul, certainly his most loyal advisor. In Rassoul's presence Karzai repeated the same message; he did not want to cling to the presidency. Rassoul seemed surprised. It was probably the first time he had heard the president speak in such terms. Afterwards, I regretted having raised the matter. I believe he was right and I had come to the same conclusion; there was no obvious candidate to succeed him.

The international community had made Karzai the target of such criticism and demonstrated such a lack of respect that I had never witnessed anything similar. He had experienced a kind of pressure we would find hard to understand. Civilian casualties worried and humiliated him. When he raised such incidents, he was told by international partners to keep the disagreements behind closed doors. Prominent international politicians could say that the problem was not the insurgents, but bad government. However, the same international politicians had never lifted a finger to marginalize the old warlords and powerbrokers, who had no interest in reforms and good governance. They criticized Karzai for corruption but continued to make contracts with well-known corrupt Afghans. There was a level of hypocrisy that made him bitter and angry; his irritation seemed to grow by the day. But encouraging the president to step down was not the solution.

CHAPTER SIXTEEN

NEW MINISTERS AND NEW EXPECTATIONS

In spite of all the conflicts and confrontations during the fall and winter months, there were promising developments as well, which gave us hope for progress in some very important areas. When I arrived in Kabul in March of 2008 as the UN envoy, I knew several of the ministers well. My preferred interlocutors were people I have already mentioned: Rassoul, Spanta, Atmar, Wardak, in addition to the minister of rural development, Mohammad Ehsan Zia, and the minister of health, Sayed Mohammad Amin Fatimi. But the overall quality of the government was very uneven. It was not a real team. One of the reasons was a general lack of experienced and competent candidates. Another was the fact that Karzai had to balance all sorts of forces and groups inside his government in order to satisfy different factions. Had he been able to freely choose his team, the government would have been quite different. But he could not ignore basic realities of Afghan political life.

Neither in the security nor the economic ministries did we see the team spirit we wanted. The minister of the interior, Zarar Moqbel, was a serious source of irritation in much of the international community because of his ineffectiveness and his acceptance of widespread corruption. Yet, the president showed no sign of wanting to replace him. The minister of finance, Anwar ul-Haq Ahadi, was competent, but not a team player, and he had irritated some of his most important colleagues. Agriculture and infrastructure were neglected by the Afghans and underfinanced by the international community. The minister for water and energy was the widely unpopular Ismail Khan, the brutal former warlord from Herat. There was no one to bring ministers together in a cooperative way. Instead, they competed for attention and resources.

During the summer of 2008, rumors started to circulate about changes in the government. I was enthusiastic since it would provide an opportunity to bring together a new team with more reform-oriented and efficient politicians. It seemed clear that a new minister of agriculture would soon be appointed. That was good news and an important first step. But we had to take full advantage of the opportunity to make further changes. I discussed the situation with a very small group of international partners. In my view it would be important to convince Karzai to replace the minister of interior. His ministry was one of the most important; there was an urgent need to clean up the high level of corruption and build a more reliable police force in order to help stabilize the country. I had a number of conversations with the president about the composition of the government. It was my opinion that he could not make changes in one or two of the ministries without also replacing the minister of interior. Doing so would send the wrong signal at a time when corruption had become one of the highest priorities of his Western partners and one of the main concerns of Afghans themselves. Karzai needed a minister who would be forceful, who could be trusted by the largest donors, and who would act quickly to respond to the deteriorating security situation in the provinces around Kabul and on the highways. The president responded that the United States trusted Zarar and worked well with him. The Americans did not want any changes. Why would he want to replace Zarar? Karzai probably wanted to keep his minister and was using the Americans as an excuse; Zarar was a prominent Tajik and represented an important constituency. And in fact, opinions about Zarar were divided among the Americans: The U.S. military who worked with him had a less negative opinion than the rest of the administration. But we had to get the police right and start cleaning up the Ministry of Interior. When I raised the issue with Condoleezaa Rice, she reassured me that the U.S. administration shared our misgivings and hoped that Karzai would replace Zarar.

After further discussions, Karzai was finally ready for a change. Now the conversations turned to who would be Zarar's successor. Several names were mentioned, but the discussions soon centered on one man, Haneef Atmar, my preferred candidate. The problem was that Atmar had become irreplaceable in every position he had held in the government. He had been a highly successful minister of rural development and lately an equally successful minister of education. Would he leave a ministry he enjoyed so much and where the results were so promising? And if he did, who could replace him and enjoy the same trust from the donors? Once Atmar was approached with the idea, he too worried about who would be his successor. And he was worried about what he could achieve in the Ministry of the Interior in the one year remaining before the presidential elections. He knew that the expectations of the international community would be high and that the key donors would be impatient and probably unrealistic in their expectations. They would be pleased, but expect too much too soon.

The annual meetings of the UN General Assembly in New York were drawing closer. There would also be a UN Security Council meeting on Afghanistan and a separate ministerial meeting among countries most involved with forces and financial resources. The debate about the government reshuffle seemed to be coming to an end, and I was looking forward to presenting some good news in New York. But on the morning of my departure from Kabul, the phone rang and a well-connected Afghan friend told me that the president had decided to delay the entire reshuffling. Was this a reliable report? After many weeks of discussions with Karzai and a sense that they were coming to a successful end, I almost wanted to postpone my trip and remain in Kabul. Most of the other news coming out of Afghanistan at this stage was negative and created a gloomy atmosphere. We needed an injection of optimism, and the cabinet reshuffle would provide that. After a few phone calls, I decided to get on the plane. The president would call me as soon as I arrived at the airport in Dubai. When he did, it was with a reassuring message. He would soon announce the changes, but it would be after my first meeting with ministers. What could I tell them? I wanted to give them good news. "Then tell them that there will be good news," Karzai responded.

A few days later, I met Atmar in New York at the UN headquarters. He was part of the Afghan delegation. He thanked me wryly for having promoted him. "Since I promoted you to an impossible job, I should have expected that you would do the same to me," he said. On October 11, Atmar was formally nominated. Following approval by the National Assembly, he moved into his new ministry and demonstrated energy and determination from the very first day. Other ministers were also appointed. Muhammad Asif Rahimi became minister of agriculture and Wahidullah Sharani took over as minister of trade and industry. Both had experience as deputy ministers and both brought a level of energy that by far surpassed their predecessors.

In February 2009 another important improvement followed. The positions of minister of finance, economic advisor to the president, and cochairman of the JCMB had been divided among two different people and lately even three. There was competition between them, which made our coordination efforts even more complicated. The economic advisor, Omar Zakhilwal, was clearly more dynamic and strategic in his thinking than the minister of finance, Ahadi, and the elderly cochairman of the JCMB, Hedayat Amin Arsala.

Above all, Zakhilwal seemed to be more of a team player. I had never been overly impressed with Ahadi. He was obviously a competent minister, but he did not share my enthusiasm for the National Solidarity Program, which I considered to be one of the great success stories of Afghan reconstruction so far. Arsala was a pleasant and aristocratic figure, but he lacked the energy and authority we now needed. Karzai had twice rejected Ahadi's resignation as minister of finance. The president knew that Ahadi was preparing to run against him in the presidential elections and probably wanted to keep him in the fold as long as possible. I expressed my frustration to him. When Ahadi announced his resignation for the third time, the president couldn't keep him any longer. Finally there was a chance for a more dynamic leadership. I strongly preferred Zakhilwal as Ahadi's replacement and Karzai knew it well. When I left his office shortly after Ahadi had resigned for the third time, Karzai told me that Zakhilwal would indeed be the next finance minister. I assured the president that his choice would be received enthusiastically by the international community.

The effects of the reshuffle came quickly. Atmar was in a hurry. He had to show from day one that he was serious about cleaning up the ministry and the police. When he arrived for his first day in the Ministry of Interior, some of the offices were already empty. Several employees had obviously decided to leave before his arrival rather than wait and face a minister determined to make serious changes. A number of higher police officers were dismissed, and illegal roadblocks where police officers could demand bribes were removed. New plans were drawn up to reform the ministry and to reorganize the police. A few months after he took over, a plan to increase the police by 15,000 officers was presented to the donors, including an increase of almost 5,000 to strengthen the security in Kabul. It was a first, urgent measure to reverse the disturbing trends in the capital and other vulnerable provinces.

The new minister of agriculture presented his first plans for modernizing the agricultural sector. The minister of trade and industry proposed new initiatives to improve working conditions for the private sector. And Zakhilwal, the new minister of finance, launched plans to increase state revenues, attack the problem of economic coordination within the government, and improve the effectiveness of the international aid community. He was now minister of finance, senior economic advisor, and my JCMB cochairman at the same time. Clearly Zakhilwal also had the president's ear.

We had experienced some unsuccessful JCMB meetings over the previous six months. Our efforts to create a more decision-oriented mechanism didn't give the results I had hoped for. There simply were no decisions to be made. Important donors started to complain again, first among themselves and then directly to me in quite unpleasant terms. During a meeting of about twenty ambassadors, some of them looked at me and said that the JCMB was now irrelevant.

Finally, after the government reshuffle, their attitudes started to change again. Political initiatives were produced by the new ministers with the assistance of the UN and other international partners. Mark Ward gave all the support he could to the ministers of finance and agriculture. And Chris Alexander worked closely with Atmar to shape his police reform. From the ambassadors we now heard praise instead of criticism. Visiting delegations of ministers and parliamentarians came to me enthusiastic about the changes that had taken place. It seemed that a long period of political standstill had come to an end.

At the time the discussions of the government reshuffle started, the UN Office for Drugs and Crime (UNODC) had presented another piece of good news. For the first time in many years, there seemed to be a positive trend in the opium production. Since

2002 the trends had gone in the wrong direction every year, with an increase in opium production from 3,400 tons to 8,200 tons in 2007. This was enormous since the annual global consumption never exceeded 4,000 tons. Afghanistan produced twice as much as the world market consumed. The latest figures showed that the production for 2008 had gone down to 7,700 tons. The number of opium-free provinces had increased from thirteen to eighteen out of a total of thirty-four provinces. Nangarhar, in the east, which had been one of the big opium-producing provinces the previous year, was now opium free. Of the total opium production in Afghanistan, 98 percent was concentrated in seven provinces, mainly in the south.

The results for 2008 also demonstrated that the eradication of opium fields and harvests, which hurt the poor farmer much more than the drug barons, had been ineffective. Only 5,480 hectares (21 square miles) of opium crop had been destroyed, which was only a quarter of what had been destroyed the previous year. But the costs in terms of human lives and economic resources had been high. Altogether, seventy-eight people had lost their lives as a result of this very limited eradication. And the economic costs per hectare had been $36,000 compared to $1,000 in Columbia. The reason for the reduction was obviously not that crops had been eradicated but that the farmers themselves had stopped growing poppies. There was a stronger leadership from a number of provincial governors. There was better support for rural development in several provinces. And religious leaders and village elders seemed to have engaged themselves more than before. Unfortunately, there was also another reason: the drought had contributed to bad harvests, especially in the north and northwest. In other words, we could not take it for granted that the same positive trends would be seen next year.

The director of the UNODC, Antonio Maria Costa, emphasized strongly that we were talking about one year of positive development, not yet a trend. We could very well witness a backlash next year. But this year, at least, we could say that opium production was not an Afghanistan-wide phenomenon, but one limited to a small number of provinces in the south of the country. And a little later, the first prognoses for the 2009 harvest were presented. They seemed to indicate that the decline in production would continue. And it did. When the final figures for that year arrived, the overall production had been reduced further to 6,900 tons and the number of opium-free provinces had increased to twenty. The most remarkable development was that production in Helmand had been cut by one-third, and this was by far the province that produced the majority of Afghanistan's opium by far.

The plans of the minister of agriculture to increase the licit agricultural production; the minister of interior's efforts to clean up a corrupt police force; the finance minister's plans for increasing the tax revenues; and the trade ministers initiative to stimulate legal economic activities: all of this affected some of the most serious concerns of many Afghans and of the international community as well—namely, corruption and drug production. Finally, we hoped to see some negative trends being turned around.

Changes had also taken place in my own office. Tom Gregg had left to marry. To succeed him I had been able to recruit the best expert on Afghanistan at UN headquarters in New York, Scott Smith. Scott had lived in Afghanistan and followed developments in the country for almost a decade. He was in charge of the Afghanistan team at the UN. His political instincts were extraordinary and nobody could match him in drafting speeches or reports. In addition, he knew the entire UN system well.

CHAPTER SEVENTEEN

OBAMA'S DREAM TEAM STUMBLES

In November 2008 Barack Obama was elected president of the United States, the first African American president in the country's history. His election was seen as good news around the entire world. He had strongly criticized the American intervention in Iraq and made Afghanistan his first foreign-policy priority. American strategy was now to be reviewed.

As early as January 10, 2009, just a week before Obama's inauguration, the new vice president-elect, Senator Joseph Biden, visited Kabul accompanied by Senator Lindsay Graham, a senior Republican. The morning before they were due to meet President Karzai, they came to Palace 7, my own residence. Within the UN Mission, we had decided to give the new administration our own input to the formation of a new strategy. First of all, we requested once again that new agreements be negotiated between the Afghan government, the United States, and NATO with regard to the presence and conduct of international forces. We also asked the Obama administration to review U.S. development policies and presented a set of concrete suggestions aimed at greater aid effectiveness. Biden was friendly, interested, and willing to listen. Since the new administration had not yet taken over and was about to undertake its own review, he did not yet wish to comment on its behalf.

Biden's meeting with President Karzai was not quite as amiable. Rumors quickly circulated among politicians and diplomats in Kabul about what had been said. Biden had made it clear that Pakistan was fifty times more important to the United States than Afghanistan. The United States was much more concerned about Al Qaeda than about the Taliban. President Karzai had once again protested the loss of Afghan civilians as a result of operations by international military forces. Both sides seemed to have offended each other. According to Bob Woodworth's book *Obama's War,* the two U.S. senators were apparently pleased with their performance. They had given Karzai a serious warning that the Obama administration's relationship to the Afghan president would not be as cozy as it had been during the Bush administration. Biden's statements sounded alarm bells among Afghan leaders and fueled Karzai's suspicions. The tone of the new American leadership was not what Karzai was accustomed to.

On January 20 Obama and Biden were inaugurated as president and vice president of the United States. The first appointments were soon announced: Secretary of State Hillary Clinton, Secretary of Defense Robert Gates, and National Security Advisor James Jones. Who would now be responsible for the everyday conduct of the United States's Afghanistan policy? A few days later came the answer that many had anticipated: Richard Holbrooke was announced as special representative for Afghanistan and Pakistan, and George Mitchell took the corresponding post for the Middle East. I had mixed feelings. Gates I knew by now and my relationship with him was excellent. Jones had been NATO's top military commander during most of my time as NATO ambassador. I had only met Holbrooke once at a breakfast meeting in New York, despite the fact that we had both been engaged in the Balkans. I had never met Hillary Clinton.

On the other hand, I knew George Mitchell relatively well. In 2000 and 2001, I had been a member of his staff on the so-called

Mitchell Commission, originally established by President Bill Clinton and UN Secretary-General Kofi Annan to present proposals that could help end the Second Intifida in the Palestinian territory. Mitchell had impressed me as a man of great integrity—determined, yet always respectful in the way he treated his interlocutors. I felt that he would have been better placed in Afghanistan than the Middle East. The Middle East conflict was deadlocked with no solution in sight. In Afghanistan, there was now a possibility to enter a new phase. I believed that Mitchell would have been much more effective than Holbrooke as Karzai's main U.S. interlocutor.

Karzai's reactions were also mixed. Holbrooke had visited Afghanistan the year before, and when he returned to the United States he had criticized Karzai sharply for failing to fight corruption in Afghanistan. Karzai had just met Biden, and that meeting had certainly not been a success. He seemed satisfied with the appointments of Clinton and Gates and wrote to President Obama to congratulate him. But it took a long time before he received any response from the new president. It quickly became clear that Obama did not intend to continue Bush's practice of biweekly video conferences with Karzai. Obama had made Afghanistan his top foreign policy priority, but there was no sign that he or the new secretary of state would visit Afghanistan in the near future. The Obama administration clearly intended to keep Karzai at arm's length. The new administration's approach to the Afghan president received broad public attention, both in Afghanistan and in international media. Karzai felt humiliated, and irritation grew in the presidential palace in Kabul.

There was a widespread impression in Kabul that Biden and Holbrooke, together with Senator Graham, were behind this new heavy-handed approach. Holbrooke was undoubtedly a person who had demonstrated that he could exercise pressure and produce rapid results. His intellectual skills were outstanding. Within a matter of a few days in Dayton, Ohio, he had negotiated an agreement between Balkan leaders that brought an end to the war in Bosnia and Herzegovina. It was a historic achievement. But in Afghanistan, external pressure could not yield the same results as in the Balkans. Quick results were simply not achievable. Obama had said that the new administration would distinguish itself from its predecessors in its ability to listen, and I was encouraged when I read that. It seemed to indicate that the new president had understood the feeling in many capitals about U.S. diplomacy. But Holbrooke was not renowned for his listening skills. The first signals did not indicate that Washington would listen more than in the past, but rather the contrary.

Already in the beginning of February, members of the new U.S. leadership were due to meet Karzai at the annual Munich security conference. Karzai also had a meeting with the NATO secretary general, Jaap de Hoop Scheffer, on his agenda. I had discussed the Munich conference with several of my closest Afghan interlocutors. None of us could afford for this to go wrong. The day before his departure, I sat down with Karzai in his office. I emphasized that this was not simply another conference, but his first real meeting with the new U.S. administration. The discussions with Holbrooke the previous year had not gone well. The meeting with Biden a few weeks earlier had been bad. I understood Karzai's feelings and concerns, but the Munich conference had to be used to establish a good relationship with Obama's people. Karzai fully agreed and he seemed to look forward to the conference. The same afternoon the NATO secretary general called. What was the atmosphere like in Kabul? Was the president in a constructive mood? He obviously shared my concerns. I gave him my impression from the meeting with Karzai earlier in the day. Karzai had seemed constructive and eager to turn this into a success. I felt fairly certain that the meetings in Munich would go well, but I added that this was my impression two days before the conference. I knew that the situation could change quickly.

I received frequent reports from the meetings in Munich from Afghans and internationals present. They were alarming. Important meetings between Karzai and the Americans had turned into confrontations. The NATO secretary general had ended up asking Karzai if he wanted the international forces to leave Afghanistan. "If so, then tell me now," de Hoop Scheffer had said. The days in Munich had reinforced international skepticism about Karzai as well as Karzai's suspicion toward the international community. And again it seemed that it was the civilian casualties that had triggered the intense discussions. From Kabul it was impossible to judge who were to blame for the confrontational meetings.

But there was something else that caught my attention from the meeting in Munich. In two of his appearances, Holbrooke had spoken about the international coordination efforts in Afghanistan. He had brought up the old Ashdown story and characterized Karzai's rejection of Ashdown as a lost opportunity for all involved. Not once had he mentioned the UN. Ashdown and Holbrooke knew each other well, as the British politician had for years been in charge of implementing the agreement Holbrooke had negotiated. In response the Afghan foreign minister, Spanta, had defended me and commented that international coordination would not have been any easier whether the international civilian leader was Ashdown or Eide. Holbrooke's comments surprised me. He had been U.S. ambassador to the UN. I had expected a commitment to work together. Instead, a story that was now one year old had surfaced again.

Irritated by Holbrooke's remarks, I sent an email to Jim Jones and Robert Gates expressing my disappointment about an entirely unnecessary and unhelpful comment. I later heard that the email had reached Hillary Clinton and was conveyed to Holbrooke. In the evening a few days later, I was sitting in Palace 7 with Alain le Roy, who was the new head of the Department of Peacekeeping Operations (DPKO). He was now my immediate superior at the UN headquarters. Hanne Melfald, my special assistant, informed me that Holbrooke was on the phone. What followed was a heated and unpleasant exchange. I complained about his Munich remarks and he complained about the fact that I had raised them with his superiors. I could see the concern in the face of le Roy sitting on the sofa next to me. The media had called me the "mild-mannered Norwegian." That was probably also the impression in New York— or at least, until this phone call. It was a bad start. Karzai was not the only one who had difficulty forming a good relationship with the new American administration.

Three days later Holbrooke came to Kabul. We were scheduled to have breakfast together at the residence of the U.S. ambassador, Bill Wood. I had to repair the damage done a few days earlier, and I asked Wood for a few minutes alone with Holbrooke before breakfast. But Holbrooke had been delayed the evening before due to bad weather and had arrived from Islamabad late in the night. He was tired when he finally joined us for our breakfast meeting. There was no time for a private discussion with him. Instead, we all sat straight down to have a breakfast, a group of Americans and my own closest colleagues. After having greeted us, Holbrooke asked me, 'When does your contract expire?" I had only recently renewed it for another year, I responded. The damage control had not started well.

Then followed the next surprise: "I understand that you're an old friend of Peter Galbraith from your years in the Balkans," Holbrooke said. Galbraith was a close friend of the Pakistani president, Asif Ali Zardari, and Holbrooke had met them both in Islamabad. "He would be an excellent number-two in UNAMA," Holbrooke added. I was in the process of interviewing candidates for that position. Chris Alexander was to leave after many years in Kabul, first as Canadian ambassador and then as deputy head of the UN Mission. My preferred choice to succeed him in the position was an experienced German diplomat named Martin Kobler. I told Holbrooke that I knew Galbraith well. We had not been close friends but had worked together in Zagreb between 1994 and 1995. We had also spent time together privately. Our relationship in Croatia had sometimes been strained, but we had maintained a professional friendship.

I had several doubts about Galbraith. I knew that he would never make an excellent deputy. He would find it difficult to adapt to being my immediate subordinate. I also thought it would be a mistake to appoint an American as the political deputy of the UN Mission. I knew that confrontations would occur between the United States and me in the future, just as they had in the previous eleven months I had spent in Kabul. I wanted to be able to think and discuss without one of Holbrooke's closest allies constantly looking over my shoulder. Moreover, I often had to spend time away from Kabul, and during such periods Galbraith would lead UNAMA and be the head of the UN family, which would mean that the three leading international figures would be the American ambassador, the American ISAF commander, and an American UN representative. That would simply be too much; the international presence would be dominated by Americans. I was concerned about the impression this would give of the UN among Afghans and international colleagues.

The ideal solution would be to find an experienced representative of a Muslim country as my deputy. We had searched for such a candidate without any luck. The second best option would be a representative of an important European country. It could not be the U.K. A German candidate seemed to be a good alternative. But now Holbrooke had put Galbraith's name on the table, and Ban Ki-moon would obviously be under strong pressure to appoint him.

However, Holbrooke's main focus that morning was another topic: Could we live with Karzai for another five years? I had just had my own conversation with Karzai regarding his thinking about the future, and I certainly did not want to inform Holbrooke about it. I expressed my serious concerns to Holbrooke. It would be impossible to live the next five years in the same atmosphere of confrontation

Visiting George W. Bush in the White House, spring 2008, with
Hanne Melfald, Tom Gregg, and Scott Smith.

General McChrystal visiting me at home in Palace 7.

The commemoration of the United Nations' International Day of
Peace, September 16, with multiple organizations present.

At a conference in Kabul, July 8, 2009. From left: Atmar, Rassoul,
Wardak, Zakhilwal, me, Galbraith, and Watkins.

Meeting of ministers of defense in Krakow, February 19, 2009.
Secretary of Defense Robert Gates is sharing some of his thoughts.

Visiting a polling station in Kabul, August 20, 2009.

Karzai announces that he is willing to take part in a second election round, here with John Kerry.

After immense efforts Dr. Abdullah and Karzai were finally convinced to meet with regard to the election.

Report on the election in the upper house of the Parliament. At the top, chairman of the upper house, Mujaddedi. In front, from left: Margie Cook and Chris Alexander.

A "private" walk in beautiful Bandi Amir.

Opening of the UNAMA office in Sar-i-Pul.

Meeting with the residents in a village outside of Jalalabad, the Province of Nangarhar.

Sewing classes for young girls in the Province of Nangarhar.

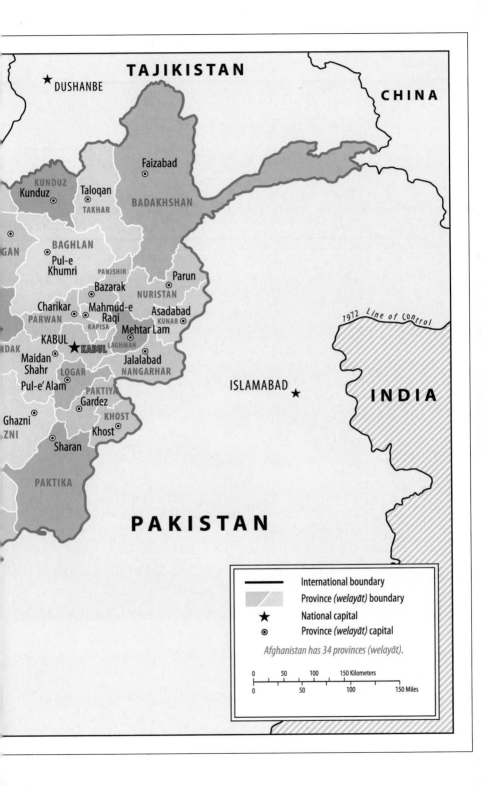

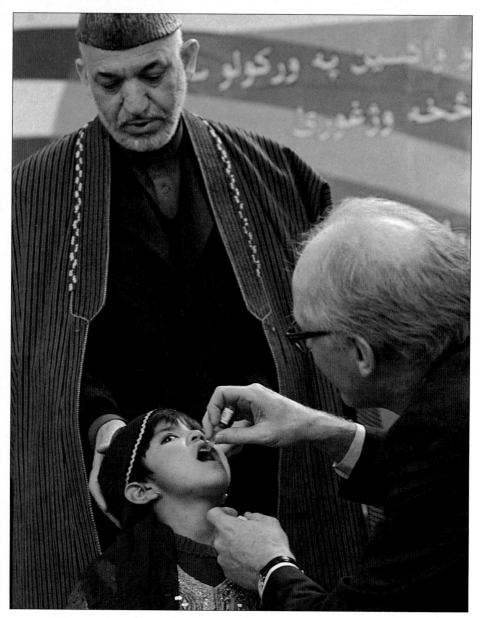

The opening of a vaccination campaign against polio, January 11, 2009.

Pervez Kambaksh, who had been sentenced to death, right before he became a free man.

The residence in Kabul, Palace 7, with the surrounding garden.

A last good-bye to one of the UN workers killed in the attack on the Bakthar Guesthouse.

Surrounded by security guards at all times.

Driving through one of the security points on my way home to Palace 7.

Press conference, August 9, 2009. On the left: the chairperson of the Afghan Independent Human Rights Commission, Sima Samar; on the right: the press officer, Nilab Mobarez.

The London meeting, January 28, 2010. From left: NATO Secretary General Anders Fogh Rasmussen, UN Secretary-General Ban Ki-moon, and US Secretary of State Hillary Clinton.

Two years have come to an end; saying good-bye to Kabul.

The never tiresome sight of the mountains of Afghanistan.

that we had experienced in these past months. But we also had our share of the responsibility for the current atmosphere of mistrust. In the end it was the Afghan people who would have to decide who would be their president for the coming five years. When Karzai was first elected, he was also the candidate of the international community—particularly the United States. This time, we had all agreed that we would show no preference and remain neutral.

Holbrooke continued and went one step further: "Who would be the best candidate to replace Karzai?" He mentioned one of my favorites in the current Karzai government, Haneef Atmar. Holbrooke had decided that he wanted to meet him the following day and raise the issue. I had serious doubt that Atmar could or would challenge the president. He was known for his loyalty to Karzai and would not be prepared to stand against him. Meeting him separately would also be a dangerous move; he would immediately inform the president. But Holbrooke arranged a meeting and raised the subject. The response was, predictably, a polite refusal. Karzai probably learned about Holbrooke's move before the day was over. In the days and weeks that followed, rumors circulated about politicians that had been encouraged by Holbrooke to challenge Karzai. The rumors included ministers as well as prominent politicians in the opposition.

One Friday morning I went to the Turquoise Mountain, a center for young craftsmen on the outskirts of Kabul. The center was founded by a British academic and politician, Rory Stewart, who made a name for himself following the publication of his remarkable book *The Places in Between*, an account of his journey on foot between Herat and Kabul. The center was having an open day with artisans and craftsmen present and had invited a number of diplomats and politicians. I spotted First Vice President Ahmad Zia Massoud sitting on a carpet drinking tea and decided to join him. It had been a long time since I had last seen him, and I asked him politely how he had been. Massoud jokingly remarked that he felt lonely. "I must be the only person in Kabul whom Holbrooke has not invited to challenge Karzai for the presidency," he said. An exaggeration, of course, but it was a clear indication of the prevailing atmosphere in Kabul.

Holbrooke's activities during this period greatly damaged the confidence between Afghan leaders and the new U.S. administration. Karzai's anger was widely shared within the Afghan government, even by those most skeptical of the president. The common sentiment was that Washington was displaying a dangerous lack of respect. The new U.S. administration was not simply trying to maintain a neutral stance with regard to who would become Afghanistan's new president. This was an attempt to sideline Karzai. He found it difficult to believe that Holbrooke's efforts to mobilize against him did not reflect the views of the entire new U.S. administration. Karzai looked at Holbrooke's activities in the context of what he had experienced over the last few weeks: the unsuccessful Biden visit and the abrupt end to the video conferences that he had grown accustomed to. The new administration did not only want to keep him at a distance, it seemed to want him out.

For some time, there had been constant speculations about the American UN ambassador, Zalmai Khalilzad. Would he stand against Karzai? Khalilzad would, of course, never admit publicly that he was thinking of running for president. But he seemed to be testing the waters or positioning himself for a future in Afghan politics. Karzai believed that such a well-known representative of the United States would never consider running for president in Afghanistan without at least the tacit agreement of the U.S. leadership.

On February 19, a few days after the breakfast with Holbrooke at the residence of the U.S. ambassador in Kabul, I met Robert Gates in Krakow, Poland. Defense ministers from all ISAF countries were meeting, and NATO's secretary general had made a habit of inviting me to such occasions. I had requested a few moments to speak with Gates alone. My questions were simple: Did he know about Holbrooke's activities? Did they really represent the policy of the new U.S. administration? Were they looking to replace Karzai? For Gates, Holbrooke's activities seemed to come as a surprise. No doubt the Obama administration had decided to keep Karzai at a distance and to show him that this would not be the warm relationship he was used to. But they had not agreed to replace him. Gates seemed surprised and concerned. It was clear that the members of Obama's team in Afghanistan were not on the same page.

Just after Holbrooke's first visit, I was called to Karzai's office. We had both experienced unpleasant encounters with Holbrooke over the last few days, and neither of us could hide our disappointment and concerns. "He is after both of us," Karzai said. He had probably heard of my own confrontation with Holbrooke from his ministers. And I agreed.

My first experience with Holbrooke had been difficult. But he also took initiatives that I fully supported. In particular, he invited colleagues from countries involved in Afghanistan to create a group of special representatives for Afghanistan and Pakistan, known as the "Af-Pak" group. Soon it consisted of more than twenty representatives. I hoped that this group could be a useful channel of communication between me and the UN on one side and political leaders in important capitals on the other.

Before the end of April, the new American ambassador to Kabul, Karl Eikenberry, was confirmed by the U.S. Senate. He had two tours of duty behind him as a military commander in Afghanistan and knew Karzai well. Eikenberry brought a strong team with him, in particular the highly experienced diplomat Francis Ricciardone as his deputy. Both were impressive individuals and both became my good friends. I had met Eikenberry several times since I took over as SRSG. During my first visit to the NATO headquarters in April 2008, we had spent an hour together. Eikenberry had shared with me his thoughts about the situation in Afghanistan and his view of

Karzai. He described Karzai with respect and advised me to seek a close relationship to him. "Whenever you travel," he said, "inform the president in advance and offer to bring one of his ministers with you. It is more important that they are seen than that you are seen." The day Eikenberry arrived in Kabul I had my weekly consultation meeting with around twenty ambassadors. Eikenberry came almost directly from the airport to Palace 7 to join the meeting. It was intended as a show of support for the role of the UN, and it made a solid impression on me as well as on the others gathered around the table.

By the end of March, Peter Galbraith had been appointed to be my deputy. This was the only time Ban Ki-moon and I disagreed during my two years in Afghanistan. The pressure on the secretary-general to choose Galbraith had been strong, and after a while, he conceded. But an atmosphere of doubt prevailed in the UN system. I told the secretary-general that I could live with the decision if he thought it was important to appoint Galbraith, but I did not look forward to having him in the UN Mission.

On March 19 I was due to brief the UN Security Council. Later in the week, I met briefly with Galbraith at the Beekman Tower Hotel. It was a polite and friendly conversation. Galbraith stressed that he would be loyal to me and certainly would not be Holbrooke's tool. But my instincts told me that my arguments against his appointment were right. During that weekend, before traveling from New York to Washington to meet the new U.S. administration, I attempted to have the announcement of his appointment postponed. I did not want it to dominate the conversations and possible media reports from my visit to Washington. I called several people who had been involved within the UN secretariat. They were all at a weekend retreat with members of the UN Security Council. Finally, I was able to speak with a senior member of Ban Ki-moon's staff. Once again I expressed my doubts, and asked that the decision be postponed for another few days. The media wrote that I had tried to block his appointment, which was not correct. But as soon as he was appointed, leading U.S. newspapers were writing about the new American "dream team," in which Galbraith would be responsible for ensuring that American policy was followed within the UN. It was a kind of story that was unavoidable, but also exactly what I had feared. It certainly was not received with enthusiasm at the UN headquarters in New York or in the presidential palace in Kabul.

CHAPTER EIGHTEEN

CLINTON'S SURPRISE ANNOUNCE-MENT AND THE HAGUE CONFERENCE

The new U.S. administration started its review of the American strategy in Afghanistan. Hundreds of pages were produced and discussed. We had given Vice President Biden our advice when he visited Kabul just before the inauguration. Now we could only observe the discussions from a distance. No serious attempts were made to consult. A group of key Afghan ministers had visited Washington in February, and it was during this visit that one of them wrote me the text message with only one word, "Neocolonialism." The Afghans did not feel that they had been consulted. They had spent one week in Washington, but they had largely been spectators.

The NATO secretary general had pulled me aside and given me a cautious hint during the ISAF Defence Ministers' meeting in Krakow; it seemed that the new U.S. administration was planning a big conference on Afghanistan in order to present its strategy, he had said. I did not hear more about it for several weeks and thought that the plan could have been dropped. However, on March 5 I was in my office at Palace 7 in front of my computer. Suddenly, I received an email from the assistant secretary of state, Richard Boucher, in Washington. He had been responsible for U.S.-Afghanistan policies in the State Department for several years but was now planning to leave. Boucher had become a good friend and was well liked among the Afghans. Now he wrote that I would soon receive a message that the United States wanted a new international Afghanistan conference and that I would be asked to chair it. That was all.

I was still in front of the computer when the first reports started to come in from news agencies in Brussels. A NATO foreign ministers' meeting had just ended and Hillary Clinton had called a press conference. She had announced that there would be a big international conference in The Hague to present the U.S. strategy and agree on the way forward. The UN secretary-general would be present and I would be asked to chair the conference. Surprised, I called Foreign Minister Spanta and told him about the news reports. What was this all about? He had just been in Washington with several of his colleagues. Why had he not informed me? But Spanta was more surprised than I was. During his stay in Washington, nobody had informed him about a possible conference. He would call Karzai immediately to check if the president had been informed. A few minutes later Spanta called back. Karzai had not been notified and knew nothing. He was not happy about receiving the news in this way. The following day I met with Karzai and some of his ministers in the presidential palace. There was great irritation, not because the administration in Washington wanted a conference on Afghanistan, but because the Afghans themselves had been neither consulted nor informed. To Karzai and his closest ministers, it was yet another example of the new administration treating them without respect. However, we had to start getting ready for the Hague conference. The date was set for March 31.

During the following two weeks, I did not have further news about the conference. Since I would be going to New York for the regular UN Security Council meeting in March, I decided to spend a day in Washington on the way to New York. Richard Boucher did his very best to help, but it was clear that the new administration had not yet drawn its conclusions from the review. The strategy debate was in its final stage, and there was not much information to give us. We were informed that President Obama himself was planning to launch the new strategy in a speech. Hopefully, the Americans would be able to give us what we needed in advance of the conference in The Hague. We had to start thinking of a final declaration from the conference. Boucher and I sat down with some of our staff to discuss an outline of a declaration and what I could say to delegations at the UN later in the week.

At the UN headquarters in New York, we brought together a large group of member states and international organizations to consult on the forthcoming conference. It became a painful event, because we had little to report. But it must have been even more painful for the U.S. representative, who knew even less than we did. As soon as our meetings at the UN headquarters were over a few days later, we returned to Washington hoping that we would now be able to learn more about the U.S. preparations. The clock was ticking fast, and we urgently needed information in order to plan the Hague conference.

Back in the State Department, it was clear that the last days had been consumed by lengthy discussions of the new strategy. Mark Ward and I had been speaking for months about a "civilian surge"— more attention to critical civilian requirements. Now the same theme seemed to be emerging from the discussions in Washington. I was enthusiastic about what I was told, even if it was still difficult to get a precise read on the strategy. The conference in The Hague was only days away. With Boucher, we continued work on a first draft for a concluding declaration. It included a statement that civilian assistance was as important as military programs and a commitment to reduce dependency on big contractors. Not only was the civilian emphasis positive, but it also seemed that the new administration was prepared to look at the effectiveness of the U.S. assistance.

Two days in Washington also gave us a chance to meet the most prominent members of the new administration and to gain greater insight into U.S. thinking. Hillary Clinton impressed me from the first moment. She asked concrete questions about requirements in agriculture, infrastructure, and civilian institutions. From our conversations with Robert Gates and others, we understood that the United States was launching an ambitious plan to recruit hundreds of American civilian experts to Afghanistan. I had never experienced any discussion in Washington with such emphasis on areas that had also become our priorities.

In almost all the meetings, my relationship with Holbrooke was raised. *The Times* of London had reported that Holbrooke considered me to be "useless and ineffective." I had little doubt that the anonymous source was either somebody close to Holbrooke or Holbrooke himself. The comment seemed to be a follow-up to our first conversations in early February. During his stay in Kabul, I had heard Holbrooke deliver unflattering remarks about several international and American colleagues, people who were among my closest partners. His superiors emphasized that the United States fully supported the UN and me. President Obama had himself given the same message to Secretary-General Ban Ki-moon in their first conversation. But Robert Gates again questioned whether I would receive the assistance I needed from the UN bureaucracy in New York. "We support you fully," he repeated. "The problem is that you are not getting the resources you need."

We returned to New York for another round of consultations before the Hague meeting. The discussions had become more concrete, but still we only had a limited impression of what the U.S. review would conclude. On March 27 President Obama gave his speech and presented the main elements of the new strategy. And when I was getting ready to leave New York for Europe and The Hague, I received a five-page document, a so-called White Paper, summarizing the new U.S. strategy.

Pakistan was now more at the center of Washington's strategic thinking. It was obvious that without an effective policy toward the insurgency in Pakistan, Afghanistan would be confronted with permanent instability. Of course there was a need for a stronger strategic engagement with Islamabad. But it would be difficult to move from declarations to concrete political steps. The Pakistani authorities had been a problem for the Bush administration and would remain a problem for Obama and his team. Political pressure had been tried and generous economic support had been given. However, there had not been any change in Pakistan's policy toward Afghanistan.

I was pleased to see the strong emphasis placed on the need to change the priorities in the civilian assistance to Afghanistan and to make it more effective. The paper said the U.S. and other development aid had been poorly organized and several key areas were seriously underfinanced. I could not have agreed more. At the same time, significant parts of the international assistance had gone to finance international consultants. There had never been a real assessment of the impact of U.S. aid programs; therefore, a total change was required. We could have written these parts of the White Paper ourselves. And the paper we had given Vice President Biden two months earlier had made the same arguments.

The White Paper also identified the areas that had to be given priority: agriculture, infrastructure, and a dramatic build-up of Afghan capacity to enable the Afghans to strengthen their institutions, in particular in the provinces and the districts. The paper called for a "civilian surge," the expression we had used in UNAMA, including a strong increase of civilian expertise paralleling the expansion of the army and the police.

I was also satisfied with the attention given to a policy of reconciliation: Mullah Omar and other members of the Taliban core could not be included in reconciliation. But the war could not be won without convincing the "nonideological insurgents" to lay down their arms. This did not go as far as my own views, since I believed that a policy of reconciliation would have to include the Taliban leadership. I wondered what precisely the United States meant by "nonideological insurgents." But Washington had taken a huge step in the right direction.

I arrived in The Hague a day before the rest of the UN team to continue work on the final declaration before the conference started. From the window of the hotel, where the conference was also going to take place, I could observe the Dutch working to get everything ready. It was like watching a movie in fast-forward, with flagpoles, conference and media facilities, flowers, and security measures being put in place in record time.

Holbrooke had asked for another meeting in The Hague the day before the opening of the conference. He had two main points on his agenda: How could we get rid of Karzai's half-brother Ahmad Wali Karzai, who was chairman of the Provincial Council in Kandahar and widely criticized for corruption? And secondly, could I help Holbrooke arrange a meeting with the Iranian deputy foreign minister the following day? I recommended against raising the question of Karzai's half-brother without having solid evidence available. It had been done before; international representatives had presented general accusations to Karzai without any proof. Karzai's reaction had always been the same: "If you give me evidence, then I will act. Without evidence, I will not." That was likely to be his reaction if Holbrooke raised the matter. He would only be angered, and the discussion would lead nowhere. I believed that the United States must have an abundance of intelligence that would prove the half-brother's involvement. Why not make use of it? After all, Ahmad Wali Karzai had been paid by the CIA for years. He owned properties rented by the United States in Kandahar. He was Washington's partner.

The most pressing topic that Holbrooke had on his mind was the Iranian participation at the conference in The Hague. At the Paris conference in June 2008, the Iranians had abstained from participating at the very last moment. Now they had decided to be represented by the deputy foreign minister, Mohammad Mekdi Akhoudzadeh. That was an important development. Could I sound him out and see if he would be prepared to meet Holbrooke the following day? All the media attention would now be on the Iranian participation and not on the conference itself, Holbrooke said. I certainly wanted to be helpful and had scheduled a meeting with the Iranian early the next morning. But I had serious doubts that he would be willing to meet Holbrooke; he probably did not have instructions that would allow him to meet a very senior U.S. representative at such short notice.

The following morning I raised the possibility of a meeting with Holbrooke during my discussion with Mr. Akhoudzadeh, and I encouraged him to meet the American envoy. However, he confirmed what I had thought already: it was not possible for him to meet with Holbrooke now. I informed Holbrooke as soon as the conversation ended. The rest of the morning I was busy chairing the conference with the Dutch foreign minister, Maxim Verhagen, and Foreign Minister Spanta. During lunch I was seated between the Afghan and Pakistani foreign ministers. Holbrooke was at the table behind me, with his back close to mine. At the end of the lunch, he leaned back and asked me where the Iranian was sitting. I told him that he was sitting right across from me next to the Turkish foreign minister, Ahmet Davutoglu. Holbrooke got up from his table and walked over to Davutoglu and greeted him. He stretched his hand across to Akhoudzadeh and introduced himself. Akhoudzadeh responded and they exchanged a few polite phrases. "We must stay in touch," Holbrooke said. The surprised Iranian did not react. And then it was over.

In less than thirty seconds, Holbrooke created the media headlines of the day. Almost without exception, the media reported about the surprise meeting that had taken place. It was seen as a symbolic first contact, an introduction to a new phase in the relationship between the two countries. Hillary Clinton emphasized at her press conference that it had not been a planned meeting. It certainly had not been—at least not for the Iranian. I was pleased to see that Holbrooke wanted to meet Akhoudzadeh. Perhaps it was a sign of a more constructive policy and a U.S. readiness to at least discuss Afghanistan with its neighbor to the west. It was a unique opportunity and I certainly wanted to assist. But I was sad to see how Holbrooke made use of this improvised contact to create a media story that had little to do with the reality. It could have been a brief and discreet confidence-building step. But the media coverage became more important than the political process. Iranian skepticism toward the United States was reinforced rather than the opposite. In Tehran the authorities denied that any meeting had taken place. Later I tried to arrange a meeting between Holbrooke and the Iranian ambassador in Kabul in my residence when Holbrooke visited during fall 2009. But again the Iranian declined, this time at the very last minute.

While the foreign ministers were making their speeches in The Hague, the concluding declaration had to be finalized for approval. We made use of the U.S. White Paper to the extent we could. And we knew that the UN positions were identical to those of the Afghan government: a better balance between the civilian and military challenges; the need for clear priorities that would form a strategic approach to the development of the country; and an impact-based policy rather than one determined by the short-term priorities of individual donors. For quite some time we had argued for ambitious national programs to build civilian institutions in the districts and provinces as well as in Kabul. Ministries suffered from a dramatic lack of qualified staff to develop new nationwide development programs. However, better institutions could not be built without educating the human resources. Additional attention had to be paid to higher education and professional training. To create sustainable growth, critical sectors such as agriculture, energy, and infrastructure had to be given higher priority. The foreign-aid programs had to aim at reducing dependency on expensive foreign contractors and ensuring equitable development across the country. We tried to have all these elements reflected in the declaration.

The last consultations took place in the meeting hall, with members of the UN delegation rushing around to get acceptance from delegations. With minor adjustments the declaration was adopted and the meeting was adjourned. Strategic priorities had been set in a much more precise way than at the Paris conference. Important principles for aid effectiveness had been included. On paper, this was a first outline for a strategic development policy. And it was a departure from the dependency culture that had become an obstacle to Afghanistan's development. In my own short speech, I urged the participants to concentrate on the priorities that had now been set and to do their utmost to put the "doom and gloom" atmosphere behind. Hillary Clinton made the same points. It was time to roll up our sleeves and get to work in a more focused way than before.

Even if the Hague declaration was promising, none of us expected immediate changes in donor policies. But we—the Afghan ministers and UN together—hoped that it could represent a turning point. Unlike the Bush administration, the new U.S. administration seemed to have a strategy, and in many ways one similar to ours. We left The Hague with a sense of relief and new energy. But we also left curious about how the U.S. administration would proceed. Would Washington listen more? The preparations for the conference had not been encouraging. Could this conference be the start of something new and different?

CHAPTER NINETEEN

FINALLY, A REAL STRATEGY?

We arrived back in Kabul determined to make the most of the results from The Hague. Finance Minister Zakhilwal, Mark Ward, and I decided to get together immediately to start the follow-up from the conference. A few days later, we met at Palace 7 with a group of other ministers. We knew that preparations were underway in Washington to recruit a large number of civilian experts—several hundred—intended for the American PRTs. There had not been any consultations with the Afghans with regard to what kinds of experts were required or where they would be needed; the risk was now that a large number of more or less qualified foreign experts would arrive in Afghanistan without an Afghan plan that could guide the donors, including the United States. We needed a preemptive Afghan program that was based on Afghan requirements. During the meeting in Palace 7, Zakhilwal gave his colleagues three weeks to formulate a list of priorities. The donors were, I think, surprised when the first draft was circulated to them, and most were pleased. Following some adjustments, the plan was presented to donors from the Ministry of Finance as well as from my own office with a strong encouragement to come up with experts and financial resources as soon as possible. It suggested, as a beginning, to provide resources and experts for fifty-five priority positions. At the following JCMB meeting, donors adopted the plan. The first promises of financial support came quickly. We seemed to be on the right track.

Following the Hague conference, Zakhilwal also developed his plan to reorganize the government, with support from Mark Ward. After the adoption of the Afghan National Development Strategy in Paris in June 2008, seventeen interministerial committees had been created. The result was, of course, that no serious coordination took place. Zakhilwal wanted to bring together clusters of ministers to address the priorities that had been defined and approved in The Hague: agriculture, infrastructure, human resource development, and, later, civilian institutions or governance.

A few weeks earlier, Mark Ward and I had brought the three ministers responsible for different parts of the education sector together. I was surprised when the new minister of education, Farooq Wardak, told me that this was the first time they had met to discuss the entire education sector as a whole. The discussion revealed serious imbalances in the education strategy and a lack of an overarching thinking. Education was one of the government's priorities. But how could we ask the donors to reallocate resources if the Afghan government and the UN did not have a comprehensive outline of requirements?

The education sector was always presented as one of the success stories in Afghanistan. But still 42 percent of all children of school age were without any access to education. Altogether, 74 percent of Afghans fifteen years or older were illiterate. Teacher training was lagging behind. Training of female teachers was concentrated in a small number of big cities. In some of the thirty-four provinces only 3 percent of the teachers were women. And in one-third of the 364 districts, there were no female teachers at all. This had a serious impact on efforts to bring girls to school. Donors had focused on the number of schools without making sure that the new schools had trained personnel and adequate equipment. In a few years, 600,000 young boys and girls would graduate from school. But universities could only absorb 60,000 of them, and public professional education would be able to accept less than half of that figure. Only 4 percent of those who graduated would be able to receive professional education. The number should probably have been 40 percent. In spite of the constant efforts of Haneef Atmar during his term as minister of education, donors had given little attention to what was needed to make education meaningful and to what would happen once these young people had finished their primary or secondary education. If these imbalances were not addressed quickly, we would soon have an enormous number of young people without opportunities for further education. Afghanistan would not be able to build the capacity required for economic development. It would become yet another potential source of disappointment and discontent.

Similar imbalances could also be found in civilian institutions, in Kabul as well as in provinces and districts across Afghanistan. Ministries had a large number of foreign advisors, but they were scattered across the government, with little thinking being given to their strategic impact. Documentation from the Independent Directorate for Local Governance (IDLG) told us that out of the 364 district governors, 184 had no office space, 288 had no vehicles, and 318 administrative centers lacked electricity. The salary level was low; a district governor could earn as little as $70 per month and have an administrative budget of $15. I repeatedly asked Popal, the director of the IDLG, if these figures were correct. And every time he confirmed them to me. How could you then believe that district authorities would deliver the services the population rightly expected of them? And how could you expect local authorities to resist the temptation of taking bribes from the population?

Another missing element was the training of civil servants. Many donors were engaged in "governance" programs, in training and support of various kinds to local authorities. But these efforts were insufficient and unsystematic. While one donor country organized small training courses in one part of the country, another donor would organize a different course in another part. Each donor provided training according to its own traditions and standards. Again, the international community contributed to the fragmentation of the civil service rather than bringing it together based on Afghan needs.

Gradually, the instruments we needed were coming into place. The government of South Korea had built a Civil Service Institute in the outskirts of Kabul. Since the Koreans only paid for the building itself, there had been problems securing resources for the operation of the institute. It had offices in thirty-two of the thirty-four provinces and could offer training courses for thousands of civil servants. During fall of 2009, we celebrated another important milestone: an Afghan curriculum for administrative functions, such as financial management, administration, procurement, and project development, had been developed. It could be used across the country, employ Afghan teaching personnel, and give all civil servants the same training. However, it was a step that received little attention from donors. At an event celebrating the completion of this work, only a U.S. representative and myself were present from the international community. The institute continued its struggle for financial resources. And donors continued to prefer their own fragmented and modest training courses.

In August 2008, Karzai, Atmar, and I had inaugurated a new National Institute for Management and Administration (NIMA). A year later, 1,700 young, future civil servants and managers attended the institute. They came from all the provinces, and almost half of the students were women. But the budget was so low that it did not even allow for proper cleaning and maintenance. With the current salary level for local civil servants, most of the students would probably not return to their own province when their education was over but would seek better employment in Kabul or the other main cities.

Salaries, training, infrastructure, and appointment policies were parts of a wider package of problems that had to be addressed at the same time. In other words, some of the critical tools required to create a better functioning civil service existed. But over and over again I found that donors were not aware of them. On two occasions toward the end of my mandate foreign ministers asked me if it would be a good idea to create an institute for the civil service. I could not blame them for not knowing that the institute already existed. On the contrary, I was pleased that there was finally interest at such a high level.

Agriculture was still at the level of the Middle Ages in many parts of the country. Afghanistan had more than 30,000 square miles of arable land, but much less than half—some estimated as little as 25 percent—were now cultivated, mainly as a result of lack of water. Only a third of the area that had been irrigated before conflict ruined the country now had such systems. By far most of the surface water was flowing out of Afghanistan unutilized. Investments in this area could more than double agricultural production and enable farmers to switch to more profitable crops. Improved infrastructure and cold-storage facilities could even turn Afghanistan from a vulnerable, food-insecure country into an exporter of agricultural products; in earlier times, Afghan raisins and pomegranates had been attractive products beyond the borders of Afghanistan. The farmers also had very limited access to loans in order to increase their production or switch to more profitable crops. Families, drug criminals, or loan sharks were the most accessible sources for loans. And they often forced the farmers to continue their opium production rather than enabling them to grow other crops.

Infrastructure needed investments that could have a positive impact on productive activities. The ring road around the country had been almost completed, reducing travel time between major cities and stimulating economic activities. But a wider plan for the country's strategic infrastructure was lacking, infrastructure that could give Afghanistan electric power and the ability to start extracting its natural resources. In June 2009 Zakhilwal, Mark Ward, and I presented a document to the big donors at the G-8 meeting in Trieste and to the group of special representatives established by Holbrooke. We identified two priority projects. The first was the extension of the power corridors from Central Asia. A first power line from Uzbekistan had now been completed and had given significant parts of Kabul power for fifteen hours a day. It had stimulated economic activities and reduced dependence on expensive and polluting diesel generators. The second priority was the construction of a rail-link across the country from Pakistan to Iran with an extension toward the north. This would link Afghanistan to all neighboring countries as well as to the sea in Iran and Pakistan and to China via the Central Asian countries. It would pass in the vicinity of vast mineral resources and facilitate economic activities inside Afghanistan and trade across the entire region.

Altogether, these areas represented a strategic approach to development. Agriculture and infrastructure would form the basis for the exploitation of Afghanistan's natural resources. They would open for real economic growth, employment, and gradual reduction in the dependency of foreign aid. Development of the educational sector would help provide the human resources to create a more competent labor market and to enhance the government's ability to administer the country.

Under the leadership of the Ministry of Finance and with UNAMA's support, we now had the strategic outline. Efforts to streamline the government were underway. It would force ministers to focus their efforts better and have a common objective concentrated around a set of priorities. But would the donor community respond and support this new Afghan approach, or would donors continue to do more of the same? The first weeks after the Hague conference had been promising. There were more reform-oriented people in the government than before. The priorities were becoming clearer. But we had only just started. The next steps would have to follow quickly: the development of national programs and projects that could force the donors to focus their resources. It was May. The elections were less than four months away. And the political temperature was heating up. My fear was now that the elections would absorb so much attention and energy that the reform process would stagnate or be derailed.

CHAPTER TWENTY

OLD WARLORDS ENTER THE SCENE

We had entered a new phase in the election process. The focus was now on how to create equal conditions for all the candidates. "Level playing field" were the buzz words among both international representatives and the Afghan opposition. The Afghans knew better than foreign representatives that this would be an almost impossible task. Our understanding of the Afghan society and what took place in villages and local communities was limited, and so was our access to them. But it was of critical importance to our credibility that we demonstrated readiness to take the challenge seriously. Hopefully our effort could have some impact and have a deterring effect on attempts to intimidate voters. In UNAMA, a set of guidelines for the conduct of candidates and authorities were formulated and presented to the president as well as to other candidates. The AIHRC and UNAMA decided to monitor the election process together and to present regular reports of our findings. I asked the president to sign a decree on noninterference in the election process as he had done during the last elections. The purpose was to deter Afghan authorities and institutions from misusing their positions to influence the campaign and the election results. I discussed the decree with Karzai on several occasions before it was issued. He insisted on one addition before it was signed: that the international community should also abstain from any interference in the election process. That was a reasonable addition in light of what we had already experienced.

It was also a period of nomination of candidates. In parallel with the presidential elections, there were elections of the thirty-four provincial councils. Since most of the attention was devoted to the presidential elections, however, I will focus on these in my account.

May 8, the deadline for nomination of candidates, was approaching fast. Among the opposition candidates it had been clear that Dr. Abdullah Abdullah would be the most prominent. He had been close to the late warlord Ahmad Shah Massoud, who was killed by a visiting television team two days before the attacks on the World Trade Center buildings in New York. He had also been Karzai's foreign minister until 2005. In addition, there were rumors about the former finance ministers, Ashraf Ghani and Anwar ul-Haq Ahadi; the former minister of interior, Ali Ahmad Jalali, who had settled in Washington; and the governor of Nangarhar, Gul Agha Sherzai, a brutal and corrupt but efficient strongman who had been the governor of Kandahar and was a politician many Americans seemed to like. The speculation about the former U.S. ambassador to Afghanistan and the UN, Zalmai Khalilzad, also continued. Would they be able to unite behind one other candidate besides Dr. Abdullah? That seemed highly unlikely. Several of the potential candidates had unrealistic views of their own chances.

During the spring, Karzai had also changed. Earlier in the year, he had been exhausted and on the defensive, but his tactical victory in the battle over the election date seemed to have invigorated him. The president was ready for a fight. Three weeks before the deadline for registering candidates, I was asked to come and see him. He wanted to talk about who he should choose as his two vice-presidential running mates. Karzai started with his candidate for second vice president. Karim Khalili, a Hazara, had served in this position the past five years. From my perspective he had been pleasant to deal with and was not a controversial personality in the international community. Karzai also mentioned other prominent and more controversial Hazara politicians, but Khalili seemed to me to be the best choice. It was obvious that the president had already made up his mind to keep him for another presidential period.

Then came the difficult part; Karzai intended to nominate Qasim Fahim Khan as his candidate for the first vice presidency. What did I think about him? Fahim was one of the old warlords, known for his involvement in drug trade and for violations of human rights on a grand scale. Fahim's men had even beaten Karzai up in 1994 when Karzai was deputy foreign minister. Fahim had been one of the main allies of the United States in the struggle to topple the Taliban regime. He had been defense minister during the interim administration. Karzai had recommended him as the candidate to become his vice president already five years ago, but the international community had reacted strongly and Karzai had dropped him. "I don't think the international community will be happy if you choose him," I told the president. But I asked him to let me come back to him the next day.

I was at a turning point in my relationship with Karzai. So far I had dealt with him as the president. From now on, I would have to deal with him as President Karzai and as Candidate Karzai. It would be a difficult balancing act. Certainly it was not my task to advise Karzai on whom his running mates should be. But if Karzai was elected for a second term—which was the most probable outcome of the elections—we would have to deal with the people he was now selecting. It was legitimate and necessary to warn him against candidates who could damage the relationship between Afghanistan and the international community. I drove back to Palace 7 and discussed the conversation with two of the most important ambassadors. They were alarmed but left it to me to communicate their dissatisfaction to the president.

The next day I saw the president again and raised the topic of Fahim's candidature. "He is a thug, Mr. President," I told him.

Karzai did not disagree. "The choice of Fahim could have serious implications for your relationship with key international partners, and it would be contrary to all the positive trends we have experienced recently: the appointment of reform-oriented members of the government; the enthusiasm of the donors that we could now see," I continued. "Why would you risk all this by selecting one of the worst candidates you could find—one of the old warlords, with a record of brutality and abuse, who would prolong the status quo? Why would you want to resuscitate a person we had hoped would disappear from the political scene?" I asked. Fahim would offend not only the international community, but also many Afghans, who had hoped that old warlords and powerbrokers could be marginalized and pushed aside to make room for more modern politicians. The discussion quickly became a repetition of arguments from both sides. Karzai claimed that Fahim would not be an important player in everyday politics, that I should not be nervous because he would not have any control of ministries. Furthermore, Fahim was not as bad as I had described him. I objected and referred to the American expression about the vice president: "He will be one heartbeat away from the Oval Office." If anything happened to the president, then Fahim would be in charge of the entire government. He would certainly not be a marginal player. Karzai objected and referred to the Constitution: if the president would not be able to perform his duties for any reason, then new elections would be held within three months. Of course, that was what the Constitution stipulated, but we both knew well that it was an impossible deadline and that it could take a year to organize and hold presidential elections in today's Afghanistan.

Karzai seemed to have made up his mind and was inflexible, at least toward me. Ambassador Eikenberry and I agreed to go to the president together. The arguments were the same, apart from the fact that Karzai now refused to accept that Fahim was a dubious individual. He was a good man, he insisted. My hope was that because Washington was now fully involved, it would be possible to change the president's mind before it was too late. Eikenberry was respectful but strong and clear in his message. Karzai did not budge, but the U.S. ambassador had one final card to play: Karzai had been invited to Washington. Eikenberry explained that it would undermine the visit if Karzai made his choice before he arrived in Washington.

Over the next few days, I met with Karzai over and over again, alone and with Eikenberry. It seemed that the president was considering delaying his decision. Hillary Clinton was now also engaged. She spoke to Karzai on the phone and urged him to delay. Eikenberry and I were invited for another meeting with him. It proved to be the last on this topic; the battle was over. Karzai informed us that he would register his candidature the same day, and that Fahim and Khalili would be his candidates for first and second vice presidents. Obviously Karzai had no intention of changing his mind. And he had calculated that it would be better to come to Washington with the decision made than to risk having the entire visit dominated by discussions on this single issue.

I was disappointed. For almost one year I had invested much energy in promoting more reform-oriented politicians, hoping that the president would bring them into the government. I thought it had been quite a successful effort. The nomination of Fahim was a serious setback. Reports of our discussions now appeared in the media, international and Afghan. I could not hide my frustration, and declarations of support came to our office from known and unknown Afghans in many parts of the country.

It was not difficult to understand Karzai's logic. Voter turnout in the Pashtun areas would be low. This was where the conflict was the most intense and the majority of the voters would probably not go to the polling stations. But it was also where he had his own constituency. He could never be reelected if he did not manage to obtain support from a significant portion of the other ethnic groups, Hazaras, Tadjiks, and Uzbeks. Karzai needed the support of prominent politicians with strong links to the former Northern

Alliance. Not many could help him or do this for him. Other leading Northern Alliance politicians had declared their support to Dr. Abdullah. The choice of Fahim was an important tactical move to mobilize the votes Karzai needed. We could hope that Fahim would not have a serious impact on policies. But there was a significant risk that the opposite would happen and that Fahim would become a strong opponent to the reform-oriented politicians that were now in the government.

Just as the discussion concerning Fahim was coming to an end, the president had invited prominent Afghans and international representatives to celebrate Mujahideen Victory Day on April 28. This year the military parade had been canceled. The security situation made it too risky. At the last minute, we were informed that a lunch would be arranged in the garden of the presidential compound. Two long tables were waiting for the most prominent Afghan guests at one end of the garden. One step down were small round tables for the diplomatic corps and less-prominent Afghans. I sat down with two of my colleagues among the ambassadors. As the lunch was about to start, the president's head of protocol rushed over to me and told me that I had been invited to sit at the president's table. Having found my new seat next to him, I greeted him and Vice President Khalili, who was seated on his other side. My attention was on the president and at first I did not notice the person to my right. Karzai wanted to introduce me and when I turned around I could see that my neighbor was none other than Fahim Khan. I greeted him, but fortunately the language barrier made it impossible to try to engage in a discussion. What could I have said? Fahim was certainly aware of my opposition to his candidature. Around the table some of my best friends among the ministers could barely hold back their laughter. The president probably understood that even if I could see the funny side, I was not pleased. To soften me up, he leaned over to me and invited me for a walk around the palace grounds as soon as the lunch was over. It was a nice gesture. We walked over to his own residence, where a couple of goats were playing and a cat was watching. Karzai's son came running out of the house. Little Mirwais absorbed the president's attention completely as I said goodbye to him and walked back to my car.

With the nomination process over, we entered the last phase of preparations before the election campaign itself could begin. The list of candidates had to be reviewed to exclude individuals with links to illegal armed groups. This work was under the leadership of one of the president's most competent advisers, Masoom Stanekzai, the chairman of the committee responsible for the disarmament of illegal armed groups. Stanekzai was a man of integrity with a clear head. In addition, the national security adviser, the ministers of defense and interior, and the head of intelligence (NDS) participated, together with the commander of ISAF and the UN Special Representative. After having collected information about all the candidates, Stanekzai and his team presented us with a list of people suspected of having links to illegal armed groups. The national security adviser, Rassoul, invited us to a final meeting to review the list.

I made one last attempt to exclude Fahim Khan, who was not on the list. The head of intelligence, Amrullah Saleh, once a close associate of Fahim, objected. Fahim no longer had any illegal militia. They had all been registered as regular forces. Among the other accepted candidates were people with depressing records of human rights violations and links to drug trade or corruption. How could we allow these people to run for an elected office? The Afghans around the table were themselves upset when they saw candidates who obviously should have been excluded for their past activities. But our mandate was limited to proposing exclusions on the basis of links to illegal armed groups. The rest was up to the ECC, and they had also little chance of excluding other offenders from the race. We all knew that there were criminals on the list of candidates, but they had not been brought to court and had not been subject to any criminal prosecution.

The president was informed about the list. He protested over the exclusion of two candidates for the provincial elections in Helmand. They were among his supporters, individuals who could mobilize for him in this southern province. But they also had links to illegal armed groups. Karzai now claimed that ISAF, which in this case would mean the British, with their large engagement in Helmand, were behind the exclusions. At the same time, he also found a minister of defense of the former Communist regime, Shah Nawaz Tanai, on the list of approved presidential candidates. How could we not have excluded him? He was responsible for the killing of thousands of civilians. It was certainly a legitimate question. If the justice system had functioned and the political readiness to address the crimes of the past had existed, then Tanai and a number of other candidates would never have been on the list. Now the criminals of the past could still present themselves as candidates for the future.

During a meeting in his office, with several of his ministers and advisers present, the president declared that he would protest publicly, in particular against the exclusion of the two Helmand candidates. I responded that the decision to exclude them from the list had been made by a group consisting mainly of Afghans, his own most prominent ministers and advisers, in fact some of whom were sitting right there in front of him. It was not foreign interference. I agreed that many others should never have been allowed to run for public office, but there was no formal basis for excluding them. If he decided to make his views about international interference in this matter public, then he would force me to confront him. I would call in the media and give them my own version: that this was not his responsibility. It was up to our group to draw up the list of who should be banned and the ECC's responsibility to make the final decision.

News about the disagreement quickly reached a few of my international colleagues. They were concerned. We had to maintain a close dialogue with the president at this critical stage of the election process. A few days later the storm seemed to have passed, primarily due to the efforts of Stanekzai, who managed to convince the candidates not to protest over the exclusion. But Stanekzai was under severe pressure. One delegation after the other came to see him and it was not a gentle kind of pressure. Among those who came to "convince him" was Moqbel Zarar. The former minister of interior engaged himself in support of people involved in serious crimes. We had certainly been right to ask the president to replace him almost a year earlier.

In the end, forty-one candidates had been registered and admitted to the presidential race, in addition to thousands of candidates for the provincial elections. I felt sad for the voters, the vast majority illiterate, being presented with a list several pages long, with photos and names of presidential candidates they had never seen or heard about in their lives. And the lists of candidates for the provincial councils were considerably longer. Even in a modern society, this would have been a huge challenge. Now the process of printing all the ballot papers and other election material could start. Two and a half months remained before the elections would take place. And all the material would have to be printed abroad, brought back to Kabul, and then distributed to voting centers across the country. I found it hard to explain to Karzai that all this material had to come from outside the country. Could really nothing be printed inside Afghanistan? I wondered myself. According to UNDP rules, it could not. The next phase would be another race against time.

I had been upset when Fahim was nominated as candidate to be Karzai's first vice president. It signaled a negative trend, even if I understood why the president had chosen him. A few days before the day of the elections, another piece of bad news emerged. There were rumors that the notorious warlord Abdul Rashid Dostum would return from his voluntary exile in Turkey to ensure support for Karzai. Dostum was well known for his brutality, not least during the bombardment of Kabul in 1994. Karzai wanted his assistance to have the votes he needed from the Uzbeks in the north. During several meetings in August, Eikenberry and I urged the president not to bring Dostum back. But it soon became clear that the president had made up his mind. Nobody could prevent him from returning, Karzai insisted. He was a citizen of Afghanistan and could return whenever he wanted. The president said that even he did not have the power to stop him. Late one evening, the very same day that the last presidential debate between Karzai, Bashardost, and Ghani took place on television, Dostum arrived at the airport in Kabul and continued to the north after a brief stop. My thoughts went back to my first weeks in Kabul, when Karzai wanted Dostum arrested. A little more than a year had passed, but coalitions change quickly in Afghan politics.

Fahim Khan was back on the scene, Dostum had returned from exile, and Ismail Khan was already minister of water and energy. These were the three main warlords that the United States had relied on during the offensive in late 2001 after the September 11 attacks. They were all known for their ruthlessness. Significant parts of the international community had for years protected them and enriched them—as well as other prominent warlords. Now we protested when Karzai needed them to get reelected. Why had we not worked to marginalize them instead of enriching them over the past years?

During the last weeks and months before the elections, there was also another debate that disturbed the president. It was initiated by some U.S. and European representatives who were convinced that the president lacked the ability to lead the government. They wanted to establish a new position—a sort of prime minister—in charge of the daily running of the government. Since the president himself chairs and leads the government and there was no provision in the Afghan Constitution for appointing a prime minister, another variation had to be found. Papers and proposals were floating around in Kabul as well as in some western capitals proposing that a chief executive position be established. One European foreign minister even presented a written proposal directly to Karzai himself. Some of the proposals included provisions that would remove the authority of appointing and dismissing governors and other key government officials from the president. Karzai's reaction was predictable; he saw these proposals as yet another example of interference by the international community intended to undermine him.

Karzai raised the matter with me several times. I found the proposals unhelpful and damaging. It was not our business to reorganize the Afghan government or to limit the powers of the president. The proposals had little chance of being considered seriously, and they only served to increase Karzai's irritation toward important international figures. During one of our meetings, Karzai asked me what was behind all of it. I told him that we both suffered from a lack of administrative talents. Finding a solution that would give the government greater coherence was a good thing and worth discussing after the elections. I asked other international representatives to stop the discussion.

CHAPTER TWENTY-ONE

COUNTDOWN TO ELECTIONS—AND THE FIRST CLASH WITH GALBRAITH

Galbraith arrived in the beginning of June, two and a half months after his appointment. To create a good atmosphere between us, I invited him to stay with me in Palace 7 until he had found suitable accommodations. However, I quickly sensed that I now had Holbrooke's extended arm in my own house. I told him repeatedly when the discussions turned difficult between us that he had to get Holbrooke off his shoulder. Galbraith protested and swore his loyalty to me and to the UN, but it soon became clear that there would never be anything resembling a trustful relationship between us, and it became particularly difficult when the conflicts and discussions took place within the walls of Palace 7. I no longer had any place to seek rest or a few hours of calm. Nevertheless, his arrival also had positive effects. His main task during this phase was to organize UNAMA's role during the last stages of the election process. Galbraith shuffled personnel in his part of our organization and did it well. He held daily meetings with his staff, meetings that had not taken place before. His contribution was in many ways positive, and I appreciated his efforts and the new energy he brought. Galbraith also spent time visiting various candidates, with the exception of the president. Karzai would, of course, not accept meetings with my deputy as long as I was in the country. I also saw other candidates, but less frequently than Galbraith did.

On July 5 Karzai organized the first meeting in the presidential palace to review preparations for the elections. He had gathered the key ministers, the IEC, the U.S. ambassador, and me around the government's huge conference table. The IEC had developed a provisional list of polling centers for planning purposes. Altogether it contained almost 7,000 centers. One center could include several polling stations, depending on the size of the population in the area the center served. It was obvious that some of these 7,000 could never be opened, primarily because of a lack of security. The list was based on previous elections. In the meantime the conflict had intensified and there were villages where the security situation would never allow elections to take place. In some other places there was no population left.

But what really worried me during this meeting was the information provided by the ministers of defense and interior as well as the head of intelligence; out of the 7,000 sites, 40 percent had not yet been visited to verify whether they could be used for polling or not. Any credible security plan would, of course, depend on sufficient knowledge of the locations where the opening of polling centers was proposed. There was little time left since the physical establishment of polling centers, recruitment of personnel, and distribution of election materials would be time-consuming logistical challenges. We had to know more about the security at the proposed sites in order to advance our planning. The head of the Afghan intelligence service (NDS), Amrullah Saleh, declared that two-thirds of the country were relatively quiet and stable. The rest was in different stages of instability or under the control of the insurgency. The IEC was impatient and complained about the slow progress. The president was also surprised. He instructed the security services to accelerate their efforts and to visit the rest of the

7,000 sites identified by the IEC immediately. We agreed to meet every Sunday to review the progress.

Since Galbraith had arrived and was now concentrating on the election process, I left for Europe for one week of vacation. During my absence Galbraith called a meeting at Palace 7 with the IEC, the security ministers, and key ambassadors. He insisted that the number of polling centers be reduced and that an agreement be made limiting the number to 5,800. He claimed that the remaining 1,200 could not be opened due to the security situation and would in reality become "ghost centers." If we tried to open these centers, they would be particularly vulnerable to fraud and irregularities. In his opinion it was a decision that should be made now and not be delayed. His proposal represented a major political initiative on behalf of UNAMA. But Galbraith had never discussed it with me before I left Kabul a few days earlier, nor did he inform me before he presented his proposal. Nevertheless, he put great pressure on the Afghan ministers present to adopt his proposal immediately. The Afghans were infuriated, both by the proposal itself and by the way Galbraith tried—just a few weeks after his arrival in Kabul—to force them to accept it.

Obviously, with fewer polling centers more voters would be excluded from exercising their right to participate. The majority of these voters would come from unstable areas in the south and the east and the largest ethnic group, the Pashtuns, who were Karzai's main constituency. If Galbraith's proposal for 5,800 polling centers had been accepted, more than a million voters—perhaps many more— would have been excluded from the very outset. It could easily have provoked riots and unrest in addition to the armed conflict that was already raging. The proposal would have damaged one candidate— Karzai—and benefited others, in particular his main opponent, Dr. Abdullah. Clearly a significant number of the 7,000 polling centers would not be opened. How many, we could not know at this stage. ISAF was, at that moment, carrying out operations to "clear" some of the areas to secure them for the elections. It was important for Afghan authorities to be seen as trying their best to give as many as possible of their citizens the opportunity to vote.

When I returned from Europe, Wardak, the minister of defense, who was usually a calm and controlled man, told me that he would never again attend any meeting chaired by Galbraith. He and other participants at the meeting were offended by Galbraith's tone and the fact that they had been surprised by the proposal and pressured to make a major decision without previous discussions. Galbraith's behavior was seen as unacceptable for a foreigner who had only spent a few weeks in the country. It was an attitude that started to spread in the Afghan leadership. The president also refused to see him despite several attempts. This could quickly affect my own access if the situation was not brought under control. The UN could not afford to end up in a situation where I no longer had a dialogue with my main Afghan interlocutors. Of course, Galbraith's attitude became known among opposition leaders. They now started to see him as their new ally. Galbraith had given me the impression that the other internationals present had supported his proposal and that they had been very close to pressuring the Afghans to an agreement. But as soon as I returned to Kabul, they approached me one after another to tell me that they had been embarrassed by what they saw as unacceptable bullying.

At the very end of July, the same group of ministers, election officials, and ambassadors gathered in Palace 7. Galbraith had left for three weeks of vacation and would not be back until ten days before the elections. The Afghan ministers now claimed that they would be able to open 6,400 polling centers, and they continued work to be able to open others. From now on we met several times a week in Palace 7, the Ministry of Defense, or the presidential palace. Three lines were pursued to expand the number of polling centers: ISAF and the Afghan army were conducting military operations to secure unstable areas; talks with village leaders were conducted to mobilize the local population to protect their villages and help open polling centers; and local Taliban fighters were bribed to withdraw temporarily from communities so that polling centers could be established. But time was running out. We were all concerned. Election staff and material had to reach the polling centers well before the elections. By then the centers would have to be secured. The candidates would have to be informed about their locations in order to organize their campaigns and send their observers. And, most important of all, the voters would need to know where they could vote.

I did not believe much in attempts to buy off local Taliban or even to mobilize local leaders. Neither voters nor observers would trust that these sites were safe enough. Not even the IEC would dare send officials to organize elections in centers that had just been cleared. The Afghan security ministers were giving a much-too-optimistic picture of the situation.

On August 2 we met in the presidential palace with Karzai. The ministers and the intelligence chief could all tell us that they were making encouraging progress. They would certainly be able to open 6,500 polling centers, possibly more. Perhaps even half of the remaining 400 could also be opened, although some could not be located exactly as planned and would have to be moved to other sites in the vicinity. In some cases two centers would have to merge. I listened to the discussion in disbelief. We were only two weeks away from the elections, and there was still no list of polling centers available to us. The final list, we were told, would be presented on August 16, four days before the elections. The logistical problems would be almost unsolvable. The IEC and our UN support team would only have a couple of days to bring material and staff to the polling centers. To believe that the most difficult and inaccessible polling centers could be reached in such a short time was delusional.

The president sat at the end of the table and I was next to him. I asked him to give me a few minutes alone with him immediately after the meeting. When we entered his office, I shared my worries with him saying this was completely unrealistic. Karzai looked at me and nodded. He knew these parts of the country, the communities and villages, better than anyone else around that conference table. What was going on, I wondered. Did the ministers really believe in their own reports? They were obviously struggling as hard as they could to open additional centers and enable voters in the conflict regions to participate. But this was going too far. Ministers had started their security planning much too late and taken the president by surprise. Now they were presenting reports that were simply not realistic—and the president knew it.

The Afghans were not the only ones having difficulties in meeting their timetables. The UNDP was responsible for procuring all kinds of material, from election ballots to indelible ink, on behalf of the IEC. But the procurement process had gone slowly, so slowly I feared that critical material would not reach the polling centers in time. Over and over again we had made the UNDP in Kabul and New York aware of the delays in procurement. It had little effect. In the end I decided to sound the alarm bell as loudly as I could and sent a confidential message to Ban Ki-moon, with a copy to the new head of the UNDP, the former prime minister of New Zealand, Helen Clark. I described the difficult situation as clearly as I could. Normally such messages would go to the heads of the different departments of the UN system. From there they would be brought to the attention of their superiors. To send a message directly and confidentially to the secretary-general was an unusual step, but at this stage I considered it necessary. The delays and complications had become a constant problem, one that could endanger the entire election process. That would, of course, have been a scandal, leaving the UN responsible for a failure. The Afghans would certainly be quick to wash their own hands and point their fingers at us. We needed a real change of pace. And we succeeded—almost immediately. But my relationship to the UNDP leadership was damaged for the rest of my stay. Again, Ban Ki-moon was supportive. He knew that I would not send such a message if it had not been a real problem.

The struggle against the clock continued. ISAF had relocated forces to the extent possible in order to reinforce support for the election process. Discussions with local leaders and Taliban fighters continued. Election material was positioned as close to prospective polling centers as possible. Ministers asked for one more day, but guaranteed that on August 17—three days before the elections—the final list of polling centers would be ready. The IEC was under strong pressure from both sides: on one hand, the logistical complication that became worse with each day of delay; on the other hand, heavy-handed pressure from ministers to wait a bit longer. I had always been in favor of trying to open as many centers as possible to give voters access. But opening additional polling centers was meaningless if voters did not know where they were located. Getting the word out in a matter of a very few days would be difficult in most societies. In Afghanistan it would be impossible.

In the end around 6,200 centers were open when polling day arrived. That corresponded to what many of us had expected and was approximately the same as in previous elections. It had been right to demonstrate to voters that we—the IEC, the Afghan security institutions, and the international community—were all determined to give as many Afghans as possible the opportunity to vote. The mistake was that the development of the security plan for the elections started too late, and the attempts to open more polling centers continued too long. The Afghan security forces obviously did not have the capacity to plan for an event of such magnitude.

While we were bogged down in the practical preparations, the election campaign raged. Dr. Abdullah impressed many with an aggressive and well-organized campaign. His main proposals were to replace today's presidential rule with a parliamentarian system and to introduce significant regional decentralization. Karzai presented a five-point program for security and economic development, but his campaign lacked drive and enthusiasm. Ashraf Ghani had the most comprehensive plan for the development of Afghanistan, as we had expected. But he gained more attention in the Western media than in Afghan society. The real surprise was Ramazan Bashardost, a Hazara and former minister of planning. He had installed himself in a small tent along one of the main roads on the outskirts of the city and focused his campaign on the fight against corruption. He was himself known to have been an honest minister, and he clearly appealed to the many who had been angered by the endemic corruption.

Huge meetings were organized in many parts of the country. Karzai and Abdullah gathered thousands in election meetings such as Afghans had never seen before. There were debates on radio and television. The last debate, between Kazai, Ghani, and Bashardost, was said to have been seen by six to seven million Afghans. For the first time, the Afghans saw presidential candidates being questioned and challenged on topics that preoccupied them every day. There had been fears that voters would be apathetic. That prediction proved to be wrong. The interest and engagement from young people was impressive. Until a few days before the end of the nomination process, the number of female candidates for the provincial councils was disturbingly low. But the women's networks across the country mobilized. And when the nomination was over there were more female candidates than during the first provincial council elections in 2005.

During the election campaign there were constant accusations of misuse of government institutions and officials. The main opposition candidates attacked the president for using the police, the intelligence service, and the local authorities to win support. The appointment of police officials became a particularly contentious topic as Abdullah criticized Atmar for replacing higher police officers with officials more loyal to Karzai. Of course, Atmar had the full right to replace police officials as a part of his reform program, but it was not helpful to continue this in the middle of the presidential contest. I asked Atmar to stop new appointments until after the elections were over in order to bring an end to the accusations. It was a request he accepted immediately.

Of course there were police chiefs, intelligence officials, and people in provincial and local administrations who violated the rules and influenced or intimidated citizens to vote for a particular candidate. For many of those who favored Karzai it was not so much a question of supporting the president as it was a way of securing their own positions for another few years. Abdullah also had his supporters among government officials. The powerful governor of the Balkh province, Mohammad Noor Atta, supported him openly and consistently throughout the campaign, in violation of the election rules. The president's loyal minister of information, Karim Khoram, made sure that state-owned radio and TV stations gave more attention to the president than to other candidates. But altogether the media coverage was varied and exciting thanks to the media revolution that had taken place since the fall of the Taliban regime.

During the last days before the election, the intimidation from the Taliban became more intense; people were constantly threatened and told to boycott the elections. Those who were found with ink on their fingers would have them chopped off, the Taliban proclaimed. On August 15 a car bomb was detonated outside the ISAF headquarters in Kabul. Seven were killed and many more were wounded. The car had managed to get through one roadblock after another in the most heavily protected part of the capital. Three days later a car with explosives rammed into an Italian military convoy a few hundred meters away from the site of the first attack, on the dangerous Jalalabad road. Two Afghan UN staff members who happened to be in a car nearby were among those killed. The security situation seemed to deteriorate from one day to the next.

CHAPTER TWENTY-TWO

ELECTION DAY AND MORE FOREIGN INTERFERENCE

Early on the day of the elections, Scott Smith, Hanne Melfald, and the head of the UN Security Office had gathered on the terrace of Palace 7. We all feared that a big and sophisticated attack, a blood-bath, could come any second bringing the elections in Kabul or other parts of the country to a halt almost before they had begun. We could hear explosions from rockets and minor incidents in various parts of the city. Reports of similar attacks came in from all parts of Afghanistan. Tension was high, but the big attack did not seem to come.

In the UN office, the election team was gathering information about the situation at polling centers. A special operations room had been set up. There was constant contact between its staff and our representatives on the ground. The UN could not function as a formal observer since we were assisting the IEC in organizing the election. To be a co-organizer and referee at the same time would have created a conflict of interest. But we could demonstrate that we were present around the polling centers to help provide at least some deterrence against fraud and irregularities—even if our staff was modest and our access limited in many parts of Afghanistan. In provinces such as Helmand, there was no UN representation. In others, such as Kandahar, UN staff was limited in numbers and its ability to move around was severely restricted. Nevertheless, our staff members were encouraged to demonstrate their presence and seek information wherever it was possible—without risking their own security. Three times that day Galbraith organized telephone conferences with our eight regional offices, each covering several of the thirty-four provinces. He reviewed the situation on the ground and listened to what our staff had seen or heard. There were reports about fraud, attacks, and low voter turnout.

During the day the big group of twenty ambassadors also gathered three times in Palace 7 to consult and share information. Apart from ISAF, only the UN had a presence in all regions of the country and could provide information of interest to all the ambassadors present. Before the final meeting of the day, I had a brief discussion with my new British colleague, Ambassador Mark Sedwill. There seemed to be a significant difference between his and our information about turnout in some of the southern provinces. The U.K. had military forces in Helmand province, where we had no staff at all and had to rely on second- or thirdhand information. He assessed the turnout in Helmand to be 15–20 percent. Our estimates were 5–10 percent, perhaps closer to 5 percent. Sedwill and I agreed that it would be unwise for the UN to present turnout estimates to the other international representatives so early. The figures simply differed too much. I knew that once such figures had been shared, they could soon appear in the media as the UN's figures. I asked Galbraith to avoid presenting turnout estimates at this stage to the ambassadors assembled around the table. He followed my advice without objections.

We all agreed that there had been significant irregularities. How significant they had been was too early to tell. Some of the information we had received was solid and based on eyewitness accounts from our own staff. There were even boxes full of ballot papers found in Kabul before the elections took place. Other information was anecdotal, stories our staff had heard from people they knew in provinces where we were not present. The most alarming reports came from provinces where observers had not been able to deploy because of the security situation and fraud could happen undisturbed.

Early in the afternoon I visited a polling center in the middle of the capital and was interviewed by Lyse Doucet of the BBC. When I returned to the office, the Afghan and international media were assembled and expected a brief comment. In spite of all the problems—the irregularities and insecurity—I thought it would be right to give the Afghans a compliment. Millions had defied the threats from the Taliban and gone to the polls. The public engagement demonstrated that the people—in particular the younger generation—wanted a democratic government. Thousands of election officials had done an excellent job. I decided to tell the media that in this sense the elections had been "an achievement." I had great respect for those who had cast their votes, for those who had organized the elections, and for those who had done their utmost to secure the process.

Some international representatives quickly characterized the elections as a success. I deliberately decided not to go that far. Lyse Doucet had noticed my caution and my choice of words. My comments corresponded to what a number of other international actors expressed, including prominent politicians. President Obama said that face-to-face with the brutality of the Taliban, millions of Afghans had exercised of their right to choose their leader and to determine their own future. He had been struck by their courage faced with intimidation and their dignity faced with disorder. The spokesman of the U.S. State Department declared that patience would now be required to allow the respective authorities to do their job and to wait until the results were made public. We had basically all said the same. Nevertheless, some media outlets quickly claimed that I had prematurely declared success. For many weeks this was repeated in the media as well as in reports from serious nongovernmental organizations.

From a security perspective it had been a difficult day, even if the big attack so many had feared had not come. The total number of security incidents of various kinds exceeded those of any other single day since the fall of the Taliban. Most of them seemed to be intended to frighten voters away from the polling centers—to intimidate rather than to kill. Because they were scattered, low level, and spread across the country, we did not realize until late in the evening, when all the reports had come in, how many incidents had taken place. Thirty-one civilians had been killed, including eleven staff members of the IEC. The army had lost eighteen people and the police had lost eight. Altogether, fifty-seven Afghans had lost their lives. That was a high price, but less than what one single attack against a target in a big city could have caused. With fifty-seven Afghans killed, I was even more convinced that it had been right to praise those who had participated, organized, and done their best to secure the elections. There were many stories of irregularities committed by election officials, police officers, and others. But the great majority had performed as best they could and deserved our recognition.

The countrywide turnout was estimated at 38.7 percent, lower than previous elections. The conflict was now more intense and prevented people from voting, and the atmosphere of intense enthusiasm that had brought so many to the polling centers during previous elections was understandably not there anymore.

Holbrooke had made it a point to be in Kabul to follow the elections as closely as he could. On the morning of August 21, he came for an early morning meeting at Palace 7. He was accompanied by Eikenberry and a few members of his staff. On my side of the table were Galbraith, Margie Cook, and my special assistants, Scott and Hanne. It was a strange constellation. Eikenberry was probably closer to me than to Holbrooke in his assessment of the situation. And Galbraith was closer to Holbrooke than to anyone on the UN side of the table.

Holbrooke's main point was that Karzai needed to be prevented from declaring victory. We should now insist on the need for a second round to clear the air after all the irregularities. I thought it was an impossible proposal (?) and told him so. Should we really ask Karzai to accept a second round even if we did not know the results from the first round? Constitutionally, a second round had to be held if no candidate earned more than 50 percent. It would be weeks before we knew the results from the first round. The spokesman of the U.S. State Department had correctly spoken of the need to let the election bodies do their work and to wait for the results. Holbrooke's proposal was exactly the opposite. He was scheduled to meet Karzai over lunch. I warned him strongly against raising his proposal with the president. "You have to understand," I told him, "that Karzai sees you as someone who wants to get rid of him." Eikenberry did not comment during the meeting, but I think he shared my view. I did not manage to change Holbrooke's mind. He insisted that he "knew how to handle Karzai." He probably saw my objection as another reflex of our own problematic relationship and not as serious advice.

When our meeting was over Holbrooke had a phone conference with members of the group of special representatives for Afghanistan and Pakistan. He made the same suggestion again, and then continued to the presidential palace. The meeting went as badly as I had expected. Holbrooke had not listened to my advice and repeated his proposal. Karzai was furious—and rightly so. The information he had received gave him a clear lead; why should he talk about a second round? Karzai saw it as yet another example of the international community—under Holbrooke's lead—trying to steal victory away from him.

Galbraith later claimed that I had called Karzai after the meeting at Palace 7 to inform him about Holbrooke's proposal. That did not make much sense. I had urged Holbrooke not to make the proposal for fear that it would complicate the process. Why would I then tell Karzai about it before he had his meeting with Holbrooke? I had no interest in any heated atmosphere.

However, I was called to Karzai's office when his meeting with Holbrooke was over. The atmosphere in the presidential palace was tense. The president was bitter after having listened to the American envoy and his closest ministers share their feelings. Holbrooke's behavior had confirmed the president's skepticism toward the U.S. administration. I tried to convince him that Holbrooke's proposal was probably again his own and not backed by the U.S. administration as such. But I fully understood Karzai's reaction.

It is interesting to see the cables that have become public after the Wikileaks affair. In the reports from Holbrooke's various meetings that day, all references to his proposal have been deleted. It is as if this most controversial theme of all the meetings that day was never raised. He must have understood how damaging his idea had been and that it was therefore not to be read in Washington. Some media picked it up, including the BBC, but in the U.S. cable traffic there is no trace of Holbrooke's proposal. After the meeting with Karzai, one of the Americans present told me that even Holbrooke had commented that he might have gone too far.

The next day the president and I were together, with some of his staff running in and out of his office and presenting him with the latest results. According to Karzai, he could have won as much as 60–65 percent of the votes, including a significant part of the votes in the northern and central parts of the country, where Uzbeks, Tajiks, and Hazaras dominated. His figures were unrealistic. I told him that even if this was early in the process, my estimate would be that he had received just above the 50 percent required to win the first round. We discussed the reports of irregularities and fraud. "Where do you believe there has been fraud?" he asked me. I thought that he would be in a better position to answer that question than I would be. He knew the country and I did not. The president pointed to some of the polling centers in Kandahar province. They were also on our list. But Karzai reiterated that he could lose a great number of votes in the south and the east and still win the first round as a result of the support he had received in other parts of the country.

Some of the information we began to receive from across the country was astonishing. Votes had been received from polling centers that had never opened. Ballot boxes were full even where few people had reportedly turned up to vote. Some had registered a number of voters that went far beyond the population of the district. One polling center had an identical number of votes in each polling station, a number that was far above the number of ballot papers that center had received. Some ballot papers were found in the ballot boxes still glued together, just as they had been received from the IEC. The officials at the center had not bothered to take the bundles apart and separate them into single polling papers. Others had been folded and stacked in a way that could not possibly have occurred had they been dropped into the ballot boxes.

The amounts of fraud and irregularity were impressive, and much of it was so blatant that it could be seen at a glance. But to say how much fraud there had been would at this stage be pure speculation. And to draw any conclusion with regard to the need for a second round was certainly premature. Furthermore, it was not my mandate. That would depend on the final numbers counted by the IEC, following the adjudication of complaints made to the ECC. I could not first appoint the majority of the ECC members and then preempt them with regard to what conclusion they would reach. That would have been unacceptable interference in their work.

On August 24 I saw the president again. He had read an article in the British newspaper the *Guardian*. According to the article, a senior UN official had said that a second round would be the best way forward—in other words, Holbrooke's message. Karzai was friendly but visibly irritated. UNAMA was now in his view infiltrated by Holbrooke and his views. The president claimed that I no longer had control over my organization. Concerned about the last days' events, I called Jim Jones in Washington to inform him about what had happened—about Holbrooke's visit and Karzai's anger. It was clear from my conversation with Jones that Holbrooke's proposal had again been a personal initiative and had not been discussed in Washington. Reactions must also have come from others. Jones seemed upset. When Holbrooke returned to Washington his tone and his media profile changed. Most likely he had been told to demonstrate greater caution.

The IEC had decided to release results in batches as information came in. The first batch of results was announced on August 25. They included only half a million votes and did not give any clear indications. Karzai had received 41 percent and Abdullah 39 percent. Four days later another set of results followed. The president had increased his lead and now had 46 percent. Abdullah had fallen to 31 percent. Ramazan Bashardost, the anticorruption campaigner, surprised most international and Afghan observers with about 10 percent support. Ashraf Ghani was far behind. That did not surprise me, since I had never believed that any of the "foreigners," those who had spent many years in the West, would have much of a chance. But the modest support for Ghani—around 2 percent—was lower than I had expected. He was popular among internationals, and foreigners therefore tended to overestimate the support he enjoyed among Afghans.

I had hoped that the most difficult stages of the election process would soon be behind us, but I was terribly wrong. The next weeks and months were the most bitter and dramatic I had experienced in my professional life. However, elections were not the only topic on our agenda, even if they absorbed by far most of my attention and energy. There were constant discussions about other critical topics ranging from the surge in the international military presence to difficult human rights cases. Some of these discussions received broad coverage in both Afghan and international media. Others were deliberately kept far away from media attention.

CHAPTER TWENTY-THREE

THE SECRET GUEST

When Holbrooke and other visitors were sitting downstairs in Palace 7 discussing a second election round, a young Afghan man was hiding one floor above them. I had first heard of him in October 2007, when I was still in the Norwegian Ministry of Foreign Affairs. A student of journalism, Parvez Kambaksh had been arrested in the northern city of Mazar-e-Sharif. He had been accused of blasphemy and sentenced to death for having downloaded an Iranian article about the rights of women under Islam. The sentence caused widespread protests in the international community—from governments, media, and nongovernmental organizations, not least the international PEN club. The Nordic countries and Canada were strongly engaged. In Kabul a number of embassies followed the case. Perhaps the most dedicated was a young Norwegian diplomat, Andreas Løvold, who worked closely with UNAMA's human rights office.

The court case had been a farce. The judge had played the role of prosecutor, and in the early stages Kambaksh had not been allowed a defense lawyer. There was also no legal basis for the charges of blasphemy. Kambaksh was obviously an outstanding student. He had dared to raise critical questions and to challenge authority. He had been accused of being an infidel and a communist. His case was an illustration of the strength of conservative forces in the Afghan society and the weakness of the justice system. This was not a question of foreign interference in Afghan affairs or lack of understanding of Afghan traditions or culture as some claimed. The Kambaksh case was a question of respect for basic international obligations Afghanistan had signed.

I raised the Kambaksh case several times with Foreign Minister Spanta during summer 2008. I also discussed it with close colleagues, in particular the head of UNAMA's human rights office, Norah Niland. Spanta proved to be an ally from the very beginning. So was the chairperson of the AIHRC, Sima Samar. When I first raised it with the president he listened politely, but that was all. Having just arrived in Afghanistan a few months earlier, I did not dare to push him further, and I abstained from commenting publicly. My fear was that public protests and comments would complicate the case and make it more difficult to make concessions. Karzai could be blamed for giving in to international pressure.

In October the appeals court reduced the sentence to twenty years in jail. Kambaksh had been transferred to Kabul. Once again, the court proceedings had been fraught with irregularities. I decided to raise the case with Karzai again. The president now had confidence in me. We had been through some difficult weeks after the U.S.-led attack on the Azizabad village, and we had stood together.

Karzai, Spanta, and I had lunch in the presidential palace. At the end of the meal I raised the topic that was really on my mind that day: I was deeply concerned about the twenty-year sentence against Parvez Kambaksh. It would be best for all if the case could be heard in the Supreme Court as soon as possible. Then, as a next step, I hoped the president could grant him amnesty. On special occasions, such as the New Year, the president would give amnesty to a limited number of prisoners. The Afghan New Year would be on March 21. I told the president that the pressure from the international community would increase in the months ahead. The political temperature inside Afghanistan would also rise considerably as the election process moved forward. The longer he waited, the more difficult it would become. Clearly the best option would be to let him go as soon as possible.

Spanta, and I were both nervous about how the president would respond. Would he close the door or would he open it slightly? Our lunch discussion had so far been open and lively. Now the president's tone changed and he became more formal. He had nothing to do with such cases. It was a matter for the justice system and not for the president. Afghanistan's Constitution was based on a division of powers. The judiciary was independent. We should turn to the Supreme Court. That was the right address for our request, he said. I told him that I would have done so if the justice system had functioned. But it didn't. This entire case had been a perversion of justice. It was shameful for the country and put the president in a very negative light.

I knew it was risky to challenge him so directly. But if this case could not be solved over the next months, I feared that positions would harden and that the international community would, instead of increasing its pressure, gradually forget about the entire case. Kambaksh could end up being imprisoned for many years to come.

Fortunately Spanta intervened. He supported me fully. This had not been a serious court case, and a young man cannot be left in prison on such charges. The pressure would increase, he noted, adding that he was getting constant calls and requests from foreign governments for the release of Kambaksh. Spanta confirmed the impression I already had of him but had never seen expressed as clearly as now. He was without doubt the most prominent human rights advocate in the Afghan government. And he was probably the only member of the government who dared to contradict the president so clearly—even in the presence of an international representative. The president's attitude changed a bit. The death sentence had been reduced to twenty years and perhaps it would be further reduced, he speculated, but he did not give me any indication of readiness to intervene.

Kambaksh now became a constant theme in our discussions. There were hints that the president was considering amnesty, but there was no breakthrough. In February came another surprise: Norah Niland informed me that the Supreme Court had already ruled in the Kambaksh case. The twenty-year prison sentence had been confirmed. Neither Kambaksh nor his lawyer had been informed of the Supreme Court's ruling. It was a demonstration of how the justice system did not function all the way to the top. I asked the president to grant Kambaksh amnesty soon and not let it drag on any longer. Finally the president seemed to be changing his mind. He agreed to discuss the case with religious leaders and try to convince them to support amnesty. I asked him if he could promise me that he would let Kambaksh go. The president nodded, and I stretched my hand toward him. Karzai reached out and we shook hands.

Norah Niland had told me there were rumors that Kambaksh was now imprisoned in the Pol-i-Charki prison on the outskirts of Kabul. It was the worst place he could possibly be, with hardened criminals and terrorists. He could be in serious danger if other prisoners discovered his identity and the "crime" he was sentenced for. I asked Karzai if he knew of the rumors and whether they were correct. The president responded that Kambaksh was at one of the guesthouses of the NDS, the Afghan intelligence service. I asked to see him. It was Saturday morning, and the president promised to call me back later in the day. A few hours later his office was on the line. I could meet Kambaksh the same afternoon at the attorney general's office. At 2:00 PM I was there waiting with an interpreter. I could hear footsteps in the hall outside the office. Kambaksh and his guards had entered the building. One of his two guards asked the other if Kambaksh's handcuffs should be taken off. "Yes, he should look as good as possible," the other replied. The prisoner entered the room, a good-looking young man, well dressed and seemingly in good shape. Kambaksh sat down in front of me. He tried to relax, but the constant movements of his legs hinted that below the facade was a very tense person.

I asked him where he was now imprisoned. Kambaksh told me he had been at a prison belonging to the Ministry of Justice, where he had shared a cell with seven other prisoners. They were mostly incarcerated for minor crimes. Two hours before our meeting, without any warning, he had been asked to collect his belongings and had been transferred to a detention center belonging to the NDS. There he shared a cell with only one other prisoner, but the inmates in this detention center were all hardened criminals or terrorists. He felt much safer in the prison he had been removed from. The other prisoners there had become his friends, and the prison director was kind toward him. I asked the attorney general to come and join us. He was flexible. Kambaksh could stay wherever he preferred. A few hours later he was brought back to the prison belonging to the Ministry of Justice. Karzai obviously had not known where Kambaksh was imprisoned. Probably his office had found out that he was not in any NDS "guesthouse," but in a prison run by the Ministry of Justice. Transferring him quickly to the NDS facility was an attempt to accommodate my concerns without knowing more about the conditions in the two facilities. At least we now knew that Kambaksh was not at Pol-i-Charki, but back in a prison where he felt relatively safe.

It was already early March. Karzai said he had consulted others as he had promised. I was now convinced that the release could happen any day. With the help of an outstanding Canadian ambassador, Ronald Hoffman, who was also strongly engaged, all preparations were made for bringing Kambaksh out of the country as soon as he was released. Then the next disappointment followed: there would be no release, Karzai told me. The rumors had spread that an airplane was on standby at the Kabul airport ready to take Kambaksh out of Afghanistan. Somebody had come to Karzai and protested. If Kambaksh was taken out of the country, this would constantly encourage new "Kambaksh cases." So Kambaksh would have to remain in prison.

Karzai's decision was a terrible disappointment and I protested strongly. It had been clear all along that Kambaksh should be taken out of Afghanistan. He would not be safe in Kabul and certainly not in his hometown, Mazar-i-Sharif. But the president was firm. We would have to wait again, probably until after the elections, I thought. How had we come to this impasse? I was certain that I had told him about taking Kambaksh out of the country. But I had not told Karzai about the fact that a UN plane was on standby at the airport during the critical days. Very few had been informed. How could the information have leaked?

In June a team from a Norwegian newspaper came to Kabul. The journalist and a photographer were allowed to be present in the president's office at the beginning of the meeting. It became one of the most difficult discussions I ever had with Karzai. First, I raised reports showing that the Karzai camp was proportionally given far greater attention by state media than any of the other candidates. The president objected. He was not only a candidate, but also the president and the media could not stop covering his presidential functions because of an election campaign. Then I raised the release of five young men convicted for drug-related crimes. They had been granted amnesty and had been released several weeks earlier. The atmosphere was already tense, and both of us were in a bad mood. Then I raised the Kambaksh case. The president had promised me to grant him amnesty. We had shaken hands. To me a handshake was just as binding as any written agreement, I told him. But Karzai showed no flexibility. The Norwegian journalists had waited outside the president's office. When it was over they asked if it had been a good meeting. "Interesting enough to write half a book," Hanne Melfald replied. I was not in the mood to give any comments. We walked through the presidential grounds to give the journalists a brief sightseeing. Hanne did most of the talking. I was too upset to say much.

However, the meeting proved to be a turning point. A few days later, the president's office called again. Karzai wanted to see me. I repeated my disappointment, but in a mild way. The NDS "guesthouse" Karzai had spoken about was certainly not a guesthouse, but I was prepared to take him to a real guesthouse: my own guesthouse, Palace 7. Karzai did not reject the proposal. Back in the office I wrote a letter to Spanta requesting permission to take custody of Kambaksh for medical examinations. The reply came quickly. Spanta could inform me that the president was ready to transfer him to me, provided Kambaksh wanted such an arrangement. A meeting with Kambaksh in his prison was organized, and he accepted my proposal.

Urgent preparations were now made at Palace 7. Ka ka Sher, the master of the house, was informed. So was the Romanian close-protection team. Ka ka Sher remembered the case, but he thought that nobody else in the house would recognize the young man or understand who he was. I notified Eikenberry and his deputy, Frank Ricciardone. They looked at me and asked me to think twice; if Kambaksh was transferred to the residence of the UN envoy and Karzai did not grant him amnesty in the end, I could be stuck with him in my house for months. For a moment I hesitated. But it was really too late to change plans.

Around lunchtime on August 18—two days before the elections—three cars with heavily armed guards entered the gates of Palace 7 and stopped in front of a side entrance. We did not want the Afghan police at the gate to see that a new guest was moving in. The prison director and several representatives from the Ministry of Justice jumped out of the cars and came to greet me. Kambaksh followed and entered the house without anything other than the clothes he was wearing. The prison director was grateful to see that the young prisoner was free. Papers were signed and the cars returned. Kambaksh was now in my custody and was standing with us in the entrance, happy, but worried. He was a free man—but not quite. Finally he was out of prison. One crucial step had been taken. It had taken longer than I had hoped. But that didn't matter much. Kambaksh was here now, and Karzai had kept his word.

Over the next two weeks, we played hide and seek with ambassadors, ministers, international visitors, and UN personnel. Whenever guests arrived, Kambaksh had to disappear up the stairs and hide in his room. He read a lot and followed the election process on Afghan TV. Hanne Melfald, Scott Smith, and I canceled evening events outside Palace 7 as much as we could in order to spend the evenings with him. His brother came to visit from time to time, and his parents were brought with a UN plane to Kabul. All knew that perhaps years would pass before the parents would see their son again. There were tears and dignified good-byes.

The president, however, had still not granted Kambaksh amnesty. I sent a second letter to Spanta asking the president to grant amnesty on a humanitarian basis. Three days later, at the very end of August, the message arrived from the presidential palace; Karzai had granted him amnesty. I went to see the president to express my gratitude, and while there, I confirmed with him that Kambaksh was now a free man. However, he asked me to let him stay with me for some time. I didn't answer. Kambaksh had been moved from one prison to another, albeit a more luxurious one. We could all feel how tired he was because of the uncertainty. How long would he have to stay?

Only a couple of Afghan ministers knew what was happening. One of my best friends among them advised me to "get him out as soon as you can." That coincided with my own attitude. I was afraid that the election process would become even more complicated and the president more reluctant to let him leave. As soon as the president had granted amnesty, Spanta, Sima Samar, and I gathered in Palace 7. Kambaksh was in the garden, and we sat down with him.

Spanta gave him the message from the president: "You are now a free man." The foreign minister had tears in his eyes, and so had Sima Samar and I. Only Kambaksh did not show emotions. How free? he probably wondered. How do I get from here to real freedom? I had no final answer to give him. But another critical step had been taken, and seeing Spanta express his emotions so clearly made me happy. Here was a man at the center of the Afghan government, close to the president, with a strong commitment to human rights. He had been a true ally from the very beginning.

Sitting there in the garden, we discussed how to take Kambaksh out of the country and where to take him. It had to happen in secrecy. And we had to be certain that it would not cause media headlines that could endanger any of his family, embarrass the president, or put Kambaksh himself under pressure he was not prepared for. Some countries had signaled that they were ready to receive him. A plan was made for taking him to Norway, where we believed he would be less in danger of media exposure. From Oslo he would be taken to his final destination, if he decided not to stay there. Everything was prepared, we thought. But then a final visa complication ruined our plan. In a hurry a new Norwegian visa was provided, but it was a visa that would not permit him to stop in any other European country on his way to Oslo. And there were, of course, no direct flights from Kabul to Oslo. How would we get him there?

The solution came when the Swedish foreign minister, Carl Bildt, arrived in Kabul for an official visit the same day. I had known Bildt since 1971, when we were both engaged in youth politics. And we had been together in Sarajevo when he was the high representative of the international community and I was the UN envoy. He had planned to return to Stockholm the next evening. It was perfect timing. I would then have to leave Kabul on my way to Paris for a meeting with Holbrooke and the other special representatives. And I could not leave Kambaksh alone in Palace 7. Bildt was contacted and asked if he could bring Kambaksh to Stockholm. He was in a meeting with Karzai but received the request. On his way out of the meeting, he consulted Spanta, who agreed that this was the best solution we could find. Late the same evening, Kambaksh and Hanne Melfald were brought from Palace 7 and led directly onboard Bildt's aircraft. "On the runway," Hanne wrote in a text message as the plane accelerated. Generously, Bildt offered to take them all the way to Oslo, where the Norwegian foreign ministry had arranged accommodations. Kambaksh had taken the decisive first step into a very different life as a free man.

In Kabul no one had noticed what had happened except a handful of internationals and a couple of Afghan ministers. The day after my return to Kabul, the group of twenty ambassadors was called in to discuss the election process. I expressed my gratitude to all those who had contributed to ensure the freedom of a young man whose name we all knew. They were all—with the exception of Eikenberry and Ricciardone—surprised when they found out that Kambaksh had been in the same house during so many meetings in Palace 7 over the past weeks. A few days later, the British newspaper the *Independent* printed a brief message that Kambaksh had been granted amnesty and had left Afghanistan. That was all. We had avoided the public attention that would endanger his family and cause protest from conservative forces or burden my own relationship with the president. I expressed my gratitude to Karzai, who had kept his promise.

In so many human rights cases I have experienced how governments become engaged for some time, and then their interest gradually disappears. In the Kambaksh case, I witnessed a constant and strong engagement from the Nordic countries and a handful of others, in particular Canada. There were also NGOs engaged, first and foremost the international PEN club. Hillary Clinton followed the case and sent me a letter expressing her satisfaction that

Kambaksh was a free man. I was grateful to her and all those who had provided their support.

We celebrated the release of Kambaksh; however, his ordeal illustrated the state of the Afghan justice system and the tremendous influence of conservative forces in Afghan society. There were so many other cases where there was no happy ending. Conservative forces are still strong and have the ability to mobilize and influence the justice system. They represent forces that are still hostile to what the international community is trying? to achieve in Afghanistan and, much more importantly, to what so many Afghans want.

CHAPTER TWENTY-FOUR

A DANGEROUS PLAN

With Kambaksh safely out of Afghanistan I traveled to Paris for the meeting with Holbrooke and his colleagues and then onward to Stockholm. The plan had been to continue to a conference at Visby, on the island of Gotland, where the chairmen of all the parliamentary foreign affairs committees of the EU member states were gathering. In Stockholm my wife and I celebrated our wedding anniversary with Bildt and his wife. But bad news reached me from Kabul. The IEC was about to issue new figures. It seemed that it had set aside its own criteria for excluding suspicious votes from the preliminary count, apparently following a protest from Bashardost, who had claimed that the IEC did not have any authority to do so. Bashardost was clearly wrong, but the IEC now decided to count such votes instead of excluding them. As a result, Karzai advanced to 54.1 percent, and Abdullah dropped to 28.1 percent. For the first time, the president was above 50 percent, the magic line to win in the first round. I called Ludin, the chairman of the IEC, and protested. He referred to the objections from Bashardost and was not interested in any discussion. We then issued a statement asking the IEC to revert to its own criteria. Shortly afterward the ECC ordered the IEC to conduct a comprehensive review of suspicious votes, essentially by reapplying the criteria that had been suspended.

Galbraith contacted me by phone. In his opinion, the entire election process was close to collapsing. The counting and verification of results would take such time that it would be impossible to hold the second round before spring 2010. He implied that we had hit the wall and had to look for ways out of the situation. I cancelled my speech in Visby, traveled to Oslo to say goodbye to Kambaksh, and from there went back to Kabul.

As soon as I reached Kabul in the morning of September 9, I sat down with our UN election experts in Palace 7 to review the situation. Contrary to Galbraith they told me that we had not hit the wall yet, but we were getting very close. The international members of the ECC agreed. But if we were to avoid a postponement of the second round until spring 2010, which could mean that Afghanistan would be in a political vacuum with a contested president for nine months or so, we would have to find other solutions than a time-consuming recount of every single suspicious ballot.

In the afternoon I met with Galbraith and some of his closest staff. Predictably, his message was the same as I had heard over the phone two days earlier: We were already in a crisis. The president had not received the 50 percent he needed to win in the first round, in spite of the figures presented by the IEC. A second round could not take place before the spring of next year. Until then, there could be a political vacuum. The consequences for the country would be serious. One of the other senior UNAMA staff members agreed that it was a crisis, but emphasized that in any crisis there is a new opportunity. We had to be bold. I was told by my closest colleagues that Galbraith had met with some of the staff in advance and agreed on the script. After a brief discussion, Galbraith turned to me and suggested we go outside and continue our deliberations. Only one person, Talatbek Masadykov, the head of our political office, was invited to join us.

As we sat around a garden table, Galbraith revealed what he thought should be the next steps. He should himself travel to Washington as soon as possible. The first step would be to arrange a meeting with Vice President Biden—well known for his skepticism toward Karzai. If Biden agreed with Galbraith's plan, they would go together to President Obama to have his approval. The plan was to convince Karzai to withdraw as president and Abdullah to withdraw as a candidate. A new government could then be installed under the leadership of Ashraf Ghani or Ali Ahmad Jalali, a former minister of interior. I listened to Galbraith and decided not to give my response there and then. The plan was simply not serious. I told Galbraith that I wanted to think and promised him a response the following day. During the evening I discussed with my closest staff how I should respond, not only to the plan Galbraith had outlined, but also to address the confrontational atmosphere that now poisoned the mission.

The next morning Galbraith and I were alone in Palace 7. I gave him my response: the proposal he had presented was totally unrealistic and would be a violation of the Afghan Constitution and the rules that had been established for the entire election process. It represented an unacceptable interference in Afghan affairs. If we were to go ahead, it would cause protests in the international community and riots in Afghanistan and discredit the UN. Galbraith then preempted me. In light of our disagreement, he suggested that he should leave the mission for a few weeks and come back when the atmosphere had calmed down. I agreed. He left the room and, a few days later, he also left Kabul and Afghanistan.

This was not the first time Galbraith had gone far beyond his mandate. His initiative to limit the number of polling centers had been taken without my knowledge or consent. Soon after the elections he had also approached Abdullah to suggest that, if he accepted Karzai's victory in the elections, Karzai could be given a more ceremonial position as president and Abdullah could become prime minister. That would require a change of the Constitution, but Galbraith said he had significant influence in Washington if Abdullah would accept. Abdullah had not responded. Some of my best international colleagues contacted me the following day and told me about the conversation. They had been informed by Abdullah himself. Obviously Abdullah was curious. Could Galbraith approach him like this without anybody else being involved? Or was he testing the ground on behalf of somebody—the United States or the UN? First Galbraith denied that the conversation had taken place. But he changed his mind and confirmed it in a letter to me. In his view it had been a "judgment call." His reactions became a familiar pattern. When the news about his proposal to remove Karzai reached the media, his immediate reaction was again to deny. Asked by the BBC in December 2009 if I had lied about the story, he hesitated for a second and then said, "yes." In other comments he confirmed that his plan was to remove Karzai, but added that it was only intended as a temporary measure. Temporary or not, his plan was in violation of the Constitution. Galbraith was freelancing in extremely sensitive matters. It was impossible for me to have any confidence in him and it was right of him to leave for some time.

The discussions with the president about the election results continued. He was increasingly impatient. On September 17 he scheduled a press conference. The day before, the IEC had presented their preliminary overall results. These results would now go to the ECC for verification and then back to the IEC for the final decision. According to the latest results, Karzai had 54.62 percent of the votes and Abdullah 27.75 percent. But these results included the votes that should have been excluded because there was suspicion of fraud. Karzai would certainly not be able to retain this percentage after the fraud investigation had taken place. I asked to see Karzai as late as possible in the morning, just before the press conference was scheduled to take place. When we met, I urged him not to declare victory but to underline that the process should move ahead to its final conclusion through the institutions that had been established. If he declared victory now, it could cause riots in Kabul and in other cities.

When our meeting was over, I rushed back to the office to watch him on TV. Karzai did not declare victory. He repeatedly referred to the important work now being undertaken by the IEC and the ECC in order to come to a final result. The process was still on track.

CHAPTER TWENTY-FIVE

A RACE TO RESCUE THE ELECTIONS

With Galbraith out of the country for a few weeks, I hoped that our work could move into a more constructive phase. As a first step, we called in some of the best experts we could possibly find. Carina Perelli, the deputy director of the International Foundation for Electoral Systems (IFES) was already in the country and had followed the process. She was one of the most respected experts we could find and had, in fact, been brought to Kabul on Galbraith's advice. She was a former director of the UN's Electoral Assistance Division. Perelli proposed that we contact Carlos Valenzuela, the head of the UN's election staff in the Democratic Republic of Congo, and ask him to come to Kabul as quickly as possible. Valenzuela brought with him rich experience from a number of complex elections in various parts of the world. The two of them allied themselves with one of the world's leading statisticians in this field, Carlos Lopez Pinto of Spain, and other prominent international experts.

Together the experts proposed a method for determining the final results in time before winter would make a second round impossible. Instead of going through each and every ballot box, we would base our work on a sample method. We would identify a representative sample of the suspicious ballot boxes, examine them, and extrapolate the figures, which would give us the results for the totality of votes. The first challenge was to identify the criteria and the size of the sample in order to have an acceptable margin of error and give the final results credibility. We discussed the methodology with the ECC and the IEC. They were both supportive in finding a way forward that was credible and fast. It was essential to us that these two bodies work together. Given the tense political climate, a dispute between the entirely Afghan IEC and internationally dominated ECC would have exacerbated the crisis. The campaign managers of the two candidates also accepted our methodology. It seemed that the crisis was over and the matter was back in the hands of the electoral institutions.

None of the participants had ever been through anything similar. It was new ground to all of us—even to the experts. The ECC had determined the criteria for the ballot boxes that now had to be subjected to new examination. The first included polling stations with more than 600 votes, since that would be more than the number of ballots each polling station had received. The second was polling stations with more than 100 votes, but where more than 95 percent of the votes had been cast for the same candidate. The third was a combination of the two former criteria: polling stations with more than 600 votes and where more than 95 percent had been cast for the same candidate. Each polling center could, as I have mentioned earlier, have several polling stations. If polling stations had more than 600 votes, the reason could be that voters had cast their votes in a different polling station in the same building. But if there were more than 600 votes combined with 95 percent of votes for one candidate, then there would be serious suspicion of fraud. There was also a number of other criteria for declaring votes invalid and there was agreement that in case of doubt, then a vote should be counted in order to minimize the risk of rejecting possibly legitimate votes.

The next step was to draw the sample. Representatives for the two campaigns gathered in the UN headquarters with the chairmen of the IEC and the ECC. For each of the three subsamples proposed by our experts, a specific number of boxes were drawn. In the beginning it seemed to work well. Having witnessed the opening, I went quickly back to my office nearby and left the others to conclude the work. It only took a minute before an agitated UNDP ELECT leader, Margie Cook, was on the phone. A quarrel had erupted between Ludin, the chairman of the IEC, and the head of Abdullah's campaign. The process of drawing the samples had stopped, and the two were shouting at each other. Ludin had called Abdullah's man a loser. Margie Cook was afraid that they could physically attack each other if it was not stopped. I ran back from my office to the meeting room. The two were standing opposite each other, so close that it was impossible to get in between them. I pushed them aside and shouted at them to sit down and continue the work. To my surprise, they immediately followed my order. We had previously discussed whether the media should be invited to the event. Fortunately they were not.

The selected boxes now had to be brought to Kabul from across the country. Altogether, 358 boxes were collected from most of Afghanistan's provinces. They represented a total of 3,498 suspicious boxes. The sample included more than 10 percent of all the suspicious boxes, which our statisticians had assured us would give a high degree of accuracy. On October 5 the complex process of going through each and every box could finally start. It was a battle against time. Every time I met the president, he insisted that we must finish the audit and make the results public immediately. I asked him to be a bit more patient, just a few more days. The same ritual continued day after day, week after week. The entire process took much longer than I had expected. Procedural mistakes were made and had to be corrected. And there was constant friction between the internationals involved: the experts we had brought to Kabul to assist us, the three internationals I had appointed to the ECC, and the UNDP ELECT team that supported the IEC. Karzai, meanwhile, insisted to me that significant amounts of money were leaving the country every day. The number of visa applications for neighboring countries increased dramatically. He was right; we were in a political vacuum, and it could quickly develop into a political storm and to riots in the streets. People sensed insecurity and prepared themselves.

CHAPTER TWENTY-SIX

GALBRAITH IS FIRED AND TAKES REVENGE

In the middle of our struggle to find a way out of the crisis in Kabul, I had to travel to New York for the UN General Assembly. The "group of friends" was to meet on September 25 at the foreign ministers' level, and my own briefing of the UN Security Council was scheduled for four days later on September 29. Scott Smith, Hanne Melfald, and I arrived in New York just in time for the meeting of the foreign ministers. Hillary Clinton had asked for a few minutes alone with me before the meeting. She immediately raised my relationship with my deputy, Peter Galbraith. Clinton was as friendly and correct as I have always experienced her to be. The U.S. administration had nothing to do with the Galbraith affair, she said. The UN could take whatever action it deemed necessary. This was the responsibility of the UN and only the UN. In other words, she would not try to defend or protect him. She reassured me that the confrontation with Galbraith had not affected my relationship with her or the United States, and that she understood what a burden it had been to me.

The other participants had gathered already when we entered the room. Galbraith was sitting in the chair behind me. He saw Clinton and I enter the room together and must have guessed what had happened. It was the first time I had seen him since he left Kabul. Galbraith had been in New York a few days already to talk to senior UN officials, but I had no information of the conversations he had held with my superiors. I informed the ministers of the election process on where we stood at the moment. There was full agreement that we all had to do our utmost to keep the process on track until the end and appeal to calm and order. As soon as the meeting was over, Galbraith and I took the elevator down to 2nd Avenue and spent a few minutes together on the street outside the Canadian UN Mission, where the meeting had taken place. Our conversation was short and not particularly friendly. When we parted, Galbraith said that he had lost this round—but the battle was not over yet. It was a warning of what was to come and what would dominate much of my remaining period in Kabul.

I left New York in the evening after my briefing to the Security Council four days later without any knowledge of what the secretary-general intended to do with Galbraith. The discussions with visiting foreign ministers and the UN Security Council debate had gone well. There was full support for the line we had been taking on the elections. But when I landed in Dubai the following evening, a storm had erupted. Galbraith had been dismissed and had sent a letter to the secretary-general, a letter that found its way remarkably quickly to *The New York Times*. After the thirteen-hour flight from New York to Dubai, I must have been the only person involved who was not familiar with his dismissal and the letter. It was a lengthy piece of accusations, lies, and slander that I was not prepared for.

Within a matter of a few days Galbraith managed to launch a media campaign covering North America, Europe, Asia, and Australia. It was no longer a debate about political issues but a bitter, public series of recriminations from a person who had experienced something as unusual as being fired from a high-level position by the UN secretary-general. It was obvious that the media would give attention to the controversy. But what surprised me was that no one—except a French newspaper—asked the fundamental question: How could it be that a prominent American UN representative, chosen by Richard Holbrooke, could be fired without even a hint of objection from Washington? How could it be that the presidency of the EU, the NATO secretary general, and the spokesman of the U.S. State Department all gave me their support and expression of confidence? They could have kept quiet, but they didn't.

When I returned to Kabul, I felt sure that the campaign would last a few days and then disappear. It seemed impossible that the media would be interested for long in a story that was so obviously an act of revenge. But the campaign did not stop and the media continued to recycle Galbraith's accusations. They were rejected from the UN headquarters in New York as well as from our own media office in Kabul. Of course, Galbraith's colorful accusations created more attention than the rather terse and formal rejections. Soon they were picked up by Abdullah. In media comments and in discussions with me, he repeated Galbraith's accusations almost word for word. After a few days I decided not to read the news summaries for a while. We were in a critical phase of the ECC's work. I had to focus my attention and energy on the election process and avoid being constantly distracted and drained by bad media coverage.

After a week of accusations that seemed to never end, I decided that silence could be interpreted as an admission of guilt. The media and observers would think that there must be something to these accusations if I remained silent. My public affairs office agreed, and we decided to call a press conference on October 11. Colleagues in the diplomatic community in Kabul had given me full support during this difficult period. When I told them about my plans to hold a press conference, several wanted to join me. And when I sat down to start the press conference I was surrounded by six of them: the French, British, American, and German ambassadors, as well as the EU ambassador and the senior civilian representative of NATO.

From the very beginning to the very end of the election process, around twenty ambassadors from Asia, Australia, Europe, and North America had met regularly in Palace 7 under my chairmanship. Together we had discussed every aspect of the elections and there had been full agreement among us throughout the entire process. Galbraith's attacks were attacks against agreed-upon international positions.

His list of accusations was partly misleading and partly untrue, but some of them contained enough grains of truth to appear convincing. It was correct, for example, that I had objected when he—acting with little knowledge and without consulting me—had tried to limit the number of polling centers. It was also correct that I had asked him not to present voter turnout figures the same day the elections took place; the polling centers had just been closed and we simply did not know.

I had not refused to share information with the IEC and the ECC. Both commissions received information from us soon after the elections had taken place. There was even a written agreement that I had signed with the ECC in May that obliged us to share information that was relevant to its investigations. Both commissions told us that the information we had—which was often anecdotal—was of limited value for their purposes.

Galbraith claimed that I did not want to admit the extent of the fraud. But none of us knew the scope of irregularities only a few days after the elections. Holbrooke and other international representatives had expressed themselves along the same lines that I had. Galbraith claimed that almost one-third of the votes were invalid. I could not give such statements, and I could not speculate without more complete information than we had at the time. That was not an attempt to protect the president. Other international representatives would have asked me for the evidence—what did I know that they did not? There was one basic difference between Galbraith and myself after his dismissal: He was a "free" man and could afford to behave even more irresponsibly. I continued to be the most senior representative of the international community in Kabul and had to behave responsibly in a very volatile political situation.

The audit and counting process moved forward slowly. Even if we still could not draw any firm conclusions, it seemed that the president had around 50 percent of the votes. It could be a little more and it could be a little less. The U.S. and U.K. ambassadors and I sat down with the international members of the ECC to review the situation. We were all concerned; what would the president's reaction be if he received less than 50 percent? We could experience the scenario that we had all hoped to avoid: he would accuse the international community—and "my" three international representatives in the ECC—of having stolen the election from him. If he decided not to accept the outcome, the opposition could react with demonstrations, road closures, and riots in Kabul and other big cities. Who would stop an angry demonstration? It would certainly not be the international military. Riot control was not within their mandate. We were all concerned that demonstrations could lead an inexperienced Afghan police force to overreact and provoke violence and chaos in the streets. The three members I had appointed felt the full burden of their responsibility. I reassured them that I would support them no matter what result would come out of their final deliberations. But inside I had serious doubts if we understood the Afghan society well enough to make the right assessment of what constituted fraud and what did not. What did we know about the life in little Afghan villages of a hundred or so voters, where nobody could read and write? How would they decide whom to vote for and how would they behave at a polling station? I was afraid that our lack of insight could lead us to serious misjudgments.

CHAPTER TWENTY-SEVEN

SENATOR KERRY INTERVENES

Finally the audit and counting process was coming to an end. Carlos Valenzuela came to Palace 7 to meet the U.S. and British ambassadors and myself to brief us of his understanding of the situation. He warned us that the president would most probably not reach 50 percent. Of course, it was not the task of the ECC to calculate the final result, but to inform the IEC of its findings in terms of invalid votes. The IEC would then calculate the final result. But when the ECC handed their findings over to the IEC, it was not difficult for any of us, including the campaign officials of Karzai and Abdullah, to calculate the implications: the president would receive 48.3 percent and Abdullah 31.5 percent. I asked for a meeting with Karzai to discuss the outcome of the review and its consequences.

Since he did not have the 50 percent required, a second round would be needed. Karzai protested intensely. All his figures were clear and pointed in the same direction; he had won more than the 50 percent, and there was no need for a second round. The blame was again placed on the international community. Now he asked for a total and complete recount of all the votes. I told him that would be impossible. A recount could take two months. He had complained that every day without clarity was a threat against the stability of the country. If that was the case, how could we now start a process that could take several months?

At this critical point the U.S. senator and chairman of the Senate foreign relations committee, John Kerry, came to Afghanistan. He quickly understood not only the political stakes but also the minute details. Together and separately we entered into three days of difficult discussions with Karzai and his team. The first evening was spent in a wider circle with the president and some of his key ministers and election officials. We had also brought our international election experts, Carlos Valenzuela and Carina Perelli, who had assisted us with the audit process.

The president opened with sarcastic remarks about the methodology for the audit and the lack of understanding of Afghanistan among international experts. Carlos Valenzuela explained how they had determined the modalities of the audit and emphasized that it had been accepted by Karzai's election team. The explanation was followed by a tough cross-examination from some of the ministers. The fact that all votes in a polling center were cast for the same candidate would be suspicious in the West, but not in Afghanistan. This was not a country where voters decided individually who they would vote for, they explained. When local elders or religious leaders decided, the entire community would follow their decision. The fact that the same tick marks were found on a number of ballot papers was not necessarily evidence of fraud. Afghanistan was a country where the vast majority of the voters were illiterate. Many had not seen the photo of the candidates before and many had perhaps never even seen a pen. They would need assistance and may have asked an election official to mark the candidate they wanted to vote for.

Our experts insisted that there were seventeen criteria. Votes would never be declared invalid on the basis of only one of them. Several criteria would have to be met before a ballot paper was determined to be invalid. But the experts had designed the methodology; they had not applied it. That was the task of the IEC and the ECC. In a late-evening meeting in the presidential palace, a bitter disagreement erupted between the two commissions about votes that the ECC had set aside.

Kerry suggested that we should organize a meeting between them to review the methodology and how it had been applied. The next morning we met at the IEC headquarters. I opened the meeting and left the other participants to discuss their disagreements. I was on my way back to my office when Jean d'Amecourt, the French ambassador, called. For the second time in a few weeks he had intervened and helped me at a critical moment. He was with his foreign minister, Bernard Kouchner, in Abdullah's house. Abdullah had heard about a meeting at the IEC, the meeting I had just left. What was going on behind his back? I was grateful to the French ambassador. Abdullah could soon have brought his irritation to the media and created a public confrontation, and our efforts to get the president on board for a second round could have failed. Within the next hour I traveled to Abdullah's house. My message to him was simple: "You have expressed doubts in the past about my impartiality, but I ask you to have confidence in me when I say that we are not going behind your back. If I turn out not to deserve that confidence, then you can feel free to criticize me as you wish. But give us one day—or two at most. We are in a critical phase." Abdullah listened and gave me the confidence I had hoped for. The meeting with him probably lasted less than ten minutes, but they were important minutes. I had to enjoy the confidence of both candidates to keep the process on track.

CHAPTER TWENTY-EIGHT

MR. PRESIDENT, I HAVE DECIDED TO RESIGN

For hours I had been sitting with Kerry and the U.S. delegation in the presidential palace. Kerry and Eikenberry had asked me to be present. Kerry's style was precisely the kind that Karzai liked; he treated the Afghan president with respect and calm. There was never an unpleasant word, just a serious and frank discussion of substance. Nevertheless, I was concerned that, as a result of the frequent meetings, Karzai would soon see me as an extended arm of the U.S. delegation and not as an independent UN envoy. That could damage my own ability to bear influence in a situation where the president so far had not shown any readiness to accept a second round. When the first day of Kerry's visit was over, I thought at length about how to manage the next meetings. The plan was to meet Karzai again with Kerry and the other U.S. participants late the next afternoon. But we had different ways to influence the president, I thought. Kerry could use the power of the United States, by far Afghanistan's largest international partner. I could rely on my relationship with him and my credibility. From the beginning of the electoral process I had always stood firmly on the ground of the Constitution and the election law, and for that reason I had gone through serious disagreements with U.S. representatives as well as my own deputy both before and during the election process. The next afternoon and the following morning would be decisive. If the president refused to accept a second round, and insisted that he was already the winner, then it would have serious consequences for the stability of the country. I thought that if once again I joined Kerry in the meeting with Karzai, it would reduce my own ability to independently influence the situation.

During the night and in the morning I thought about my options at length, and I discussed with Eikenberry whether I should join the Americans or not. Finally I decided to go to the president alone and not join Kerry and his team. I asked for a meeting with the president before Kerry's return from a visit to the south of Afghanistan. It was late afternoon when I walked into Karzai's office. Apart from him only Spanta was present. I told Karzai that I wanted a confidential talk with him and asked if we could use a very small office on the ground floor instead of his official office. The three of us walked down the staircase and into the little room. Here the risk of being disturbed or intercepted was limited compared to the office upstairs.

I informed the president of the conclusion I had reached: The next day would be decisive. If the president did not accept a second round, I would have to announce my resignation. Throughout the election process, I had based my thinking on respect for the Constitution and the rules of the game. I had taken a serious burden and faced criticism for that attitude. If Karzai could not accept the second round that the Constitution required, then my approach would have failed. It would mean that the president himself did not follow the rules. That would be such a serious blow to the line I had taken that I could not remain as UN envoy.

This was probably the most difficult conversation I experienced with Karzai. I was exhausted after a long election ordeal and weeks of attacks from Galbraith and some media outlets. Many months of efforts to help bring us through the entire process had sapped me of my energy. Karzai could see how tired I was and hear that my message reflected a sincere conviction. I had thought the meeting would take fifteen minutes. But we sat in the small office for almost an hour, going through some of the experiences we had shared and the frustration and even anger we had felt over the behavior of some of our international partners. He spoke quietly and I think he respected the decision I had taken and saw what it had cost me to come to this conclusion.

Kerry and Eikenberry continued the discussions with the president during the evening without me, as I had wished. They seemed to make progress. But when they started again late in the morning the following day, the president had again insisted that he had received more than half of the votes. Kerry had made it clear that he only had a few hours before having to leave Kabul. If it proved impossible to solve the problem now, then it could take a long time and the risks of further instability and unrest would increase. I spent a few minutes with them around noon, then returned to my office. I did not want to be a spectator to a discussion between Kerry and Karzai after what had happened the previous evening.

After a while I was asked to come back to the presidential palace. When I arrived it seemed that a solution had been found. But I was surprised when I heard what had been agreed. According to the IEC, forty-three of the boxes that had been set aside during the counting of the ballots failed to meet the criteria for invalidation. Kerry had agreed to include them as valid votes. The result would be an increase in the president's figures. To me it was a difficult compromise. It would mean that I distanced myself from the ruling of the ECC after having promised its members my full support. I expressed my misgivings to my U.S. colleagues, and there was a moment of nervousness. Was the UN envoy going to spoil it, after all these efforts to convince Karzai to accept a second round?

It was not hard to understand Kerry's thinking. The critical question was not if Karzai would receive 48 percent or 49 percent. If the president could be brought to accept a second round with a face-saving maneuver giving him marginally more than the ECC had given him, then it would be a price worth paying.

The representatives of the IEC now returned to their office to calculate the final results. The rest of us left the president's office and were waiting in the garden outside. Karzai and Kerry went for a "private" walk, with a long trail of security and advisors following them. I was standing with a group of Afghan ministers. They now all argued for a second round and insisted that no deal could be made with Abdullah before it had taken place. They wanted the president to obtain the 50 percent required to give him the legitimacy he needed for another demanding presidential term.

An hour or so later, the final results reached us. According to the IEC, the president had received 49.67 percent. He did not object, but accepted a second election round. We had come to the end of yet another painful chapter of the election process. Karzai and Kerry were getting ready for the press conference that had been delayed for several hours. They both wanted me to join them. I was not enthusiastic, but I decided to participate provided no one mentioned any figure. If anyone had referred to the 49.67 percent, it would have put me in an awkward position. That figure was based on a decision to move ballot boxes that had—rightly or wrongly—already been declared suspicious. It was a decision made by the U.S. delegation and one of the candidates.

The press conference took place, and Karzai made it clear that he would accept another round of elections. Kerry expressed gratitude and characterized the president's decision as statesmanship. I emphasized that the next round would have to be better than the first, and I commended the ECC members on their work. Three days of difficult discussions were over. Kerry could catch his plane and return to Washington. The rest of us would have to start the preparations for the next stage of the presidential-election saga.

I admired Kerry's performance. He had handled the president with respect. For the Afghan president, this was a very different behavior from what he had become accustomed to from Holbrooke and some other U.S. visitors. *If this had been the Obama administration's approach from the outset, then much of the tension and suspicion between Kabul and Washington could have been avoided,* I thought. Later Karzai said that the only U.S. representative whose advice he trusted was Kerry.

The date for the second round was now set for November 7. The procurement process was already under way. I had informed the president a long time ago that ballot papers and boxes as well as other critical material had to be ordered, printed, and brought into the country. Now the discussion over the security plan started all over again with ISAF, the Ministries of Defense and Interior, the NDS, and the IEC. Once again we had to decide on the number and location of polling centers. The discussion followed exactly the same lines as it had two months earlier. Once again election material would have to be distributed to districts and villages. Personnel would have to be recruited and trained. Those who had been guilty of fraud would have to be replaced. But there was one major advantage compared to the first round: we would only have two presidential candidates and no parallel provincial elections. That would make the operation easier. But it was nevertheless a challenging operation—and it would all have to be organized in less than three weeks.

I had gone through a difficult period in my relationship with Karzai, but I had won the confidence of Abdullah. During a press conference on October 21, he praised the UN and me for the attitude we had taken and stated that we had worked effectively to ensure transparency in the election process. He presented a set of clear conditions for a second round and said that from now on he would only relate to the UN and not to an IEC he could not trust. His demand that Ludin be replaced as IEC chairman before the next round was understandable but unrealistic. And his request for the removal of key ministers seemed more to be a tactical move to prepare for a possible withdrawal from the entire process. For me it was important to see the dramatic change in Abdullah's attitude; a few weeks earlier, he had echoed Galbraith's criticism. Now he had seen and understood that he could trust me.

The chances that Karzai would lose a second round were slim. Of course Abdullah understood the situation better than we did. His main supporters could also see that it would almost take a miracle for him to win a second round. Abdullah's most powerful ally, Professor Rabbani, did not want to be on the side of the loser; he would rather see what he could get out of partnering with the president. In the international community there was an increasing concern that a second round would lead to violence and instability in Kabul and in some other cities. The best would certainly be if the president and Abdullah could reach some kind of understanding. If Abdullah was to withdraw from a second round, it would be important that it was not seen as a boycott that could lead to demonstrations and violence. Clearly there were people among . Abdullah's supporters that were ready to take to the streets against an election they saw as without legitimacy. Karzai could help avoid such a situation by stretching out a hand to his opponent.

I went to the president to see if he showed any sign of readiness to reach out to Abdullah. During some of these meetings I was alone with the president. On other occasions Eikenberry and I talked to Karzai together. The president had nothing to offer. Karzai did not want a government of national unity to be forced on him, and that was not our intention. Even Abdullah did not want to become a minister in the government of a president he had characterized as being without legitimacy. Unfortunately, several international representatives and commentators had used precisely the term "government of national unity" or "coalition government" in their comments. Karzai saw this as yet another international attempt to interfere.

We asked the president to offer Abdullah a role in Afghan politics, but outside the government. A number of proposals were made, including appointing him as chairman of a reform commission. Abdullah had made reform his main theme during the election campaign. Understandably, the president was not interested in making any such concessions at this stage.

During one of these discussions between the president, Eikenberry, and me, the atmosphere became particularly heated. I said that the UN secretary-general was thinking of coming to Kabul and that he would be prepared to be helpful if an arrangement between the president and Abdullah was within reach. At first, the president did not respond. I was ready to bring the discussion to an end and leave the office. It was useless to continue. Then the president exploded; not only had we stolen the first round from him, we were now trying to cancel the second round and asking him to form a coalition with his opponent. My suggestion to make use of a possible visit by Ban Ki-moon made Karzai even more irritated. This was an election process that had to be brought to an end and not a conflict like the one between Fatah and Hamas in the Palestinian territory. I had never seen Karzai so angry.

Clearly it was not the president's fault that the meeting ended in a confrontation. I had to take the responsibility for what had happened, and I understood his reaction. I apologized as soon as I could for having provoked him.

During the last days of October I had urged the two candidates to at least get together in order to calm down the atmosphere and reduce the danger of unrest. Neither of them showed any willingness to meet. Not until October 28, the day which for me was to become the most dramatic day of my two years in Afghanistan.

CHAPTER TWENTY-NINE

ATTACK ON THE UN!

Security for the UN had gradually deteriorated both in Kabul and other parts of the country. Of course, it was a development that reflected the general security situation in Afghanistan. But it was also clear that the UN increasingly was seen as a legitimate target for the insurgency. In Kandahar, Herat, Uruzgan, Kunduz, and Kabul, UN offices and officials were either targeted or found themselves close to attacks by the Taliban. The direct threats against us became more frequent: threats against offices, residences, and Afghan staff members. We had accelerated our efforts to improve security. The number of armored vehicles increased dramatically, but the number of companies producing such vehicles was limited and could not meet the growing demand from so many parts of the world. During summer 2009 the first group of Nepalese Ghurkas also arrived to provide additional security for our offices in Kabul.

Around 5:30 in the morning on October 28, intense gunfire woke me up. It could not be far away, probably just a few hundred meters. We had experienced similar shooting before during the night or in the early morning hours. It was not necessarily a Taliban attack, but could be a feud between Afghan groups or criminals. This seemed to be different. The shooting continued. There were loud explosions. Then the first text message came from the head of the

UN Security Office. The explosions and the shooting came from one of the UN residences, the Bakhtar guesthouse.

Our guesthouse had been attacked by a group of insurgents at the worst possible time of the day. The staff was still asleep, and the security forces outside were tired and unprepared after a sleepless night on duty. This was not one lonely suicide bomber entering the compound and blowing himself up. There were several, with suicide vests and automatic weapons. It was a well-prepared and sophisticated attack. A few minutes later the message came that Afghan security forces had reached the site, but the shooting continued. The attackers seemed to be alive and fighting inside the guesthouse compound. Then a third message arrived; injured UN staff members had reached the American base, Camp Eggers, and were being treated for their injuries.

In Palace 7 we had all gathered in the big meeting room on the ground floor: Hanne Melfald, the Romanian close-protection unit, our Afghan staff, and I. Security at the gate was strengthened. Cars blocked the entrance from both sides. A second attack against another UN target could not be excluded. Thick smoke came from the area where the guesthouse was located. A BBC team had arrived close to the scene and reported. The entire guesthouse was on fire. It seemed that around thirty UN staff members could have been in the house at the time of the attack. When the noise from gunfire started to die down, I was informed that most of the staff seemed to have escaped from the scene by climbing over a wall to the neighboring property. But three of them had been killed. We all feared that the number of casualties would climb. Soon it was confirmed that five had died. The injured had been taken to hospitals. Seventeen of our staff at the guesthouse had belonged to UNDP ELECT, the unit responsible for working with the Afghan IEC. Could the attackers really have known that much—not only that this was a UN guesthouse, but actually who lived there and what their functions were? If that was the case, where did they get the information?

At Palace 7 we were given the green light to drive to our offices. The first survivors were expected in a few minutes, and I had to be there. Small groups entered the meeting room, probably ten to fifteen people in the end. All were in a state of shock, some talking quietly, others silent. Most had been able to get out of their rooms and the house. They had crossed the wall to the neighboring house and escaped. From there they had heard the shooting continue and seen the fire blazing through their building. Five staff members had been killed, but it was a miracle that more lives had not been lost. By coincidence some of the UN close-protection and security staff were living in that very guesthouse. They had grabbed their weapons, attacked the terrorists, and managed to stop them in the courtyard in front of the house.

Over the course of the day it became clearer what had happened. Three insurgents had been able to reach the entrance to the guesthouse in a police car and dressed in police uniforms. When they stormed in, they were met by our own security. Suicide vests exploded, probably earlier than the attackers had planned. A fire started in the basement and quickly engulfed the entire building in flames. The first group of Afghan security forces had arrived quickly but had withdrawn. They lacked the weapons to engage the attackers. Later, forces from the army and the police arrived and attacked.

At this point the suicide bombers were probably all defeated and killed by their own suicide vests or by our UN staff. One of our own close-protection officers, Louis Maxwell, had seen the attackers and had stopped them from his position on a rooftop. Then police entered, wearing the same police uniforms as the attackers. The police saw a dark person with a gun inside the compound. Was he one of the terrorists? There must have been total confusion as the fire raged and hundreds of bullets were fired at the building.

Weeks later, I saw a video recording published by the German magazine *Stern*. It showed a dark-skinned, unarmed man on the street outside the guesthouse. Could it be Maxwell? He walked calmly with an Afghan police officer in front of him. Then two shots were fired from a person outside the video. The unarmed man fell to the ground, dead. It was a shocking scene. As time passed, new information provided a more precise picture of what seemed to have happened. When the police had entered the guesthouse grounds, the fighting between our security and the terrorists was probably over. The attackers were killed by their suicide vests or by the UN security officers. Maxwell had probably been killed by Afghan security outside the compound. But there were compelling reasons to believe that another three were killed by Afghan forces sent to save them. One of our five victims probably died from the fire inside the building. Maxwell and our other security people in the guesthouse had demonstrated unbelievable bravery; they had given most of our staff the time they needed to reach relative safety and saved their lives.

The Taliban quickly took responsibility for the attack. They must have surveyed the area well. On earlier occasions when the UN had been attacked, we had not been able to confirm whether the UN had been the intended target. This time it was a direct attack against the UN, and our role in the election process had triggered it. The guesthouse was in ruins. I wanted to see it with my closest staff members without any media and attention. When we drove up to the building, a group of journalists was nevertheless waiting outside. I greeted them and walked inside the building. The sight was horrendous. We walked from the ground floor up to the second. Everything was burned. The windows were shattered and there was glass everywhere. The walls were riddled with hundreds of bullet holes from the security forces. They must have directed their fire at everything and every possible target without discrimination. It was hard to imagine the ordeal our staff must have gone through before it was all over. We left the building and passed the journalists waiting in the street outside. There was not much to say and not much I managed to say.

The next day I was sitting in my office with Margie Cook, the head of the UNDP election team. I called the relatives of those who had lost their lives—those we could find: a mother, a father, or a spouse. We paused between each call to gather strength for the next. Some were overwhelmed with sorrow, and others seemed not quite to understand what they were being told. Some seemed to find comfort in their belief, others in the knowledge that their spouse or child died trying to make a difference for people in need far away from his or her own country. Then came the good-byes, memorial ceremonies at the UN headquarters outside Kabul, and, finally, at the airport before the victims were sent home to their respective countries and families. Among the five we had lost were two election workers, two security officials and one member of the UNICEF staff. The survivors were sent to Dubai and onward to their homes to be with their families and friends.

Two days after the attack, Ban Ki-moon spoke at a ceremony at UN headquarters in New York. The hall was packed. It was an expression of respect for those who had been so brutally killed. And it was an expression of togetherness, of belonging to a wider family. The secretary-general then boarded a plane for Dubai to meet the survivors. The Korean struggled to maintain control of his emotions as he sat with them, comforted them, and heard their stories. He was deeply moved, and I was grateful to him for showing his solidarity in such a way. Together we flew to Kabul early the next morning. He wanted to be with his staff and share their grief and despair. The UN headquarters in New York often feels far away, but in this situation we had the genuine feeling of sharing our loss with those who had sent us to Afghanistan.

The two women who had lost their lives were both so-called UN volunteers, people who decided to be recruited to the UN without a normal salary and the compensation that other staff receives. Perhaps adventurism is the driving force for some of them. Others come to have experience that will be valuable to them later in their professional careers. But many of them simply come as a result of dedication to service. I have met a number of them. At social occasions at the UN headquarters, they were often the most enthusiastic organizers. They were staff members with an unusual ability to inspire others—and certainly they inspired me. Therefore I was grateful to receive a message from the Philippines two weeks later. Each of the coffins was accompanied to its destination by a UN staff member. The person who had accompanied the coffin with Jossie Esto to her country told us in an email how she had been received. The message described how she had been taken to her final resting place with a twenty-one-gun salute. It was an honor normally only given to the highest state leaders. A UN volunteer had been received as a hero with the deepest respect. I read the email with tears in my eyes, but also with profound gratitude to those who had received her. There was silence in my office as I read the email to my closest staff.

The story of the heroic battle of our security people went around the world. We could have lost many more that day. Maxwell and his colleagues had not only saved lives at the Bakhtar guesthouse, they had probably also rescued the UN presence in Afghanistan. If this attack had ended with tens of victims, then it could have led to the same result as the attack against the UN in Baghdad six years earlier: an evacuation of the UN presence. Our international partners understood how close we had been to an even more dramatic situation that would have affected the entire international presence in Afghanistan. After the Bakhtar attack I experienced a very different respect for our security requirements, not least from ISAF. The international military leaders in Kabul understood that another serious attack against the UN could have far-reaching consequences—not only in loss of lives, but in political terms.

We entered a difficult phase in our relationship with Afghan authorities as we started to understand what had really happened. The Afghan intelligence chief, Amrullah Saleh, said that he had received warnings about an imminent attack and had passed it on to Atmar, the minister of interior. He blamed his colleagues in the government for not having taken action to prevent the attack. In meetings with the minister of defense, General Wardak, he admitted that there had been a lack of coordination between the security forces. He promised full cooperation with the UN. At first, Atmar responded differently. He could not accept that we criticized him and his ministry for having reacted slowly when the attack took place. I asked him to calm down and work with us, which he did. At first, my criticism—and that of Ban Ki-moon—was directed against the hesitant and slow arrival of Afghan police on the scene. When I saw the guesthouse, I was shocked about the unprofessional way the security forces reacted once they arrived. And when I learned the entire story—that Afghan security forces had probably killed four of our five victims—my bitterness took another direction; if they had not arrived at all that early morning, then at least four lives could have been saved. Probably our own security officials had already defeated the attackers—only to be killed by our Afghan partners.

In the immediate aftermath of the attack, some staff members decided to stay and sleep in their offices—for security reasons and to support each other. Late one evening when I was out of the country to meet Ban Ki-moon, I received a message from Margie Cook. It read: "If you were in Kabul now, we would have invited you over to our office. We have twenty-six election staff here. We will sleep on the floor. And we have food, wine, music, and a strong sense of solidarity with each other." I wished I could have been with them. And I was deeply grateful to Margie, who played such a critical role in helping us overcome the worst tragedy the UN in Afghanistan had experienced.

It was a period of constant threats against the UN and UN staff, threats of abductions and of attacks against the residence of a prominent staff member. The Afghan security services had arrested several networks of potential suicide bombers in Kabul. Tons of explosives had been found in trucks approaching the capital. In June there had been a threat of a large vehicle-borne bomb, and the UN seemed to be the target. A truck with two tons of explosives was stopped in the Logar province, a short distance away from the capital. If it had reached Kabul and been able to detonate its deadly load, the impact would have been catastrophic. The security services—police and intelligence—had become more effective. A so-called "ring of steel" had been established around the center of Kabul. But to seal a city of four million people and to prevent every potential attacker from reaching his target would be impossible.

In January a group of insurgents attacked government buildings in the center of town. The exchange of fire was intense and seemed never to end. A few days later suicide bombers blew themselves up outside an Indian guesthouse in the center of Kabul—inside the ring of steel. The insurgents had proven that they were still able to strike at the very center of the Afghan capital and that even the most stringent security measures could not stop attackers that were well armed and determined.

CHAPTER THIRTY

ELECTION ENDGAME: KARZAI'S TROUBLED VICTORY

For weeks since Karzai accepted a second round I had tried to organize a meeting between Karzai and Abdullah to see if some sort of understanding could be reached between them that would reduce the danger of political instability. We had discussed possible times and venues for a meeting. It was important to avoid either of them claiming credit and giving the impression that one had come at the invitation of the other. Abdullah insisted that it should be organized under the auspices of the UN. Karzai was reluctant toward UN involvement. In the end, both accepted that they were responding to a UN initiative. However, they could not agree on the venue for a meeting. Karzai wanted a meeting to take place at his own presidential palace. Abdullah preferred to meet at Palace 7. Both were sticking to their positions. Such discussions may seem absurd, but in the heat of the struggle, every detail becomes a question of demonstrating strength and avoiding signs of weakness. On October 28, the day of the attack on the Bakhtar guesthouse, Abdullah took the decisive step. At the end of a telephone conversation he conceded, out of respect for the losses the UN had suffered, to remove the last obstacle by agreeing to meet in a building on the presidential compound. His words made an impression on me. Abdullah demonstrated respect and a sense of dignity. We communicated the response to the president's office. An agreement had been reached.

Hanne Melfald and I drove to the building where the meeting was to take place to see that everything was in accordance with our agreement. The residence was on the outskirts of the palace grounds. It was already evening, and the meeting was set for 8:30 PM. Abdullah arrived at Palace 7 and was taken in a UN car to the presidential compound. His arrival and handshake with the president was photographed with me between them to make it clear that it was a UN initiative. Both of them seemed relaxed. They had known each other for many years; Abdullah had been Karzai's foreign minister. But it was the first time in more than six months that the two of them had met each other.

I returned to Palace 7, where Abdullah had also left his car. Two hours later he came to give us a briefing. The meeting with the president had not produced any concrete result, but it had taken place. It was almost midnight. None of us had any energy left for long discussions. Abdullah departed and Hanne, Scott, and I remained in Palace 7 reflecting on the most difficult day we had experienced in Kabul: from the drama at the Bakhtar guesthouse early in the morning to yet another chapter in the election saga late in the evening. It was hard to believe that this had been only one day.

It seemed increasingly clear that Abdullah would withdraw his candidature for a second round of the presidential elections. Several ambassadors urged him not to present a withdrawal as a boycott that could inflame the atmosphere further. When Abdullah—overwhelmed by emotions—held his press conference on November 1 to announce his withdrawal, he was as cautious as we could have hoped for. He did not intend to participate in a second round and did not see the elections as legitimate, but he abstained from any inflammatory language. I admire Abdullah for his performance that day. He understood that he would not be able to win a second round, but he could have chosen a more combative exit from the election process.

His calm withdrawal was an important contribution to keeping the political temperature under control and demonstrators away from the streets. Therefore, the unanimous reaction from the international community was one of respect.

Karzai had shown his strength as a tactician. Why would he give his opponent added legitimacy by offering him a prominent position and lending credibility to his reform agenda? Why would he enter into any sort of understanding with Abdullah before a second round? Karzai was not interested in Adbullah's withdrawal. He wanted a second round that could give him the 50 percent he had not achieved in the first round. Only then would he have the full credibility that he needed so much, and only then would he be willing to consider any concession to Abdullah.

Two days after Abdullah's withdrawal, Ban Ki-moon came to Kabul to pay respect to the victims of the Bakhtar guesthouse attack and to show solidarity with the UN staff. I accompanied him to the presidential palace. While we were waiting outside the president's office, the IEC called me. Would the UN have any objections to canceling the second round and declaring Karzai the winner? This was in my opinion the only reasonable way forward. To organize a second round with only one candidate—and with prospects of more violence and lives lost and at a cost of tens of millions of dollars—did not make much sense. The Constitution was clear: in the absence of one candidate achieving 50 percent, a second round would have to be organized. But now there was only one candidate. The president should be declared the winner and the process finally be concluded. I saw no reason to consult other international colleagues. Certainly, they would share my view. I think the IEC was relieved. The second round was canceled. A long and painful election process had come to an end.

I spent much time afterward reflecting on the election process. At one stage during spring 2009, I had wondered if it would be at all possible or advisable to hold elections in the middle of a conflict that would disenfranchise so many voters, particularly members of the largest ethnic group. I voiced my concern to some of my main Afghan interlocutors. The national security adviser, Rassoul, was right, I believe, in insisting that the elections had to take place, even if the conditions would be far from ideal. Without elections the democratic processes in Afghanistan could have collapsed. Now, the country had hopefully—and not without difficulty—consolidated this process in the minds of its people. Many asked me if Afghanistan was mature enough for democracy. In my opinion, that was an insult to millions of Afghans—in particular the younger generations— who wanted to see progress in their country and who demanded a say in its development. If we had canceled the elections, and I don't know how we could have done so, then it would have been a tremendous setback for those who wish to see a more modern Afghanistan emerge. But in Afghanistan the process of building democratic institutions and the rule of law will take much longer than we would like.

The presidential elections were fraught with irregularities and fraud—as were the parliamentary elections one year later. But at the end of the day, the institutions established to detect irregularities functioned, forcing the process to a second round. That does not happen in many of the countries surrounding Afghanistan, countries that from institutional, economic, and social perspectives are much more advanced. In Afghanistan's immediate neighborhood, rulers receive the overwhelming support of their population—often more than 90 percent of the votes, as in the old Soviet days. And if the results are questioned, those who object are brutally brought to silence. Eikenberry once said that in the 1990s the Katusha rockets decided who would rule Kabul. Now it was the ballots. It is important to maintain this perspective.

We spent much time and energy on addressing fraud and irregularities. And it was right to do so. But both we and the international media gave little attention to Karzai's claims of foreign interference. Looking back, there can be no doubt that foreign interference was blatant and unacceptable. The encouragement given to other politicians to run against Karzai was particularly serious. Then followed attempts to influence the way Karzai would organize a future government, and to convince him to accept a second round whatever the outcome of the first would be. Galbraith's various initiatives contributed to an atmosphere of bitterness that heightened the temperature of the final stages of the election process.

Furthermore, none of us had any experience with the very complicated audit that was chosen to avoid a political vacuum until summer 2010. Mistakes were made and had to be corrected to keep the process on track. There were disagreements within the international community over one of the criteria chosen by the ECC, namely that all ballot boxes with as few as 100 votes and 95 percent given to one candidate should be considered suspicious and be included in the audit.

President Karzai claimed that victory in the first round of the elections was stolen from him. Is it possible that he was right? In light of all that happened, I cannot say with any certainty that he was wrong. The fact that he did not receive the 50 percent required to win the first round clearly affected his legitimacy and made him a politically more vulnerable president.

CHAPTER THIRTY-ONE

THE MILITARY BUILDUP

In June 2009 General Stanley McChrystal arrived in Kabul and took command over ISAF and U.S. forces. He brought new energy and new thinking to ISAF. On August 30, 2009, he delivered his "commander's initial assessment" after a lengthy and thorough process involving a group of independent U.S. foreign and security-policy experts. It was a document intended for internal use, but it quickly leaked to the media—in a slightly censored version. His assessment was a departure from earlier thinking. First of all, he underscored the fact that "neither success nor failure can be taken for granted." It was a reflection of what had also been stated in the Obama White Paper in March. But now it came from a commander on the ground. McChrystal pointed at the negative trends. It would simply not be possible to turn them around by doing more of the same. Quick-fix solutions would not work. So far, his thinking coincided with ours at the UN.

McChrystal argued for a new approach to the conflict. Not only did ISAF lack the resources required, but, as he emphasized, there was a lack of understanding of the Afghan society and its culture. A precondition for winning over the insurgency would be to get closer to the people. Until now ISAF had operated in a way that created distance to the very people the international forces had come to protect. Instead of being seen as occupants, the international forces had to be seen as the guests of the Afghan people and their government. When ISAF forces drove through even the safest places, hidden in their armored vehicles with full body armor and turrets mounted, they communicated an impression of high risk and fear to the people. ISAF could not expect unarmed Afghans to feel safer before heavily armed ISAF soldiers did, he wrote. McChrystal argued strongly for reducing the number of civilian casualties. But he also placed the military behavior in a broader context. The crisis of confidence between the people and its government was a result of weak institutions, the culture of impunity, corrupt civil servants and powerbrokers, a widespread sense of political alienation, and a lack of economic opportunities. ISAF's mistakes made these problems even more serious, he had claimed.

I was pleased when I read his assessment. Finally the problems caused by the international military presence were fully recognized by the top military commander in Afghanistan. And finally they were placed in a wider context, underscoring the need to complement military efforts with a comprehensive civilian offensive. There was no spin and no wishful thinking of the kind we had become so used to. I expressed my satisfaction in the UN Security Council and any other forum I addressed during this period. It was easy to like McChrystal. I felt that our Thursday breakfasts together with the NATO senior civilian representative, Fernando Gentilini, were useful and stimulating. McChrystal was open to discuss his own concerns and he was genuinely curious about political developments. For the same reason, Karzai also liked him.

The next phase of the debate was more troublesome. McChrystal needed additional military forces in order to build the Afghan army and police and to push the insurgency back until the Afghans could take responsibility for their security. From now on the discussion focused almost exclusively on the number of military forces and counterinsurgency strategies. That made me worried. I understood the need for additional soldiers. But I was concerned that in this debate the broader context McChrystal had outlined was pushed aside. In an October 2009 speech in London, he asked for a reinforcement of 40,000 additional U.S. troops. His request was badly received by President Obama and other key members of his administration. McChrystal had publicly and without warning his political masters presented his own view in the middle of a difficult internal debate.

Eikenberry and Ricciardone now entered a period of video conferences with Washington—almost daily at one point, it seemed. I could see how the long hours and the intensity of the discussions had an impact. Eikenberry and Ricciardone had problems with the direction of the debate and its narrow focus. It had in essence become a debate about number of military forces and withdrawal dates. The other components that MChrystal's assessment had also emphasized so strongly seemed to have disappeared from the horizon. Eikenberry and Ricciardone had made their views clear in the discussion. On November 6 they expressed their views and reservations in writing again via secret cables from Eikenberry to Hillary Clinton. The cables soon found their way to the media. Eikenberry feared that the United States was now making decisions about a very significant increase in the U.S. military presence without having considered the alternatives. An increased U.S. and international engagement in the security area would not only cost enormous amounts of money but would also increase the Afghan dependence on the foreign presence and strengthen the military engagement in a conflict most of us did not believe could be solved by military means.

Eikenberry pointed to the astronomical costs of the planned military buildup and asked for greater attention on civilian alternatives. To send additional combat brigades would cost many tens of billions of dollars over the next few years. The embassy had proposed $2.5 billion for its budget for governance and development. That, however, had already been debated at great length in Washington and turned down. Eikenberry claimed that it would probably take more time to train the Afghan security forces than expected. They suffered from a high attrition rate and low recruitment among the Pashtun part of the population. In my opinion he was right.

Eikenberry's cables also sent a clear message about the political situation in the Afghan capital: he wrote that Karzai was not a strategic partner, that there was no political elite with an adequate sense of national identity that was above local interests. Eikenberry asked Washington for a broadly based review of alternatives to implement the strategy Obama had presented on March 27, 2009. McChrystal was taken aback by the cables sent from the U.S. embassy a few hundred meters away from his office without his prior knowledge. I was not surprised by their contents. For weeks I had seen how Eikenberry, Ricciardone, and I shared the same concerns.

On December 1, 2009, and after a lengthy and sometimes confusing debate, President Obama concluded in a public speech that the United States would send more than 30,000 additional troops. At the same time he announced that the United States would start withdrawing its forces from Afghanistan in July 2011. Other ISAF countries soon decided to strengthen their military presence with 10,000 military personnel altogether. Over the next year, we could expect an increase of more than 40,000 international troops. That was a dramatic military surge. But where was the civilian surge that the Obama administration had emphasized so strongly in March?

His speech had an immediate effect on the debate in almost all other ISAF contributors, including those that had decided to send additional forces. The debate over withdrawal of forces accelerated. When the U.S. president could announce initial withdrawals from mid-2011, it meant that other NATO countries should be able to do the same. The U.S. administration had not only further militarized the strategy but also given allies with a troublesome public opinion a signal that they could now start preparing for exit from

Afghanistan. Suddenly, a debate was raging across Europe and North America about the level of ambition in Afghanistan and what would be required to declare "mission accomplished" and leave the country.

The debate had an immediate impact on Afghans—the leaders as well as the population. To Karzai it was a clear warning that he would soon have to manage with much less international support. He had also been concerned with the trend toward a further militarization of the strategy. But he became even more uncomfortable when he heard the U.S. administration declaring publicly that the clock was now ticking fast and that the speed of withdrawal was dictated more by a U.S. election calendar than by realities on the ground in Afghanistan. He also wanted Afghan security forces to take greater responsibility. However, he knew well that the timetable drawn up for the recruitment and training of tens of thousands of police and army was unrealistic. For the Afghan people, in particular in the conflict regions of Afghanistan, Obama's message was that "we are leaving you soon." In its White Paper in March 2009, the U.S. administration had written that it must overcome the confidence deficit it was facing both in Afghanistan and Pakistan, where so many did not believe that the United States was a reliable long-term partner. The decision to start withdrawing in July 2011 confirmed to many Afghans that they were right in their skepticism.

The Taliban and other parts of the insurgency certainly saw hope in Obama's decisions. They knew that the military surge would give them a difficult couple of years. An increase of 30,000–40,000 troops would have an impact on the ground, but if they could get through the next two years, the balance of forces could move in their favor. Those who had decided to announce a date for the first withdrawal could not possibly have understood the negative impact on the ground—among their allies as well as their enemies.

The pressure of new deadlines reinforced a trend where military leaders—American in particular—sought simplistic solutions to complex problems in areas where they had little knowledge or experience, such as the development of civilian institutions and economic development. During the preparation of the U.S. offensive in Marja in Helmand province in February 2010, military leaders spoke of bringing in "government in a box," as if it were something that one could fly in under a helicopter, place on the ground, and have it met by a population filled with trust. It was wishful thinking and had nothing to do with Afghan realities.

The Obama strategy was built around the "clear-hold-build" concept, to which the fourth element of "transfer" was added. In brief, it suggests that the military "clear" an area of rebel insurgents, which police and civilian administration can then "hold" with the assistance of a limited military presence. That in turn creates an environment where it is possible to develop and "build" the area and to eventually "transfer" responsibility to the Afghans.

But the strategy overlooked fundamental shortcomings of the Afghan society. There were often no local civilian institutions that could inspire confidence and bring effective governance. As a result, it was almost impossible to hold an area in a way that would allow sustainable development to start. In Afghanistan insurgents slip unnoticed in and out of the local population, sometimes in significant numbers. They maintain their grip on the people through their presence and the danger of reprisal. There is an absence of visible and competent institutions and a presence of invisible insurgents. Instead of "clear-hold-build-transfer," international forces ended up in a situation where already moving from "clear" to "hold" became a daunting task and where "build" and "transfer" was mostly out of reach.

The new U.S. strategy rightly placed more emphasis on transferring responsibility to the Afghans. However, training between 350,000 and 400,000 Afghan army and police—mostly illiterate—through courses of a few weeks duration and enabling them to take responsibility for Afghanistan's security by 2014 was simply an illusion. And again, the focus was primarily on building Afghan security forces and less on the need for stronger civilian institutions. Already in 2002 the senior U.S. diplomat responsible for Afghanistan, James F. Dobbins, had in vain urged the Bush administration to invest in building civilian institutions in addition to the army. Instead, the international community—led by the military—had positioned itself between the Afghan people and its government, ending up as the Afghan government's rival and effectively taking charge of civilian development. The process of transferring responsibility to the Afghans had been slowed down rather than accelerated. What surprised me more than anything else in international policy making during my two years in Kabul—and in particular during 2009—was the remarkable lack of readiness to listen to the Afghans. Thousands of miles from the reality of daily life in Afghanistan, strategies were formed and decisions made by military people and their political masters without the participation of their Afghan counterparts. Behind the walls of international military bases, projects were planned without genuine consultations with central or local Afghan officials. There are many examples of how the Afghan leadership was surprised by decisions made in Washington and other European capitals. I have mentioned the text message I received from a prominent Afghan minister when he visited Washington for consultations. The critical strategy debate during fall 2009 was also conducted behind closed doors in Washington. I doubt if any other country was seriously involved and consulted. The UN certainly was not, nor were Afghan authorities provided the opportunity to participate as an equal partner.

After the meeting in The Hague in March 2009, I had great expectations with regard to the U.S. strategy. Emphasis had been placed on the civilian components. There seemed to be an understanding—finally—that stronger institutions and real economic growth were as important as the military component. Now we had again taken an important step in the wrong direction.

CHAPTER THIRTY-TWO

OFFENSIVES IN THE SOUTH

In mid-February the big Marja offensive started in Helmand. Marja is a small district but was seen as a Taliban stronghold. Altogether, 15,000 international and Afghan soldiers participated in an operation that was so well published that most Taliban fighters had already left the area. It was the first offensive after the buildup of international forces had started. And it was to be the best-planned offensive ever carried out during the conflict based on the current counterinsurgency strategy.

Just as the offensive was launched, I was with General Wardak, the Afghan minister of defense. He reviewed the plan with me. I expressed my strong doubts. Of course, 15,000 soldiers could force a few hundred Taliban out of Marja in a relatively short period of time. But what about the other critical elements, those that were needed to move from the "clear" phase to "hold" and "build" and "transfer"? Had qualified personnel been recruited and trained for this operation? Had experts been mobilized to take over from the military, to govern and police the district, and to gain the support of the population? Why would the population of Marja believe that this time the Taliban would be driven out for good and not only for a few weeks or months? It all seemed quite unrealistic to me. Wardak understood me well and perhaps shared some of my skepticism. "It is a good plan on paper," he said. He was right; a good plan on paper, but one that did not fit the Afghan terrain.

I admire General Wardak for his efforts over years to build the Afghan army. In meeting after meeting with defense ministers from ISAF troop contributors he had underscored the obvious: that for the Afghan army to take over the responsibility for Afghanistan's security, it would take more than the right number of troops; it would take the right training on the ground where his troops operated, and it would take the right kinds of weapons and equipment. He had detailed knowledge of what kind of equipment NATO countries had and no longer used—equipment that was obsolete for allied forces, but that would have helped him tremendously. So often he had emphasized that Afghan forces could take losses in a way international forces could not. His troops were not fighting on foreign soil but in their own country. And so many times the answers to his reasonable requests had been negative and left him empty-handed.

As the Marja offensive was launched, I told him that his army lost soldiers every day not only because of lack of weapons and equipment but also because nobody, Afghans or internationals, had paid sufficient attention to building civilian institutions that the people could trust. He would save the lives of many Afghan and foreign soldiers if he would also become a stronger advocate of improving the civilian government. Military forces were tied down because there was no one to continue when the military had done their job. He agreed, but he had more than enough on his plate with mobilizing support required for his army. Others had to take their share of the responsibility.

When I was first briefed on the Marja offensive I was told that results would not come quickly. It could take up to ninety days—three months—before we would see if the Marja operation had been a success. The ninety days passed and then another ninety. There was no talk of success. Large military forces had been deployed, but

Afghan officials brought in to establish local institutions lacked the confidence of the population. It was hard to get civilian projects under way. The number of displaced people was more than what had been expected. This did not bode well for the larger operation in Kandahar, Karzai's own home province and the Taliban's birthplace, which was set to follow the Marja offensive.

My doubt concerning this strategy was further strengthened when Major General Michael T. Flynn, who was responsible for intelligence at ISAF, published a report about U.S. intelligence efforts up to 2009. The report was made public in January, a couple of weeks before the Marja offensive was launched. I was impressed by its openness and direct language, as well as by the fact that it had been made public. But the content was deeply troubling. It described how the United States had focused by far the largest part of its intelligence work and analytic capacity on insurgency groups and how, as a consequence, the intelligence community was still unable to answer fundamental questions concerning the broader environment in which ISAF operated and about the people it aimed to protect. In reality Flynn said that ISAF understood neither the people the international forces had come to protect nor the insurgency they had come to fight. It was a hard-hitting assessment of eight years of intelligence gathering. For years politicians and military had made statements about winning the hearts and minds of the people and helping them out of the grip of the Taliban. Now, a few weeks before the largest and best-planned operation so far, ISAF acknowledged that it knew neither the opponents nor the people.

The offensive in Marja started just as I was about to make my last trips abroad as UN envoy. A meeting of ISAF defense ministers was scheduled for February 5 in Istanbul, to be followed by the annual security conference in Munich. In Istanbul, General McChrystal gave ministers a briefing about the buildup of Afghan security forces and about the forthcoming offensives in Helmand and Kandahar. McChrystal was an excellent presenter, good at creating enthusiasm and at inspiring confidence. He had to bring ministers behind him and make sure that they shared his determination. NATO's new top commander (SACEUR), Admiral James G. Stavridis, followed McChrystal and told the audience of defense ministers—somewhat prematurely—that the Taliban was now on the run. The atmosphere around the table was almost euphoric. One of the ministers proclaimed enthusiastically that we finally had a vision and a plan for the troops to succeed. We could now go home and explain to the public that we will defeat the Taliban.

I listened to the debate with surprise and confusion. Did the ministers really mean what they were saying? When I was invited to speak, I thought it would be right to throw some cold water into the debate. There was no lack of military forces on the ground, I told them. That was not the problem! The problem was that we would not win over the people by relying so heavily on military assets alone. The key requirement was the population's confidence in the government and local authorities. Military gains would be short-lived if that was not given greater attention. When the meeting was over, I sat down with a few defense ministers individually for bilateral talks. One of the ministers that I had known well for some time looked at me and said jokingly, "Why did you have to ruin the atmosphere?" And I felt almost guilty. McChrystal and Stavridis had given the ministers a sense of optimism and confidence that the strategy would work, but this was my last meeting with ISAF defense ministers and I could not hide my doubts from them.

Over the last few years I had so often listened to overconfident reports from Afghanistan, Iraq, or elsewhere. The trends were almost always positive. The increasingly asymmetric warfare from 2007–2008 was a clear sign that the Taliban was weak, we were told. The attacks against Afghan institutions showed that it was desperate. The Taliban had never achieved any of its strategic objectives, I often heard as NATO ambassador and later as UN envoy. Well, neither had the international community.

Two days later we stopped in Munich for the annual security conference. The new NATO secretary general, Anders Fogh Rasmussen, proclaimed that there was a need for a cultural revolution among NGOs that were still insisting on their independence. They had to work more closely with the international military forces. He used the World Food Program (WFP) as a good example of how cooperation could and should be. According to the secretary general, ISAF was escorting food convoys for the WFP. I had never heard about any such escort arrangements. ISAF was informed about where the convoys were moving; sometimes international forces were in the vicinity and could assist if the convoys were attacked. But they were not escorting. On the contrary, we repeatedly appealed to the Taliban to provide free access for the WFP convoys. The NATO secretary general's statement was the kind that could damage our independence and add fuel to the Taliban's arguments that the UN was little but an extension of the international military.

A few days after the secretary general's statement, a message was posted on a Taliban website claiming that the humanitarian work of the UN was part of the military offensive. The timing was probably—and hopefully—a coincidence. But it demonstrated how difficult it was to build the confidence the UN needed to have the access it required. I often said to military representatives that the best cooperation sometimes was to keep a healthy distance between us. But it seemed almost impossible to make the military understand our concerns.

CHAPTER THIRTY-THREE

AN AGENDA FOR AFGHAN OWNERSHIP

With the election process finally over, we could all start looking forward to a demanding series of events. Karzai's inauguration for a second term was scheduled for November 19. A significant number of foreign ministers and dignitaries were expected to attend. His inauguration speech would give the first signals about his readiness to pursue a reform agenda. The next step would be Karzai's choice of ministers for his new government. Had he been forced to make too many deals with old warlords and powerbrokers during the election campaign? Would they tie his hands and force him to make unpleasant compromises? The following year would also be packed with important events. The 2010 agenda included the Peace Jirga Karzai had promised to organize in order to discuss reconciliation with the insurgency. Elections to the lower house of Parliament would take place during the summer. And we were all, Afghan leaders as well as key internationals, starting to discuss the possibility of another international conference—perhaps even two—during 2010. In parallel, the international military buildup would continue, and new offensives would be undertaken in the south.

We had discussed this program for some time among a very small group of ambassadors. Our aim was for each event, including international conferences, to reinforce the others. We worked on a concept called the "sovereignty agenda," an excellent term that I believe was first used by the U.K. ambassador, Mark Sedwill. The objective was to enable Afghan authorities to take full responsibility for their own security and development and thereby exercise full sovereignty over their own country. The agenda consisted of five elements: a strong buildup of Afghan security forces, a similar strengthening of civilian institutions, sustainable economic growth, a peace and reintegration policy, and the question of defining Afghanistan's future status in the region. Each had been discussed separately many times, but they had to be brought together better than in the past and enable us to get away from an overly militarized strategy. The last element, Afghanistan's future status, would be difficult and controversial, but the issue had to be raised in light of the critical need for genuine Pakistani and Iranian support for stabilizing the country.

Based on these five elements, we had started to plan another international conference at the level of foreign ministers. It would take place during the first quarter of 2010, preferably in Kabul. To hold a big international conference inside Afghanistan for the first time would in itself be a strong signal that we had entered a period of transition to Afghan ownership. We could then organize another conference later in the year—in a European capital—when the Afghans had formulated national programs that could be supported and funded by the donor community. I raised this agenda and the proposal for a conference in Kabul with Spanta and then with Karzai. Both were supportive and enthusiastic.

On November 5 I organized a press conference to look ahead to the next months and present the outline we were working on. The press conference coincided with our decision to reduce the number of UN international staff as a result of the attack on the Bakhtar guesthouse. In my introduction I outlined how I saw the next stages in the Afghan political calendar (the inauguration speech, the composition of a new government, and the holding of a Kabul conference) reinforcing one another. I emphasized the need for more reform-oriented politicians and used rather strong words about the old warlords and powerbrokers. In particular, there was a need to come to grips with the prevailing culture of impunity. Having reviewed the five points in our "transition agenda," I mentioned the importance of defining the future status of Afghanistan in the region in a way that enabled the countries here to live in peace with one another. In describing Afghanistan's future status, I carelessly used the word "neutrality."

The media did not pay much attention to our five-point agenda, but there were articles about my attack on warlords and corruption in addition to the inevitable focus on the evacuation of our staff. I then left the country for a conference abroad. But the next day I received a sharp reaction from the presidential palace, with accusations of interference. It was made public by the president's office and in a statement from the foreign minister. Most observers thought that the president had been upset with my accusations of corruption and impunity and my criticism of warlords. That was also what most embassies seemed to report to their capitals. But Karzai's reaction had been provoked by something very different. He had heard me criticize corruption and warlords before. He was used to my public comments, and he had never complained to me. This was different; I had used a press conference to reflect on the future international status of Afghanistan. I had even used the word "neutrality." He found that to be totally unacceptable. It was a question that first had to be discussed behind closed doors, and it was not a matter for initiatives by foreigners. The president was angry because I had raised the question of Afghanistan's international status without having discussed it with him in advance. I could only agree with him, and I apologized to Karzai for my lack of judgment.

Three days later I read an interview Karzai had given to the U.S. radio channel PBS. Karzai was asked about the withdrawal of UN personnel following the attack on the Bakhtar guesthouse. His reaction was brutal: "They can go!" It wouldn't make any difference! For the UN staff in Afghanistan his statement was insulting and demoralizing. Many of them had taken far greater risks than members of Karzai's own government. Karzai had criticized the UN—and in particular Galbraith—for interference in the elections. And he was convinced that key personalities in the international community, including the ECC, had stolen a first-round victory from him. I had now been careless in my comments about Afghanistan's future status. But to say that the UN could leave and nobody would notice—less than a week after an attack where five of our staff had lost their lives—was simply unacceptable. I never raised my disappointment with him. He had reacted in anger, and I would not gain anything from a confrontation at this stage.

CHAPTER THIRTY-FOUR

THE INAUGURATION AND A NEW GOVERNMENT

On November 19 Karzai was sworn in for a second term as president of Afghanistan in the presence of President Zardari and a number of foreign ministers, including Hillary Clinton. With one important exception, the entire Afghan political elite were also present. However, Dr. Abdullah had decided to abstain. Until now we had praised him for his responsible behavior. Of course, he had already characterized Karzai's election as illegitimate when he had withdrawn from the second round. Nevertheless, it would have been wiser and more dignified if he had now buried the election dispute and attended the inauguration.

The president's speech lived up to our expectations. He underscored that the voters had cast their votes in a way that transcended ethnic lines much more than during the first presidential election five years ago. Karzai invited all candidates, including his main rival, to come together for the sake of national unity. At the same time, he emphasized the need to draw lessons from the election process, from its good and bad sides. The attention had to be focused on "Afghanization" of future elections. In other words, the Afghans should now take full responsibility. There had been enough foreign interference.

Peace and security could not be created through fighting and violence. Karzai welcomed all Afghan citizens who felt alienated (but were not linked to international terrorism) and wanted to return to their homes, live in peace, and accept the Constitution. He promised to call a Loya Jirga to discuss the peace process.

He addressed complaints about the quality of governance and the need to ensure that both the government and the citizens enjoyed equality before the law. After the many years of conflict, people did not feel safe in their homes, and they feared the government's security institutions. Karzai promised to put an end to the culture of impunity and to prosecute those who spread corruption and misuse of public property. He committed himself to securing the rights of women in all three branches of government so that their position in the Afghan society could be further improved.

The next part was devoted to the need for economic growth and strengthening of agriculture, energy, and education. The young generation had to be given vocational training based on the requirements of the country for its development purposes. He asked donors to increase assistance given through the government's budget to 50 percent over the next two years and to be transparent in the use of aid resources. And he emphasized the need to develop the region's infrastructure.

Karzai was grateful to countries that had participated and made sacrifices to strengthen Afghanistan's institutions. Afghanistan hoped to achieve a status of non-NATO U.S. ally, he said (very different from my own remarks about Afghanistan's future status). And to open a new chapter in the relationship between Afghanistan and the international community, he announced that an international conference would soon take place—in Kabul.

It was a good and reform-oriented speech, drawing on the priorities we had agreed on during the conference in The Hague and the transition agenda we had drawn up together with key Afghan ministers over the last months. The speech was welcomed by internationals as well as Afghans. The first step had been taken to move out of the gloomy atmosphere of the election ordeal and recreate a sense of optimism. But it was only the first step. The next would be the formation of the new government.

In the morning before the inauguration, Hillary Clinton assembled a group of ministers in the U.S. embassy. She invited me to go through our priorities and focus the minds of other foreign ministers on the most essential parts of our agenda. In the afternoon, Spanta invited me for a meeting with all foreign ministers that had come to attend the ceremony. Both meetings were encouraging. I could sense that the agenda we had tried to establish and the priorities we had set were finally being noticed by our main international partners. The constant repetition was starting to yield results. The Spanish foreign minister, Miguel Angel Moratinos, argued strongly for better support to farmers and, in particular, the establishment of a mechanism for farm credits. His Italian colleague, Franco Frattini, expressed his support for stepping up the training of civil servants. The proposal for a conference in Kabul as a demonstration of a new phase of transition to Afghan ownership gathered broad support. If the statements made during these two meetings could be translated into support and cash for concrete programs, then this day had been very useful.

A year earlier, reform-oriented politicians had injected new energy into Karzai's government and created optimism among Afghans as well as international representatives. The transition agenda the president had drawn up in his inauguration speech would more than ever require competent people. However, most of the reformoriented technocrats lacked a domestic constituency. Several of them had come back after many years in the United States, Canada, Germany, or the U.K. They had little in common with traditional Afghan leaders who commanded the support of the population in significant parts of the country. There was a concern that the president would now have to pay too much for the deals he had made with this old guard to win the elections. Of course, he would have to include individuals who were seen as legitimate representatives of the main ethnic communities. He would bring in conservatives and reformers and hopefully a good number of women. Forming a government in Afghanistan is a matter of stitching the country together and satisfying a number of constituencies representing very different parts of the Afghan society. But would he include a sufficiently strong group of reformers that could carry the process of modernization forward?

When Karzai presented his new government it looked better than many of us had feared, although several of the candidates were new and unknown to us. Most of the reformers of the old government had been reappointed. The members of the security team—the ministers of defense and interior and the head of intelligence—were all there. The ministers of finance and agriculture were on the list, and the economic team seemed altogether strengthened. As I had expected, Karzai had decided to keep the minister of water and energy, Ismail Khan, the powerful old warlord from Herat. I had asked the president many times to remove him, although I knew it would be an uphill struggle. Karzai's calculation was probably that he would do less harm inside than he could potentially do outside the government.

However, there were also serious disappointments: first of all that the minister for rural development, Zia, and the minister of health, Fatimi, had been replaced. Both had enjoyed broad support from the international community and had been assets to Karzai's government. While most ministers loved to travel abroad, Zia had visited by far most of the provinces and knew the country and the rural communities well. He was clean and dedicated. Fatimi had played an important role in the development of the health sector, one of the few successes after the fall of the Taliban. On the other hand, I was happy to see that Karim Khoram, the conservative, anti-Western minister of culture and information, had also been removed. Other ministers had urged me many times to convince the president to replace him.

Even if he was on the list, I was concerned about Atmar. There were bad vibrations between the president and him. When I heard that Karzai had doubts about Atmar, I went to see him. He confirmed that he would keep Atmar in the new government, but I could sense that Atmar was no longer the star he used to be in the president's eyes.

On January 2 the president was traveling to Helmand when Parliament voted over his new government. I was about to start exercising at Palace 7 with Radha Day, who had just taken over Hanne Melfald's position in my office. Radha came from DPKO in New York and knew the UN system well. She had worked with Scott for years. In addition to her intimate knowledge of the UN and of Afghanistan, she was one of the most pleasant and entertaining people I have ever met, with a unique talent for imitating prominent politicians. She also had the rare ability to bring Scott and me to the improvised exercise area of Palace 7. Sometimes late in the evening we would receive text messages calling us to come and exercise within the next ten minutes. We rarely objected.

Working out together in the exercise area that evening, we started to receive text messages that were quite different. We were kept constantly updated as Parliament voted over Karzai's candidates. Some of my best interlocutors were approved: Atmar, Wardak, Zakhilwal, Sharani, and Rahimi. But one by one, Karzai's other candidates failed to get the number of votes required. When the final results were clear, Karzai was facing a major crisis: seventeen of his twenty-four candidates, including Ismail Khan, had been turned down. For five years Karzai had chosen to ignore Parliament. Now, on the very day when Parliament was voting over his government, he had left the capital. The opposition had united against him and rejected two-thirds of his candidates. Karzai was seriously damaged, and he was shocked when he returned to Kabul later the same evening and received the final count. When I met him the next day, he was still angry but did not say much. He needed a fresh start with a new government—and we, the international community, had hoped that after a promising inauguration speech we could have a government in place quickly. That would have allowed us to focus on the agenda the president had outlined in his inauguration speech and to put a long and troubled period behind us. Now the president would have to present another list of candidates and hope that the National Assembly would be more cooperative.

I had to express my reaction to the media. I said that the vote had been a setback but that the National Assembly had made full use of its authority and demonstrated that it was not a rubber-stamping Parliament. I wish it had been that simple. The rumors about money trading hands and of various demands from parliamentarians in exchange of support were widespread. A *Washington Post* editorial criticized me for characterizing the vote as a setback. The *Post* seemed to think that the Assembly was acting in the name of reforms. That, I believe, was wishful thinking. The Assembly was acting more out of a desire to weaken the president than to promote a reform-oriented government.

Two weeks later Karzai presented a new list of candidates for the remaining ministries. Again, seven candidates were accepted and the remaining ten were rejected. Zalmai Rassoul had become foreign minister, and Spanta would soon take his position as national security advisor. As he had promised, Karzai had proposed three women as candidates for his new government, but the National Assembly had turned two of them down. And there was more bad news: the National Assembly had voted to bring Zarar Moqbel back to the government as minister of counternarcotics. I remember the long battle to get rid of him as minister of interior. Now he had returned to a related ministry and had received the highest number of votes of all the candidates the president had put forward. The rumor was that he had also paid the highest amount for the votes he had received.

Obviously Karzai was shaken and had no desire to present a third round of candidates and go through the same ordeal again. Ministers and deputy ministers from the previous government continued as acting ministers, month after month. Some of them had been rejected by Parliament and would probably not be presented for approval again. It was a temporary government without the strength we needed at this stage.

The next new appointments did not come before June 2010, when Haneef Atmar resigned as minister of interior—or rather, Karzai "accepted his resignation." I happened to be in Kabul for the first time since I had retired as UN envoy. The big Peace Jirga was taking place in the capital as Karzai had promised in his inauguration speech. On the opening day, a grenade exploded outside the big tent where hundreds of delegates were assembled. There were no casualties, but the incident must have brought the tension between the president and Atmar to a new climax. At least the president decided to make use of the event to get rid of his interior minister. I had an appointment to meet Atmar that afternoon. He called me to say that he had just come from meeting with the president but had now been asked to come back. Our meeting had to be postponed. It sounded suspicious, and I decided to turn on the TV in my room in the Norwegian embassy. Immediately there were photos of Atmar and Amrullah Saleh, the intelligence chief. Even if I could not understand the news presenter, it was obvious that they had both been dismissed. *What a horrible mistake*, I thought.

There had been policy disagreements for quite some time between the president and Atmar. He was also disliked by some of Karzai's "new" allies from the north and even by some other reformers. He was called a "Pashtun nationalist" and was accused of corruption by his rivals in the government. Was there any truth in such accusations? Atmar had, in my opinion, tried to attack corruption more vigorously than others in the government. Accusations about corruption had become a political weapon that government ministers and presidential advisers used against each other in an increasingly vicious internal power struggle. Saleh was known to have been critical of Karzai's reconciliation policy, which he thought was naive. Atmar was also skeptical of the president's peace offensive, but less pronounced than Saleh. Both were impressive members of Karzai's cabinet with excellent relations to key Western countries. But their good relationship to Western partners also made the president suspicious. I had always found Atmar to be loyal to Karzai whenever there were disagreements between the president and his most important international partners. When we were alone, Atmar could be concerned about confrontations between Karzai and his U.S. or U.K. partners, but he never spoke badly about the president behind his back as some of the other ministers and advisers did. Even when he resigned, Atmar abstained from criticizing the president publicly even though he was bitter in private.

Zia and Fatimi had already been dropped from the government in December 2009. In June 2010 Atmar and Saleh were also gone. All four had been highly respected among Afghans and among international partners. Since late 2008 I had been enthusiastic about the number of new reform-oriented politicians in key government positions. That trend now seemed to have been reversed. Conservative forces had grown in strength. Fahim Khan seemed to have gained more power than Karzai had predicted in May 2009. It was left to a smaller group of ministers to carry the reform agenda forward.

CHAPTER THIRTY-FIVE

THE BATTLE FOR ELECTION REFORM

In the international community as well as the Afghan opposition, discussions had now started over election reforms. In his inauguration speech, Karzai emphasized the need to establish Afghan ownership over the process. I agreed; our transition agenda should include full Afghan responsibility for future elections.

We were soon in the middle of preparations for the elections to the National Assembly. Once more, the date for the elections had to be determined. Ideally I would have preferred them to be postponed until 2011, and most of our international partners agreed. That would have given time for more comprehensive electoral reform and for providing better security than in 2009, but it would have violated the Constitution. And it was unrealistic to believe that the Afghans—the president as well as the opposition—would accept a postponement beyond 2010. I thought we should aim at a date sometime in the fall as that would make it possible to at least carry out some modest, but necessary, improvements of the election process and then plan for more ambitious reforms for the next round of elections. The president seemed to agree that fall 2010 would be the most reasonable time. That would also give us time for logistical preparations.

Suddenly, the IEC announced that the elections would take place on May 28. It was a totally unrealistic date. Not only would it be impossible to discuss and implement a minimum of reforms, but we would now have at least six months less time available for preparations than we had for the presidential election. Again, meetings were called in the presidential palace with all the relevant Afghan authorities, Ambassador Eikenberry, and me. The discussion was calm and very different from the acrimonious debates we had experienced the previous year. After having listened to the participants, the president concluded that there seemed to be a consensus for a date around mid-September 2010. The next day the IEC announced that September 18 had been chosen. We seemed to be repeating each and every debate from 2009 and the preparations for the presidential election.

A few days later, on January 17, it was the president's turn to surprise us all. Karzai signed a decree that explained what he had meant when he had talked about Afghan ownership of the election process in his inauguration speech; according to the decree, all members of the ECC would now be Afghans appointed by the president. There would be no more foreigners. A new and separate committee would be established for vetting the candidates, and it also would have only Afghan members. Karzai had certainly strengthened the Afghan ownership, but he had done little to ensure that the credibility of the elections would be improved. In reality he had given himself greater control over the entire process. And he had preempted the National Assembly, which was about to return from its brief recess the next day.

Following discussions with some of the ambassadors in Kabul, I presented a list of four requests to Karzai. The first was for changes in the composition of the IEC—in other words to remove its chairman and others considered not to be impartial—to ensure its independence and credibility. The second was an amendment to the president's decree that would give internationals two out of the five places in the ECC and require the agreement of one of them for any decision to be valid. The third was that there should still be international representatives in the committee mandated to discuss the exclusion of candidates from running for elected office, and the final request was the establishment of a reform commission to propose more comprehensive electoral reforms for the future.

The president was quite clear with regard to the ECC: there would be changes in its composition, including its chairmanship. But he would not dismiss Ludin, the controversial chairman. For years, Ludin had fought bravely for his country, and the president would not humiliate him. He would wait for Ludin to resign, and Karzai was sure that he would. The president seemed to agree that I could appoint two of the members in the IEC and that one of them in reality would carry a veto. I told him that we were already in touch with two candidates: a South African, who had been close to Nelson Mandela, and a Palestinian. Karzai was skeptical of letting the UN or ISAF have any influence over the vetting and exclusion of candidates but wanted more time to reflect. He liked and trusted the ISAF commander, General McChrystal, but it was still unclear who would be my successor as UN envoy. I had from the outset made it clear that I would stay in Kabul for two years and in a few weeks my term was coming to an end. The president said the proposal for a reform committee was a good idea, but I could hear that it was a proposal he did not intend to discuss seriously with me so close to my departure.

A few days later I was called back to continue the discussions with the president. He had now taken one step backwards. He could accept two internationals on the ECC—in particular, with the nationalities I had mentioned—but he was skeptical of giving one of them a de facto veto, and he was reluctant to give any role to the UN and ISAF in the process of vetting the candidates. The discussion continued for the next couple of weeks without any real changes in his position. It seemed clear that he was not prepared to give any concessions to me just before my departure and the arrival of my successor. If he had a small "gift" to give to anybody, why give it to the outgoing UN envoy? The date for my successor's arrival had already been set.

CHAPTER THIRTY-SIX

ANOTHER CONFERENCE—BUT WHERE?

As the difficult year 2009 ended, the preparations for a new conference continued, along with the discussions about election reforms and Karzai's struggle to have his new government approved. All of us—Afghans and internationals—now aimed at a conference in Kabul, probably in March or April 2010. There was also a discussion about holding a second conference later in the year, probably in Europe. Nothing could symbolize Afghan ownership better at this stage than to see the Afghans host their first big international conference in their own capital. Prime Minister Brown, President Sarkozy, and Chancellor Merkel had proposed the holding of an international conference in Europe some time ago, but I believed that our proposal for a meeting in Kabul first had now been accepted in all the key capitals. President Karzai had even stated his intention to hold a conference in Kabul in his inauguration address.

But I was wrong. During a meeting of the British Commonwealth on November 28, Prime Minister Gordon Brown proposed to hold an international conference on Afghanistan in London. He had convinced Ban Ki-moon to cosponsor the proposal, which he demonstrated by having the secretary-general stand next to him during the press conference. The date was set for January 28. Kabul had been overruled by London. Again a decision had been taken without consulting the Afghans. This was in a way worse than Clinton's announcement of the conference in The Hague. At that time there was no planning for any other event. Now Karzai had practically invited the international community to come to Kabul. I was surprised and embarrassed after having been the first to propose a Kabul conference.

Karzai and his closest ministers commented sarcastically on Brown's proposal. The Afghan president had been accused of misusing public funds for election purposes. Now it was obvious that Brown's proposal was driven by the forthcoming British elections and the Labour Party's low standing in the opinion polls. One of Karzai's advisors told him Brown was doing exactly what he blamed the president for. And would it help Brown win the elections?

Nevertheless, we had to get on with the preparations. The British were now firmly in control and left less room for the Afghans and the UN than we had experienced in Paris and in The Hague. London drafted the concluding statement and Finance Minister Zakhilwal and I struggled to the very end to amend some of the paragraphs. However, a number of the key decisions required to give the London Conference substance had to be taken in Kabul. A few days before we left for London, the JCMB decided to increase the size of the Afghan army and police. The hope was now to reach 171,600 for the army and 134,000 for the police by fall 2011. This would send an important message from the London Conference: that the Afghans wanted to take responsibility for the security of their own country and that the international military presence would gradually play a supporting role.

Another important initiative for the London Conference was the establishment of a fund to facilitate the reintegration of Taliban fighters and other insurgents. Masoom Stanekzai, the president's adviser, had presented an outline of a peace and reconciliation policy. He underscored that the fund for reintegration of local Taliban fighters could only succeed if it was accompanied by a political reconciliation process that included the Taliban leadership. However, there was no consensus on this wider reconciliation policy. Therefore, the reintegration fund was pushed to the center; if Taliban fighters could be offered a future, security, and employment in their own villages, then they would turn their backs on the Taliban and return to normal life. It was a simplistic approach based—in my opinion—on a misguided assessment that a significant number of Taliban recruits were driven by economic motives. However, the establishment of a reintegration fund was also driven by the need to demonstrate concrete results from the London Conference.

President Karzai had already announced a conference in Kabul. It would now have to take place later in the year. The London Conference had primarily dealt with security matters. A Kabul conference would have to cover a wider range of topics related to the transfer of responsibilities to Afghan authorities. I left Kabul in March and was succeeded by Staffan de Mistura as UN envoy; however, I continued to follow developments in Kabul. The minister of finance, Zakhilwal, took the lead in preparing for the Kabul conference. He focused his attention on the four civilian priorities that the government had agreed on: agriculture and rural development, infrastructure, human resource development, and governance. After thorough preparations, the conference took place on July 20, 2010. The Afghan government presented a broad plan for implementation of the Afghan national development strategy, the most detailed and prioritized plan the Afghan government had ever presented to the donor community. The wider objective was, as Zakhilwal, Ward, and I had described so many times, a national growth strategy focused on a limited number of critical areas that would have an impact across the board. The next stage would be to transform the ambitious planning papers into national priority programs that donors could focus their attention and resources on.

The Kabul conference was a success in several ways. It was the first such conference—with more than seventy delegations at the level of foreign minister—ever to take place in the Afghan capital, and the concluding declaration contained commitments that went far beyond any similar conference in the past. First and foremost, Afghanistan's international partners gave strong support to channeling at least 50 percent of their development aid through the Afghan budget over the next two years. Resources spent outside the budget would also align with Afghan priorities. Donors agreed that over the next two years, 80 percent of their assistance should be directed to support the priority programs outlined by the government. Procurement processes should be made transparent and the number of subcontractors reduced to improve aid effectiveness.

But even if the Kabul conference was a success, I had several concerns. First of all, there were numerous (and more or less artificial) deadlines and target dates for reviews and progress reports. If taken seriously, poorly staffed Afghan ministries would spend much of their time preparing reports for donors. Furthermore, Zakhilwal had put together his "clusters" of related ministers during summer 2009—before the presidential elections. After the elections, new ministers had come into the government and demanded their share of attention. A new turf battle had erupted. Consequently the number of national programs had increased. Some donors also could not accept that their own national priority had not been included and insisted on additions. In the end, what should have been fewer than ten programs had increased to twenty-two. As one official in the Ministry of Finance told me during my visit to Kabul in February 2011, with so many priorities donors can continue as before to invest in maternal health and primary education—in the "low-hanging fruits," as Mark Ward had called such projects. Too many priorities would again make it difficult to concentrate donor resources around a real growth strategy.

CHAPTER THIRTY-SEVEN

A COMPLICATED PARTNERSHIP

The first weeks after Obama's inauguration marked, as I have mentioned, a significant change in the relationship between the U.S. and the Afghan government. Biden's visit just before the inauguration had been a failure, but the new administration seemed not to understand that Biden had offended Karzai in front of many of his most trusted ministers. Holbrooke's first visit in February made matters even worse.

The regular video conferences that the Afghan president had held with President Bush were discontinued. Relations were from now on to be handled at a lower level and with greater distance.

If the Obama administration believed that Karzai would listen more to Washington by talking less to him, then the new team was making a serious mistake. Every day during this period, Karzai became more skeptical of the Obama administration and certainly not more inclined to listen to Washington's advice or instructions. President Bush had been criticized for the frequent video conferences. I found it quite natural that the U.S. president would talk regularly and at length to the president of the country where the United States had its largest military and political engagement. The United States spent billions of dollars every year and would soon have close to 100,000 soldiers in Afghanistan. Why shouldn't Obama be able to pick up the phone regularly and have a continuous dialogue with Karzai? To me, this early decision of the Obama administration was a serious mistake.

In his recent book *Decision Points*, President Bush describes his relationship to Karzai: "I made it a priority to check in regularly with Karzai. I knew he had a daunting task, and I wanted to lift his spirits and assure him of our commitment. I offered advice and made requests, but I was careful not to give him orders. The best way to help him grow as a leader was to treat him like one." Bush was right to treat Karzai in a respectful and supportive way. I had looked forward to Obama continuing the video conferences, but perhaps in a more forward-leaning way than Bush had.

It was clear who had given Obama the advice of keeping Karzai at a distance. Biden had played a critical role and had been supported by Holbrooke when he joined the Obama administration. But what had been the advice of the other members of Obama's team? I found it difficult to believe that Secretary Gates or Secretary Clinton had been supportive of this tougher approach to Karzai.

Washington's relationship to Karzai had been troubled from the very beginning. Donald Rumsfeld provides interesting insight in his book *Known and Unknown*. He describes Operation Jawbreaker, where CIA forces had linked up with General Fahim Khan, Massoud's successor and the de facto leader of the Northern Alliance, and other northern warlords. On November 5, 2001, forces under General Dostum began their assault on Mazar-e-Sharif. Meanwhile, General Fahim Khan's troops moved to seize the northern cities of Taloqan and Kunduz. General Ismail Khan captured Herat in the west. All three were, as I have described, personalities that still played prominent roles during my period in Afghanistan many years later. When we complained about the continued culture of impunity in Afghanistan under Karzai and the influence of old warlords and powerbrokers in Afghan politics, these were among the people we had in mind.

Rumsfeld went on to describe a story from April 2002. A Pashtun warlord, Pacha Khan Zadran from Gardez, threatened to ignite a civil war against Kazai's new administration if Karzai did not recognize him as a provincial governor. Karzai responded by telling his opponent to surrender or be annihilated. Since Karzai did not have any forces at his disposal, it was obvious that he would have to rely on U.S. support to meet the challenge. Rumsfeld discussed the incident with President Bush and other leaders in the Bush administration. He wrote in a note to Bush that "the issue is whether the Afghan government will be required to take responsibility for its actions—politically and militarily—or whether it will be allowed to become dependent on U.S. forces to stay in power."

It was clearly Rumsfeld's view that Karzai would have to learn to solve his own problems with political means rather than rely on the United States to help him solve them with military forces. Rumsfeld was convinced that Karzai needed to learn to govern "the Chicago way." In the 1960s, he wrote, Mayor Richard J. Daley ruled Chicago—a city of many diverse and powerful elements— using maneuver, guile, money, patronage, and services to keep the city's fractious leaders from rebelling against his authority. Karzai should learn to do the same. Rumsfeld's conclusion in his note to President Bush was that "a Karzai tempted to overreach could drag us into reliving the British and Soviet experiences of trying to use outside force to impose centralized rule on the fractious people of Afghanistan." Bush agreed and Karzai was told that he would have to manage on his own and learn the tough lessons of governing without invoking U.S. military power.

The incident illustrates the political atmosphere in the aftermath of the fall of the Taliban. Dostum, Fahim Khan, and Ismail Khan had helped the CIA overthrow Taliban rule. And they had helped ensure a transition to the new Karzai regime—together with leading Northern Alliance politicians, such as Qanooni and

Dr. Abdullah. But these and other warlords had also played the leading roles in tearing Afghanistan to pieces almost a decade earlier during the civil war of the early 1990s. They all had somber human rights records and were known for their brutality. They also had assets that nobody else possessed at the time: the military muscle required to overthrow the Taliban without a major deployment of U.S. forces. When Karzai moved into the presidential palace in Kabul, he did not have any military forces at his disposal. He had no instruments of power and no institutions, civilian or military. The armed forces belonged to the warlords.

James F. Dobbins, the leading U.S. diplomat during the Bonn conference in December 2001 and the following period, tried as I have mentioned to convince the Bush administration to invest in building the new institutions the Karzai administration needed to extend its influence in the country. But the response was modest. "In their first year of reconstruction," Dobbins writes in his excellent book, *After the Taliban,* "Bosnians received sixteen times more international assistance than did Afghans." And there was little interest in civilian institution building.

Karzai had been disappointed as a young man when the United States turned its attention away from Afghanistan as soon as the Soviets left the country. He had he tried in vain to convince the United States and other countries to provide support in the struggle against the Taliban. Now he experienced hesitation and reluctance again. He had been brought to Kabul to lead his country, but received little assistance in creating the tools required to govern. Gradually, the international community increased its assistance and its military engagement. But it was dominated by foreign agendas and priorities—and not by those of the Afghans. Karzai wondered what would have happened if international assistance had arrived earlier and allowed him to expand his authority—perhaps in time to prevent the return and explosive growth of the insurgency.

When Obama finally made his first visit to Afghanistan, more than a year after his inauguration as U.S. president in March 2010, Karzai's irritation peaked. Comments made by the president himself and remarks made to the media by Obama's national security adviser, Jim Jones, were seen by Karzai as condescending toward him.

A few days later his frustration again boiled over when he blamed the international community—and he still mentioned Galbraith's name first—for having interfered in the presidential elections. It was on this occasion that Karzai proclaimed that he was ready to join the Taliban. Of course, it was an unwise statement. It reinforced the impression of an unpredictable president and had a demoralizing effect on those who risked their lives in the fight against the Taliban every day. There were rumors that Karzai's planned visit to Washington in May could be canceled. Karzai's attitude was that he would certainly not beg for a trip to Washington.

The Obama administration must finally have understood that this tension could not continue with such enormous human and economic resources and political capital invested in the conflict in Afghanistan. The tone changed when Karzai went to Washington on May 9, 2010. The red carpet was out, and the visit was carefully planned and managed from beginning to end. It was a serious effort from both sides to put the relationship onto a more constructive track. The need to renew the partnership had become acute. When I talked to Karzai's advisers they quickly characterized this as the best visit he had ever had to Washington. The American side had produced the script, and Karzai visited the right places and said the right things; he expressed gratitude for U.S. sacrifices in Afghanistan and visited soldiers injured in battle and soldiers planning to leave for combat in his country. There was agreement—at least in general terms—about a new strategic partnership, a reduction in civilian casualties, transfer of responsibilities for detainees, and the reconciliation policy. The United States also promised to spend more money through Afghan budgets. All were issues the Afghans had been pressing for a long time.

But even if the atmosphere had changed, the new and improved partnership remained shaky and vulnerable. One serious incident of civilian casualty caused by U.S. troops or one careless remark could trigger new confrontations. Furthermore, even if there were agreements in general terms, the specifics remained to be hammered out. How far did the U.S. agreement on reconciliation go? And what would the new strategic partnership look like? President Karzai's confidence in a long-term U.S. commitment to Afghanistan had been shaken. Underneath the harmonious surface during Karzai's visit there was a sense of nervousness on both sides.

The U.S. "dream team" was no longer such a dream. The friction between Eikenberry and McChrystal was well known after the media leaks of Eikenberry's cables to the State Department. Holbrooke's behavior had made him unpopular among Afghans as well as in the international community. The dismissal of Galbraith certainly had also damaged Holbrooke since Galbraith was seen as Holbrooke's man. I raised again the question of replacing Holbrooke with Jim Jones in the beginning of February during his last visit to Kabul before my departure from the scene. The same complaints had been made by others. I told Jones how many of us felt uncomfortable in Holbrooke's presence and how he complicated otherwise open discussions by his inability to listen and his abrasive style. Jones returned to Washington the following day. Back in the White House, he sent a reassuring message to Eikenberry: Holbrooke was on his way out. In the State Department, the message was widely distributed and became well known instantly. Obama had agreed that time had come to let Holbrooke go. Following Jones's last visit, it was my impression and that of Eikenberry, that Holbrooke would resign within days. But as days and weeks passed, it became clear that he would not be pushed aside. Hillary Clinton had protected him.

Replacing Holbrooke would certainly have been seen as a defeat for the secretary of state.

Summer 2010 brought new turbulence to the U.S. team: *Rolling Stone* magazine published a lengthy article by a journalist who had accompanied General McChrystal and members of his closest staff for two weeks. The article contained critical comments about the president, the vice president, and other top U.S. officials, mostly from McChrystal's staff. McChrystal's team had been careless and had trusted a journalist they should have known could not be trusted. Obama had no other choice than to dismiss him. But the incident again illustrated the tension inside the U.S. team. Some of the top people in the administration looked nostalgically back at Iraq and the teamwork between Ambassador Ryan Crocker and General David Petraeus. There was an urgent need for changes that could bring greater cohesion and predictability in U.S. policymaking.

McChrystal was quickly replaced by Petraeus. The man who more than any other had shaped the strategy was now in charge of implementing it. For Karzai the loss of McChrystal was a disappointment. He genuinely liked Stan McChrystal, as I think we all did. Stan was certainly a uniquely competent and inspiring commander, and he would always ask questions and be curious to hear the views of his Afghan and international interlocutors.

By fall 2010 the relationship between Karzai and the international community had again deteriorated. When Eikenberry had arrived in Kabul in April 2009, Karzai had been pleased. But the leak to *The New York Times* in November 2009 of his cables to Secretary Clinton, where Eikenberry concluded that Karzai was not a strategic partner, hurt the relationship. A few months later, when Karzai could read more of the cable traffic from U.S. embassies via Wikileaks, his trust in the U.S. administration was further damaged. With McChrystal's departure Karzai lost an interlocutor he liked.

His replacement, General Petraeus, was not the listener Karzai had become used to. With McChrystal gone and Eikenberry sidelined, the United States—and the international community—no longer had the dialogue they needed with the Afghan president.

Karzai's frustration with the Obama leadership ran deep. He was angered by the lack of understanding when U.S. operations caused civilian casualties. So many visiting U.S. delegations seemed not to understand the impact such casualties had on Karzai's standing, in particular among his own constituency, the Pashtuns. He was one of them but unable to defend them against his foreign partner that was increasingly seen as an occupier.

The Afghan president had been the target of daily criticism from foreign politicians, the media, and commentators. Sometimes it had been justified. On most occasions it had been simplistic and without understanding of the Afghan context.

On March 2, 2011, Secretary Gates also reflected my views when addressing lawmakers on Capitol Hill: "I think we have done a lousy job of listening to President Karzai because every issue that has become a public explosion from President Karzai has been an issue that he has talked to American officials about repeatedly in private. . . . in most instances there is a basis for [such explosions]." I was pleased to read these remarks. There was also another important and positive development; during spring and summer 2011, President Obama spoke directly to Karzai over video link—as his predecessor had done. Perhaps Washington had come to realize that the initial strategy toward Karzai had failed. Hopefully, there was a new thinking in the Obama administration.

By summer 2011 a new team was in charge of U.S.-Afghanistan policies. Only Hillary Clinton remained from Obama's inauguration in January 2009. The new team will have to improve relations with President Karzai before it is too late and the political leadership in Kabul has imploded. It must do so while at the same time managing expectations in the United States for significant reductions of American forces. It will not be an easy task. Afghanistan cannot wait until Karzai's successor has been elected in 2014. After a decade of troubled relations between Afghanistan and the country's by far most important partner, Washington must recognize that it is on Karzai's watch that the conflict will have to be brought to an end.

CHAPTER THIRTY-EIGHT

THE FRAGMENTED REGION

The UN Security Council had given us a mandate to promote regional cooperation. At the Bonn conference in December 2001, when the Afghans agreed on a new interim administration under Karzai's leadership, Afghanistan's neighbors had played an important and constructive role. Iran had been particularly helpful in ensuring the agreement of the Northern Alliance. Almost a decade later it was clear that a regional involvement would again be required to bring the conflict in Afghanistan to an end. Countries around Afghanistan were also suffering from the impact of the conflict in terms of refugees and drug trafficking. Insurgents crossed the border to Pakistan unhindered and found sanctuary on Pakistani territory. The Central Asian countries were deeply concerned about a potential spread of extremism from Afghanistan and Pakistan. Even China followed this challenge closely with its millions of Muslim Uigurs in the Xingkiang province, close to the border to Pakistan.

There was also a vast potential for cooperation. Afghanistan, Pakistan, and India needed energy from Central Asia. The Central Asian countries would benefit from corridors for transportation to the coasts in Pakistan and Iran. And the Afghans could soon need outlets for their own export of mineral resources. In the north was the impressive river Amu Darya. During the Soviet era there had been an agreement between the Central Asian Soviet republics and Afghanistan regulating their respective rights to the water. But as the Soviet Union collapsed so did the agreement. If the Afghans could make use of these water resources, vast agricultural areas would have been irrigated, reducing Afghanistan's food insecurity and perhaps even making the country self-sufficient in food production. The constant armed conflicts, the political rivalries, the lack of infrastructure, and the mountainous terrain hindered economic integration that could also have a positive political impact.

To explore our potential role I wanted to make regular visits to the countries in the region. It was important to be aware of the limitations. All the neighbors were affected by developments in Afghanistan, but Afghanistan was not the primary security concern of any of them. For Pakistan and India, the conflict over Kashmir remained the main security challenge. Afghanistan had become an arena for bilateral competition with India.

Pakistan could not accept a government in Kabul that was seen as pro-Indian and regarded the significant Indian involvement in Afghanistan with great skepticism. India had increased its economic engagement and its assistance to building Afghan institutions. There was a close friendship between India and prominent Afghan leaders. Karzai himself had received his education in India. At the same time, Afghan politicians were deeply suspicious of Pakistani intentions.

For the Iranian government the main focus was on the conflict with the United States over the Iranian nuclear program. If the leaders in Tehran felt that the pressure from Washington was increasing, they could in return step up their involvement inside Afghanistan. The Iranians did not have any interest in seeing the Taliban come back in Afghanistan, but they could make life more unpleasant for the United States and calibrate their involvement, including modest arms deliveries to the Taliban, in a way that would annoy the Americans. The Iranians had, as I mentioned, been helpful in bringing about the Bonn agreement in 2001. They were offended when President Bush, a few weeks after the Bonn conference, characterized Iran as part of the "axis of evil."

The Iranians were heavily engaged in Afghanistan with trade and a variety of development and cultural projects. And they were deeply involved in the political games in Kabul. A significant portion of Iranian support had gone to the Shia population in the central parts of the country and to leading politicians of the Northern Alliance. But Tehran also cultivated close relationships to the Karzai government. During the presidential elections, the Iranians probably contributed to both the main candidates.

The Central Asian countries mainly had their attention focused on each other. Water from the Amu Darya had been an explosive topic for decades. The upstream countries, Tajikistan and Kyrgyzstan, collected huge amounts of water during the summer in order to have enough for power production in the winter season. The downstream countries, Uzbekistan and Turkmenistan, needed water during the summer for cotton production. This was not a conflict of the past but colored their present relationship.

We started our round of visits with a trip to Tehran in May 2008. I was taken straight from the airport to the presidential office. The president, Mahmoud Ahmadinejad, had an aura of self-confidence and received me in a friendly way. His main message was crystal clear: that the international community should establish a timetable for the withdrawal of all its forces. Only Afghans could find a solution to Afghanistan's conflict. Ahmadinejad's concern was obviously that the U.S. military involvement would be turned into a permanent regional presence, a presence that could also be used against Iran. He spoke about Afghanistan's future, but had his own country's security and relationship with the United States in mind.

At the same time he warned strongly against any dialogue with the Taliban. I had already on several occasions argued that such a dialogue was critically important. According to Ahmadinajad it was an illusion to believe that there were moderate Taliban that could be meaningful interlocutors. Rumors about deliveries of military equipment to the Taliban were false, he claimed, and Iran had no interest in supporting the insurgency. (Later the rumors of deliveries to the Taliban were confirmed to me from a surprising source. A Taliban contact told me that he had been present when small equipment had been unpacked inside Afghanistan. I found it hard to believe that he was bluffing.)

The Iranians expressed deep concern about the smuggling of opium across the border from Afghanistan. The Afghan border police were almost nonexistent, to the extent that they did not show up at a planned border-police exercise with Pakistani, Iranian, and Afghan participation. The Afghans were also slow at implementing agreements reached under the auspices of the UNODC. Iranian authorities had taken a number of initiatives to engage the Afghans more vigorously, but the Afghan response had been slow and ineffective. The Iranians were paying a high price for the drug trade. Several hundred of their security forces had lost their lives over the last years in confrontations with drug traders and other criminals trying to cross the border. According to the Iranians, more than 1.5 million of their citizens were drug addicts. If this was the official Iranian figure, then the real number was probably significantly higher.

Of course, the Iranians also saw the potential for economic cooperation with Afghanistan and the wider region. There were plans to construct a railway to the Afghan border only sixty-two kilometers from Herat. Modern infrastructure projects could open up licit trade and the shipment of products from Afghanistan— and the entire Central Asian region—to the Iranian port at Bandar Abbas. The border areas between Iran and Afghanistan also had mineral resources that were of interest to the Iranians. I left Tehran impressed with the problems the Iranians were facing and the costs to their society of the conflict in Afghanistan. On the other hand, the potential for regional cooperation, which could provide economic benefits, was obvious.

Our first visit to Islamabad followed a month and a half later at the beginning of July. We had planned to visit Pakistan earlier; however, the Pakistanis had offered us a program in Islamabad that did not include any high-ranking official, and we decided to postpone the visit and try again later. Following a controversy with my predecessor, Tom Koenigs, it seemed that Islamabad still wanted to minimize our involvement in Pakistan's relationship to Afghanistan. I had already met the foreign minister, Shah Mahmoud Qureshi, several times at international conferences and found him to be a pleasant and open interlocutor. When we finally met in Islamabad he confirmed his readiness to work closely with us. But we could sense that his senior staff was more reluctant. The prime minister, Yusuf Raza Gilani, was a more enigmatic figure. When we waited for him in his office, a large Pakistani delegation was standing lined up on one side of the room, with my small team standing on the other. It was a sharp contrast to the more informal, but dignified way Ahmadinejad had received me alone in Tehran a few weeks earlier. The discussion was also very different. Ahmadinejad had been focused, asked questions, and been ready to listen. Gilani spoke at length, and after a while, I wondered if he had brought speaking notes intended for another meeting—perhaps with a U.S. military official.

Nevertheless, our meetings with Pakistani officials were interesting because of their offensive approach. They would certainly not tolerate that a UN official came to Islamabad to criticize them and instead preempted any such criticism. Afghan refugees had come in millions across the border to Pakistan since the Soviet invasion in 1979. Young refugees had been radicalized and represented a threat to the stability of the Pakistani society. Drugs were smuggled across the long border and were contaminating Pakistani youth. The Pakistanis rejected any hint that their authorities were providing safe havens to Al Qaeda, Taliban, or Haqqani networks on their territory. Tens of thousands crossed that porous border every day, they said. It had always been like this, and the conflict in Afghanistan had made it even more difficult to keep this constant migration under control. However, the Pakistanis were concerned about the Indian involvement in Afghanistan. According to our Pakistani interlocutors, India had increased its presence significantly and used its presence to incite instability in the border areas of Pakistan.

Contrary to the visit to Tehran, the Pakistani did not have an agenda for cooperation to present to us. They were planning to offer Afghan students scholarships in their country and to offer training of government officials. But there was no need for UN involvement in such areas. The only request I received was to help speed up the return of Afghan refugees that were still in Pakistan—and many of them had been there for decades now.

In late 2008 and early 2009 we visited the Central Asian neighbors Uzbekistan, Tajikistan, and Turkmenistan. All of them saw a great potential for infrastructure projects such as roads, railroads, and delivery of energy to Afghanistan and, farther to the east, to Pakistan and India. Some of these projects, such as the TAPI—the Turkmenistan, Afghanistan, Pakistan, and India gas pipeline—would be impossible to realize as long as the conflict was raging. Others were implementable and could provide energy to Afghanistan that would stimulate economic growth and employ tens of thousands. The first power line was already under construction from Uzbekistan and was about to become operational. That was a promising development. However, the Central Asian leaders also looked at developments in Afghanistan with nervousness. They feared that the conflict could again lead extremist movements to cross the border from Afghanistan and bring instability to their own countries.

In UNAMA, we were looking at the potential for using experts from Central Asia, Iran, and Pakistan to strengthen Afghan capacity in a number of areas. There were experts in agriculture, infrastructure, and education, who not only knew the languages of Afghanistan but were also familiar with the culture and the traditions. They shared the same religion. They even knew the soil and had in the past worked together across the borders to fight the same plagues, such as cross-border locust swarms. These experts had little need for interpreters or security. They would not demand the same salaries and would be able to stay for longer periods of time than Western experts.

The neighbors to the north all wanted to play a role in a political process to solve the conflict. In Dushanbe the Tajik president, Emomali Rahmon, recalled the bloody civil war of his country in the 1990s. Tajikistan had found its own solution—with the assistance of the UN. Perhaps there were lessons that could be useful to the Afghans. Following the first meeting with President Rahmon, the Tajik foreign minister, Hamrokhan Zarifi, folded out a huge map of the region in his office and outlined possibilities for energy and water projects. I had known Zarifi for more than ten years. We had become friends when we were both serving as ambassadors to the Organization for Security and Cooperation in Europe (OSCE) in Vienna. The Turkmens had maintained relations to the Taliban during its regime and were also prepared to assist in a peace process. I discussed their offer repeatedly with the Turkmen leader President Gurbangulu Berdimuhammedov as well as Foreign Minister Rashid Meredov. The Turkmens offered to provide a venue for meetings to initiate a dialogue with the insurgents or for the establishment of a Taliban office. It seemed to me that the Turkmen capital, Ashabad, would be a better venue for contacts with the Taliban than Dubai,

Qatar, or Turkey, where hundreds of intelligence officers from many countries would follow every move and the media attention would be more intense.

The Uzbeks were more complicated interlocutors. Considering himself as the dominant leader of the region, the Uzbek leader, President Islam Karimov, presented a proposal for the establishment of a new forum, which he called the 6+ 3 group. It was based on a group named 6+ 2 that had been established in 1999 during Taliban rule including all Afghanistan's neighboring states (Iran, Pakistan, China, Uzbekistan, Turkmenistan, and Tajikistan) as well as the United States and Russia under the aegis of the UN. Now the Uzbek president wanted to bring NATO into the framework. The Uzbeks had decided not to include Afghanistan itself and the proposal was therefore quickly rejected as a propaganda initiative. However, it probably had some merits—provided Afghanistan would be included. During the Bonn Conference, the 6+2 format had been useful for mobilizing the assistance of Afghanistan's neighbors in bringing the Afghans to an agreement.

There were countless conferences on regional cooperation from late 2008 until early 2010. The first of them was probably the most promising of all. Foreign Minister Kouchner had invited a small group of his colleagues to get together in a castle in the outskirts of Paris, La Celle-Saint-Cloud, on December 14, 2008. Kouchner wanted to create an atmosphere for open discussions and avoid the reading of prepared statements. He had insisted on keeping the number of participants at a minimum, thereby irritating a good number of countries—including Turkey. With the exception of Iran, all neighboring countries participated, in addition to India, the United States, the U.K., Germany, the EU Commission, and the EU "Foreign Minister" Solana. After having received mixed signals, Kouchner in the end was informed that there would not be any Iranian representative. The reason was probably that President

Sarkozy shortly before the conference had declared that he would neither shake hands with nor sit at the same table as Ahmadinejad because of his views on Israel.

We were disappointed about the Iranian absence, but we were all the more pleased that the Indian minister of state for external affairs, Mr. Anand Sharma, was present. The terrorist attacks in Mumbai had taken place three weeks earlier, on November 26, and indications already pointed to Pakistani terrorists. It was certainly a good sign that the Indian government would be ready to sit down next to a Pakistani foreign minister so soon after these attacks.

Kouchner and I took turns in chairing and introducing the various topics. The best of the sessions was devoted to infrastructure. Vadim Nazarov, one of the most qualified political officers in our UN Mission and formerly a senior diplomat in the Russian embassy in Kabul, had prepared a list of promising projects. Some were not implementable at this stage due to the ongoing conflict or political sensitivities among neighboring states. But others were doable and would bring significant advantages to a number of the states in the region. We had to pick a small number of high-impact projects that could boost regional trade as well as the Afghan economy. The World Bank had given us existing documentation about huge natural resources in Afghanistan as well as their locations and estimated value. To start exploiting these resources, railways and electrical power would be required. We were not talking about the "low-hanging fruits" any more, but of costly infrastructure investments. Most ministers were probably surprised to hear that Afghanistan had the largest iron-ore resources in Asia, in addition to copper, gold, precious stones, and hydrocarbons. The EU commissioner, Benita Ferrero-Waldner, reacted with enthusiasm and invited experts to a follow-up meeting in Brussels.

I also mentioned the river Amu Darya and the division of water resources between Afghanistan and its Central Asian neighbors. The Central Asians recognized that Afghanistan had a right to its share of these water resources and two of them mentioned a figure of 20 percent. The figure was obviously too low, but it would take years before Afghanistan would get close even to that figure. The topic was at least on the table, and there had been a first exchange of views, albeit brief.

The meeting outside of Paris had been a success and the discussion had been constructive and concrete. Since Kouchner had excluded a significant number of countries from the conference itself, he decided to organize a dinner in the evening at the French foreign ministry with ministers from other interested states. At dinner Kouchner praised the Indian decision to participate and the harmonious discussion with the Indian minister of state and the Pakistani foreign minister so soon after the attacks in Mumbai. In his desire to be kind to the two participants, Kouchner went one step too far in his enthusiasm. The Indian felt obliged to intervene to avoid an impression that it was business as usual in spite of the attacks. He warned that next time any such incident took place, India would not be able to show the same restraint. The atmosphere around the table suddenly became tense. The meeting itself had illustrated the potential for cooperation. This brief exchange over dinner illustrated some of the tension that made such cooperation so difficult.

A range of regional conferences now followed; first in Tehran, then in Moscow, Istanbul, The Hague, and finally in Islamabad—to mention the most important of them. They all took place within a period of two months. It was simply too much. The same small group of Afghans and UN staff had to prepare most of them. Instead of devoting time to bringing a limited number of strategic projects forward, time was spent preparing speeches and concluding statements for conferences.

On May 13–14, 2009, the countries of the region and the donor community met in Islamabad for the Third Regional Economic Cooperation Conference on Afghanistan (RECCA). It resulted in a concluding document that was at least somewhat more concrete than the outcome from other, similar conferences. Mark Ward had worked hard to help draft the document and put some concrete substance into it. The most important outcome was probably an agreement to launch a comprehensive study on a future railway network linking Afghanistan to the wider region. But apart from that, the conference was a disappointment. When the Afghan delegation arrived for the opening ceremony with the president and a dozen ministers, I was impressed. This level of participation went beyond my expectations. But my enthusiasm was short-lived. When the opening ceremony was over and the real deliberations started, not a single Afghan minister was in the hall. The entire delegation had left with Karzai on his round of bilateral meetings with Pakistani leaders. High-level Pakistani government officials waited with us for hours for their Afghan counterpart to appear. Mark Ward and I made numerous phone calls to ministers traveling in their cars behind the president to his meetings across the city. Finally the Afghan minister of economy, Jalil Shams, appeared. He had not been involved in preparing the conference but had now been sent to the conference center to represent the Afghan government. The others were already on board the plane back to Kabul with the president. A big group of international representatives had been waiting for hours, together with the Pakistani hosts. We had worked for weeks and months to get something out of this conference for the Afghans. Instead of a good discussion that could have brought us forward, we had spent most of the time waiting for them.

There is no lack of promising economic projects in the region, but the political obstacles are significant. Washington is skeptical of Iranian involvement and influence. The Pakistani thinking is influenced by Islamabad's relationship to India. It took more than a year beyond the agreed deadline of December 31, 2009, to sign the transit trade agreement between Afghanistan and Pakistan allowing goods to be transported between Afghanistan and India. The prospects of additional power lines from Central Asia are hampered by continued rivalries between Uzbekistan and Tajikistan and by the ongoing conflict in Afghanistan. Hopefully economic requirements will force the countries in the region to think in a more cooperative manner. Afghanistan, Pakistan, and India share a growing need for energy, and the gas pipeline from Turkmenistan is one of the main projects that can provide it. The potential for regional cooperation is impressive. However, as long as the conflict in Afghanistan and old regional rivalries over water and energy continue, the chances of overcoming the fragmentation of the region are modest.

CHAPTER THIRTY-NINE

NEGOTIATE WITH THE TALIBAN?

Long before I came to Kabul I was convinced that the conflict could not be solved by military means. Karzai had been speaking out publicly in favor of a dialogue with the Taliban already for some time and was obviously trying to reach out to the insurgents. The international military talked about fighting the "bad guys," meaning the Taliban and other insurgents. It was a terminology that gave the simplistic impression of a fight with evil fanatics. When they had been eliminated, the conflict would also come to an end. However, it was not only a question of defeating Taliban fighters but of including and empowering a part of the population that felt alienated after the Bonn conference. That was a very different challenge—and not primarily a military one.

The UN was mandated to support a policy of reconciliation, provided the Afghan government requested such support. This was one of the questions I had raised with Karzai in my first meeting with him in March 2008. Karzai was against any initiative that was not in advance approved by him or his national security adviser, Rassoul. He had seen foreigners make mistakes in a complex Afghan environment where relations and motives were often hidden from international newcomers. In December 2007, a few months before I arrived in Afghanistan, he had declared two international representatives persona non grata and expelled them as a result of what Karzai claimed to be unauthorized contact with the Taliban. One of them, Michael Semple, had worked for the UN and now belonged to the EU Mission in Kabul. He was probably one of the best international experts on Afghanistan.

I raised the need for a reconciliation policy in a number of speeches and meetings during the first months in Kabul and in my first regular statement to the UN Security Council later in the year. At that time, any dialogue with the Taliban was a controversial theme, and my statement to the UN was met with skepticism by some of the permanent members of the council in meetings I had with them separately. However, there were also firm supporters of a peace policy already at that time. The French foreign minister, Bernard Kouchner, wanted a statement of support for reconciliation in the declaration from the donor conference in Paris already in June 2008. At that time, it would have been difficult to obtain support from other permanent members of the Security Council participating at the conference. Even among leading Afghan politicians there was limited enthusiasm for Karzai's reconciliation initiatives. In Kabul, the British ambassador, Sherard Cowper-Coles, and EU representative, Francesc Vendrell, were among the few internationals that had constantly argued that the solution would have to be political and could not be found on the battlefield. Outside Afghanistan, Professor Barnett Rubin at New York University—later one of Holbrooke's closest advisers—was the most prominent advocate of a reconciliation policy.

UNAMA officials had cultivated contacts with Taliban representatives and middlemen for a long time. They had spent years in UN field offices in the south and east of Afghanistan and at the UN headquarters in Kabul. Some of them had been in Afghanistan since 2003. The most prominent was Talatbek Masadykov, a Kyrgiz and a Muslim, who knew both languages of Afghanistan and impressed Taliban interlocutors with his detailed knowledge of villages and families in southern provinces. But staff members with good Taliban contacts had serious doubts when I asked them if the UN would be an acceptable interlocutor. UNAMA was seen as too close to the Afghan government and, even more important, to the international military forces. In public statements during those first months I tried to demonstrate our commitment to a policy of dialogue to indicate to the Taliban that the UN could be a trusted intermediary. The Taliban was reluctant to talk directly to the Afghan government. At least during an initial phase a channel would be required that could facilitate communication and gradually bring the government and the Taliban together. There had already been several attempts to create such channels through foreign governments and NGOs. During fall 2008 much attention was given to the so-called Saudi channel. A group of prominent Afghans had met with top Saudi officials in connection with the celebration of Eid, and unconfirmed rumors said that a Taliban representative had been present. I had serious doubts about the readiness of the Saudis to engage in an Afghan peace process. It would be a high-risk game with a serious chance of failure; a risk the Saudi royal family would probably not be ready to accept.

During early 2009 our UN contacts with Taliban representatives and middlemen became more frequent. At this stage the discussion focused on the need for confidence-building measures that hopefully could pave the way for a dialogue between the Afghan government and the Taliban.

I emphasized the need for such measures both in the UN Security Council and in other public appearances. In our contacts with Taliban representatives two areas seemed to be particularly important. The first was the delisting of individuals that had been placed on the so-called 1267 list, the UN Security Council resolution from 1999 that had frozen the assets of a number of terrorist suspects and banned them from traveling. There was no ban on talking to these individuals, but the fact that they were on the 1267 list made contacts difficult—from a political as well as a logistical perspective. In addition to the 1267 list, there was a separate U.S. blacklist, with rewards promised to anybody who could deliver the blacklisted individuals. Under such circumstances few insurgents with authority would risk traveling or meeting international representatives. I had met with members of the so-called 1267 committee—the committee charged with reviewing the UN sanctions list—already in 2008. At that stage the atmosphere among the permanent members of the Security Council did not allow for meaningful delisting, I thought.

Toward the end of 2009 the atmosphere had changed. The 1267 committee was about to review the list again. Removing some of the listed people would now be symbolically and politically important. During a meeting at the Afghan foreign ministry at the end of December 2009, with Spanta and Rassoul present, I suggested that the Afghan ambassador to the UN should formally ask for delisting when the Security Council met again on January 6, 2010. There was immediate agreement among the Afghans. When the Security Council met, the very competent Afghan ambassador, Zahir Tanin, formally asked for the delisting process to be accelerated. It was an important political signal to the Taliban.

Shortly afterwards, five individuals were taken off the list, including Mullah Muttawakil, the former Taliban foreign minister. Later another five names were delisted, this time including Mullah Zaeef. Both were now living in Kabul and had reconciled with the government. I was pleased to see them delisted since they were both useful interlocutors and helpful in providing understanding of Taliban thinking. Both could also be useful in transmitting messages and establishing contacts between Afghan and international representatives and the Taliban movement.

In contacts with Taliban interlocutors, the UN was also asked to give attention to insurgents detained by the United States and by Afghans. A number of them had been detained for insufficient reasons—or even no reason at all. Many lived in conditions that could only breed more opposition to the government as well as to the international military presence. I raised the question of visiting detention facilities with the Afghan intelligence chief, Amrullah Saleh. His response was quick and fully cooperative. During the following weeks I visited several prisons and detention centers, where the conditions were appalling.

I made a similar request to the U.S. military. The request was transmitted to Washington since the decision could not be made by U.S. military or civilians in Kabul. As time passed, I decided to make my request public. I wanted to signal publicly to the Taliban and our middlemen that I had been to Afghan centers and intended to visit Bagram as soon as permission was granted. A few days later I was invited to visit anytime I wanted.

Two helicopters picked us up at the Afghan defense ministry and brought us to the enormous Bagram base. The first part of the visit concentrated on the new detention facility, with spacious cells, modern equipment for health care, and visiting rooms for meeting with families. It would open shortly and signaled a new U.S. thinking: it was an effort to bring detainees back to normal life with the assistance of village elders and families. The old detention facility was very different. Originally built by the Russians, it was overcrowded and unpleasant, but nevertheless better than any of the Afghan facilities I had seen. I was warned that the prisoners could try to throw their own excrement at us. Glass walls had been erected to make it more difficult for the detainees to hit their targets. But nothing happened. I walked as slowly as I could, knowing that the visit could soon be known outside Bagram and among Taliban representatives.

At a press conference I described my visits to the Afghan detention centers. Some of the media reported about my visits, and one journalist asked me why all of a sudden I had decided to go there. I told him I had been thinking of this for some time and had decided to do it now. The media coverage was quickly picked up by our interlocutors.

Our ambitions with regard to confidence-building measures also included humanitarian access to the population. Food convoys had to reach or pass through districts and villages where the Taliban was in control. And there were still new polio cases, mostly concentrated in conflict areas or in areas controlled by the insurgents. In 2008 the results of our efforts had not been promising. Food convoys were looted in significant numbers. The following year the situation improved. Access for vaccination programs was particularly encouraging. We communicated written lists of districts where access was required to the Taliban leadership and local commanders. The program was implemented by the WHO and UNICEF and had tens of thousands of local volunteers. Of course where fighting was ongoing, access could not be obtained. But altogether only 3 percent of the children were not reached. That was an astonishing achievement.

Was it a response to the requests we had made to the Taliban at different levels of the UN system or a result of local efforts by the two organizations on the ground? It was impossible to verify. But late in the fall of 2009, I was approached and told that the Taliban was unhappy with me for never having given public credit for the assistance the movement had provided. My answer was that it was not easy to give credit publicly if you risk that the next day there will be a brutal Taliban attack somewhere with many civilian casualties. Nevertheless, I decided to express such recognition in the UN Security Council on September 29, 2009. I voiced gratitude to all who had assisted in securing access, including the Taliban movement. It was probably the first time that such gratitude had been expressed publicly to the Taliban and certainly the first time by a UN envoy in the UN Security Council.

However, I was also convinced that confidence-building measures should include steps within the security field. It was unlikely that a productive dialogue could be established on the basis of one side being humiliated and in a position of weakness. Both would need some sense of mutual respect. Well ahead of the UN Peace Day, September 21, 2008, we made requests to the ISAF commander, President Karzai, and the Taliban to abstain from offensive operations on that day. Karzai first instructed his Afghan forces to comply with our request. Then a similar message followed from the ISAF commander. And finally Mullah Omar stated that the Taliban would also abstain from offensive operations. When we later looked at the statistics for that day, it seemed that the number of security incidents reported had dropped by around 70 percent. That was more than I had expected. A total cessation of hostilities was unrealistic, since some of the insurgent forces were not under Taliban control and others had probably never heard about any Peace Day or received a message from Mullah Omar. But a 70 percent reduction seemed to reflect that there was a command structure of some kind on the other side and that it had responded.

I wanted to go one step further and identify steps that would de-escalate instead of escalate the use of force. One such step would be cease-fire arrangements that could be limited in time and space. Cease-fires are difficult to establish, even in conventional warfare. It would be much more demanding in the context of asymmetric warfare and would have to be prepared well through discussions leading to agreement on areas to be included as well as the time frame. If successful, it could be expanded in time and area. The main purpose of such measures would be a mutual demonstration of a commitment to a peaceful solution. Having mentioned my thinking to Afghan and international partners, I quickly found that it was premature. The minds were now more on new military offensives than on a de-escalation of the use of force. Mullah Zaeef told me that the Americans wanted to fight and not to talk. As long as they did not demonstrate on the ground that they were committed to a dialogue, the confrontation would continue.

When I left Kabul, prominent people on the Afghan as well as the international side continued to work on further confidence-building efforts. Perhaps most remarkable was the information that the Taliban had allowed the opening of schools in some areas under its control. These were said to include schools for girls. If correct, such steps would be a valuable sign of readiness from the Taliban to meet basic concerns of those who feared that any dialogue would lead the country backwards with regard to the rights granted by the Constitution. And it would be a dramatic departure from the Taliban's behavior on the ground.

Early in the summer of 2009, during a meeting with Taliban interlocutors, we were warned that further discussions would have to wait until the election process was over. It made sense and made me believe we were talking to serious people. At that time none of us would have thought that the election drama would drag out for so long and delay almost all other activities. Toward the end of 2009, the situation started to look promising again. There seemed to be a genuine interest in moving from sporadic contacts to a more regular dialogue. Meetings were tentatively scheduled and practical preparations made.

But there were new setbacks. First, incorrect reports of a meeting between me and senior Taliban commanders in Dubai on January 6 started to circulate and received front-page attention in the media the day after the London Conference on January 29, 2010. The source, unfortunately, seemed to be another UN official. For the first time, my name was directly linked to a specific meeting with Taliban representatives in the major international media. I had always refused to comment on any such contacts whenever there were media questions, and we had managed to avoid any speculations. Now our Taliban contacts became more cautious. Nevertheless, we continued our effort with them to find a suitable date and venue. The most devastating blow came only a few days later when the second in command of the Taliban, Mullah Abdul Ghani Baradar, was arrested in Pakistan. His arrest was soon followed by the disappearances of other Taliban representatives. Among them were people who were strongly engaged in trying to shape a dialogue. Suddenly, all contacts were interrupted. The phones and other means of communication simply went dead. When the military offensives in the south started in mid-February, we knew that it was too late to organize any further meeting—certainly for me since I only had one month left of my time in Kabul. Our Taliban middlemen were bitter. They had taken serious risks and knew that the prospects of any dialogue at this stage had diminished dramatically.

There was no doubt in my mind that the Pakistani Inter-Service Intelligence (ISI) was well informed about contact between Taliban representatives and international and Afghan interlocutors. I was convinced that the Pakistanis had taken action to prevent the continuation of such discussions. When I was interviewed by BBC's Lyse Doucet soon after my return to Norway in March 2010 and blamed the Pakistani intelligence service for having interrupted the contacts, I quickly received an expression of support and gratitude from Taliban middlemen. Certainly the Pakistani intelligence service were not the only obstacle. Al Qaeda represented a constant threat to those Taliban who were ready to talk.

The prospects of a more systematic dialogue with the Taliban were also seriously damaged by the military offensives in the south early in 2010. The theory that greater military pressure would break the back of the Taliban movement and soon force those who remained to the negotiating table was based on a serious misunderstanding of the mentality of the insurgents. Of course, the Taliban felt the impact of the U.S. troop surge, but the offensives did not deal a decisive blow to the Taliban nor did they persuade the population to support ISAF and the Afghan government. The number of civilian casualties caused by international and Afghan forces had been drastically reduced, but the destruction of properties, farmland, and livelihood by international military forces had increased. Taliban fighters may have been killed, but the anti-U.S. attitude of the population in the south and east remained.

The military offensives and the loss of Taliban fighters and midlevel commanders could also have another negative impact on the possibility of a dialogue. There was a fear that the younger generation of commanders would be more irreconcilable and less responsive to the Taliban leadership structures. The Taliban movement could become more fragmented and, as a result, more difficult to bring into the political process.

In the absence of a political consensus in Washington about a wider peace and reconciliation policy, the United States in particular had pushed for the establishment of a fund to reintegrate local Taliban leaders and fighters in their communities. Following months of preparations, an agreement to establish the fund was applauded at the London Conference in January 2010. The ambition was to mobilize $500 million. Japan and the United States committed significant amounts of money. When the "Af-Pak group" of international special representatives met in Abu Dhabi in October 2009, Richard Holbrooke characterized the fund as a "game changer." He estimated that 60 percent of the Taliban fighters had joined the insurgency for economic reasons and could be convinced to reintegrate in the Afghan society through economic incentives. We all agreed—the Afghan government and the international community—that serious financial resources would be required to end the conflict and bring the insurgents back to society. But the Afghans and the UN, as well as experienced diplomats such as Sherard Cowper-Coles, warned against relying on the potential impact of economic resources alone. Reintegration of lower-level Taliban fighters and commanders had to go hand in hand with a strategic dialogue involving Taliban leaders. Attempts to "buy back" Taliban fighters with Western money would be seen as an attempt to convince Taliban fighters to defect for money. It could harden Taliban positions instead of making them more open to reconciliation.

One year after it was established, very few Taliban had come forward to make use of the fund and little money had been dispersed. Setting up the organizational structures in Kabul and across the country proved to be a time consuming and cumbersome process. There were even rumors of Taliban fighters who had tried to be integrated, but found that nobody was ready to receive them and provide the support that had been promised.

The discussion about the reintegration fund revealed the lack of knowledge and understanding of the Taliban. Both Holbrooke and Major General Flynn, ISAF's head of intelligence, had complained about the lack of reliable intelligence. How could we explain that the Taliban had been able to come back in such strength? Were they religious fanatics, young men looking for a decent salary, or were they coerced to join the ranks of the Taliban? There were certainly elements of all these factors. But each and every Taliban representative, sympathizer, and expert I met cited two other reasons as driving forces behind the last year's recruitment: first of all, the lack of law and order in their own society, with institutions that were seen as predatory rather than serving the population; secondly, an occupation by foreign infidels—not only an occupation in military terms, but an invasion of their culture, traditions, and religion.

Afghans can be uniquely generous and hospitable to foreigners who come as their guests and respect them, but few are more merciless once foreigners cross the line of perception between guests and intruders. When international military talked about "killing the bad guys," they addressed the symptoms and not the illness. And the illness was the alienation of people in the south, Pashtuns who had grievances about a corrupt government and the sense that they had been pushed out of Afghanistan's political life. And the international military presence was perceived as reinforcing their problems. Of course, Taliban fighters carry out attacks so heinous that the expression "bad guy" is often justifiable, but the Taliban movement would never have been able to recruit on the basis of fear alone.

Gradually the number of channels—or would-be channels—between the international community and Taliban contacts of different kinds had proliferated. Some internationals paid money to their Taliban interlocutors as an "entrance fee" or for travel costs. Some talked to real Taliban middlemen and others to imposters. It almost became a competitive market and when I left Kabul there must have been as many would-be channels as I have fingers. But in all this confusion there was also a positive sign; a policy of peace and reconciliation had gradually been accepted as inevitable in almost all parts of the international community.

This change of positions included the United States and the international military. I had already left Kabul when reports surfaced during fall 2010 about talks between ISAF and the Taliban in the Afghan capital. I was surprised that the Taliban would engage in such talks in the middle of the military offensives in the south. It was reported that a very prominent Taliban leader had been in Kabul twice for meetings at the ISAF headquarters—and had even been observed at a distance by the commander himself. Well-informed Afghans and internationals claimed that he had even met President Karzai in a building in the presidential compound. The information seemed to have been leaked by high-ranking ISAF representatives eager to demonstrate that their strategy worked; if you put increased military pressure on the insurgency, they will be more inclined to talk. According to Western media, half a dozen European ambassadors could confirm that there were contacts with the Taliban at a high level. I was suspicious since so many would normally not be aware of contacts at this level. Media representatives in Kabul called me to ask if I knew what was happening. Was it serious? Based on what credible international and Afghan representatives could tell me, I replied that most likely very little—if anything—serious was happening.

My theory was that it was media spin intended for the U.S. public to give an impression that the current offensives were having the intended impact. Then an article followed in the *Washington Post* with the information that the White House was holding back the names of Taliban participants in order to protect their security. Another round of phone calls followed from Afghanistan, Pakistan, and contacts in Europe. Now the message was different. My Afghan and international friends continued to insist that nothing was happening and that they had verified their information to the best of their ability. But why was ISAF leaking all this misinformation? People who really sought to promote a dialogue were concerned that the U.S. military could not keep such contacts secret.

Suddenly, the real story reached the media: The high Taliban representative, believed to be Mullah Mansour, now number two in the Taliban, wasn't Mullah Mansour after all. He was a shopkeeper from Quetta and had been able to conduct several meetings before being stopped by an Afghan who had known Mullah Mansour in the past. The shopkeeper had collected important amounts of money and fooled significant parts of the international community. But the incident also confirmed that there was now a readiness in the international community to engage in talks with the Taliban.

New reports surfaced in early 2011 about talks between German and American representatives and senior Taliban interlocutors in Germany and in Qatar. This time the interlocutor was serious and no imposter. Tayyab Aga, the Taliban representative, was a well-known name from our own attempts to organize meetings in early 2010. He had for years been very close to Mullah Omar, the Taliban leader. Again the talks were leaked to the media. Some reports claimed that the leaks came from prominent Afghan officials concerned that Karzai had been sidelined or who were simply against any reconciliation policy.

I had for a long time argued that while there must be "red lines" with regard to the outcome of a dialogue there could not be preconditions for beginning talks. To demand that the Taliban denounces Al Qaeda as a precondition for a dialogue, as the Saudis seemed to have done, was as unrealistic as asking for agreement on a total withdrawal of international forces before such talks could start. The only meaningful precondition I could see was a guarantee for the security of those who took part. Mullah Zaeef, had repeatedly stressed that a dialogue has to start without any preconditions. By doing so he also distanced himself from the position expressed regularly by Taliban spokesmen: that all international troops would have to leave before talks could start.

President Karzai had underscored that there would have to be red lines that could not be crossed in any political settlement. First of all, any settlement with the insurgents would have to be based on the Afghan Constitution, respecting the rights of each and every Afghan citizen—man and woman—to education and to participation in public life. A peaceful settlement could not undermine or remove what millions of Afghans saw as their most important achievements since the fall of the Taliban. In the many discussions I had about a peace process, none were more concerned than the women's networks. Their fear was that the government—under the influence of conservative forces—would abandon their rights in the name of political compromise.

Any peace settlement would also have to include a decision by the Taliban and other participating groups to distance themselves from Al Qaeda and to abandon the use of force as a means to achieve their political objectives. I have never believed that this should be a serious obstacle to a peaceful solution, even if the wider Taliban movement also included elements that are still close to Al Qaeda. While Al Qaeda is a terrorist network with global ambitions, the Afghan Taliban movement was founded in Kandahar in 1994 and originated from local grievances and from the activities of warlords and criminal gangs in the chaotic early 1990s. In a document from 2002, a high-ranking German UN official, Michael von der Schulenburg, wrote, "I recall the often deep feelings of mistrust and even outright rejection among most Afghan commanders vis-a-vis foreign (especially Arab) jihadist fighters in their midst. . . . In addition, Arab and, to a certain degree, Pakistani jihadists feel superior to their Afghan brethren, an attitude that creates considerable resentment among the proud Pashto tribesmen. All this makes foreign jihadists and Afghan Taliban strange bedfellows."

A report by Alex Strick van Linschoten and Felix Kuehn published in February 2011 ("Separating the Taliban from Al Qaeda: The Core of Success in Afghanistan") argued in the same direction. They claimed that "an undifferentiated response by the United States—as expressed in the Bush doctrine—that one was 'with us or against us' promoted the perception that the Taliban and Al Qaeda were integrated into one group."

The Taliban regime certainly provided a safe haven for Osama bin Laden and his followers. And Al Qaeda certainly provided training and experience to Afghan Taliban fighters. There were personal bonds among their leaders at the time, but I have never heard any past or present Taliban comment favorably on Al Qaeda. On the contrary, Taliban representatives or middlemen constantly explained how they feared the brutality of Al Qaeda in opposing any attempt to establish a dialogue with the international community or the Afghan government. In his Eid statement of September 2010, Mullah Omar declared, "We want to frame our foreign policy on the principle that we will not harm others nor allow others to harm us." The Taliban did not have ambitions that went beyond the borders of Afghanistan itself.

From the Taliban the main demands have been the total withdrawal of international forces from Afghan territory as well as their own return to the Afghan society in safety and dignity. As recently as spring 2011, Taliban spokesmen repeated that a total withdrawal had to take place before a dialogue could even start. I believe that Taliban leaders also know that this is an unrealistic position. Paradoxically, a gradual and well-orchestrated withdrawal linked to the conclusion and consolidation of a peaceful settlement may even be in their interest.

During his inauguration speech in November 2009, Karzai announced his plan to hold a Peace Jirga the following year. When it was held in June 2010 he did not succeed in establishing the broad consensus he needed inside Afghanistan. A number of his main opponents from the former Northern Alliance abstained from the gathering. As a result of the Peace Jirga, a High Peace Council was appointed, chaired by the former Afghan president and Northern Alliance leader, Burhanuddin Rabbani. His appointment was met with disappointment by reformers and by prominent human rights advocates, especially in women's networks. Rabbani's strictly conservative attitude, including the role of women, gave them ample reason for concern. However, Karzai's move was primarily motivated by the need to create a consensus among Afghanistan's ethnic groups. Not many could help him forge such a consensus. Rabbani was—at least for now—loyal to the president, but he was also the most senior and respected among Northern Alliance leaders.

On September 21, 2011, Rabbani was killed in his own house. It was the most devastating blow Karzai had experienced to his reconciliation policy. Aside from Rabbani, there was probably no other politician who could help him forge the national consensus he so desperately needed in order to proceed. The future of a peace process now looked uncertain.

The killing of Rabbani was the last in a series of killings of prominent Afghan government officials, including Karzai's half brother Ahmed Wali Karzai. These killings raised the question of whether the Taliban was really prepared to seek a peaceful solution to the conflict. I am convinced that many of the contacts that have taken place would not have been possible without the agreement of the Taliban leadership. However, the Taliban have to find ways to demonstrate a commitment to a reconciliation process. I expressed this view long before the killing of Professor Rabbani. When an eight-year-old girl was used to carry explosives to the target and then detonated, killing her, or when a twelve-year-old boy was turned into a suicide bomber, that was certainly not confidence-building. One prominent Taliban intermediary reassured me that this was not the work of the Taliban and that the Taliban was against such action. It would have been helpful to see the Taliban distancing itself from such acts in public. That did not happen. And after Rabbani's death it became even more critical to see clear signs of commitment to a dialogue.

Even after the killing of Rabbani there is no acceptable alternative to a policy of reconciliation. The Afghans can choose between trying to negotiate a peace or seeing the country slide toward an even more damaging conflict. Forging a national consensus among Afghans will be tremendously challenging, but necessary. It cannot happen without the involvement of the United States. For years Washington's attention has primarily been focused on Karzai. To relaunch serious peace efforts, pressure would also have to be put on the leaders of the other ethnic groups and on Karzai's opponents.

Just as the neighboring states, in particular Pakistan, have contributed for years to Afghanistan's instability, their involvement will be required to bring the conflict to an end. By arresting Taliban representatives that were willing to discuss, Pakistan made a statement that cannot be ignored. Islamabad can prevent a dialogue, but can also promote one—provided Pakistan's interests are taken into account. A solution to the conflict will have to be a solution that the neighboring states can live with and that they do not see as being detrimental to their vital interests.

Afghanistan sees a need for a long-term partnership with the United States that can guarantee its stability. But credible guarantees are difficult to establish without some sort of continued U.S. military involvement. Shaping a strategic relationship to Washington that could deter interference into Afghanistan's affairs, reassuring Iran that Afghanistan would not be used by the United States as a launching pad for engagement outside Afghanistan's borders, and at the same time satisfing the Taliban's demand to see the last U.S. soldier leave the country seem to be impossible tasks. It is a dilemma that illustrates the need for a process of consultations, where the neighbors are able and willing to participate.

The lessons of the last couple of years underline the need for bringing international initiatives and channels together. In April 2011 a panel established by the Century Foundation proposed that the UN secretary-general, in consultation with the Afghan government and the permanent members of the Security Council, should appoint an international facilitator to help move a peace process forward. It would have to be a person who enjoys the confidence of all sides. But no interlocutor can replace the Afghan government. Any sustainable solution to the conflict will primarily have to be negotiated by the Afghans themselves with regional and international support.

Hopefully the killing of Rabbani will not lead to the conclusion that a peaceful solution cannot be found. The trends of the last years have demonstrated beyond any doubts that a military solution does not exist. Just as many Afghans and internationals do not believe that the Taliban wants an acceptable peaceful solution, many Taliban believe that the international community—and in particular the United States—prefers to fight rather than to talk. The challenge is to move out of that destructive mindset and continue to explore avenues for dialogue.

CHAPTER FORTY

WHO IS KARZAI?

Thousands of articles have been written over the years about Hamid Karzai. During his first years in power, the media treated him with fascination and the expectations were high. Since 2008 the coverage has changed and become more critical of him. Few internationals have spent more time than I have with Karzai in recent years. Normally we would have weekly meetings. In more hectic periods, I would meet with him every day, sometimes three times a day. Most of the time, it was a relationship of trust and open discussion. In my final months in Kabul, the relationship became more complicated. I always liked Karzai as a person: his frankness with me, his hospitality, and his sense of humor. Politically I supported him on many occasions, and when I disagreed, I nevertheless often understood his thinking. I cannot provide an in-depth analysis of the Afghan president, his strengths and his flaws. But I believe there is a need to correct the mostly critical impression of him that has come to dominate many political circles, media outlets, and commentators. Much of the criticism has been misplaced and based on unrealistic expectations of what Karzai could achieve in an extremely complex political setting. Some of it has been hypocritical and even vulgar.

It is impossible to understand him without at least a brief look at his background. Karzai was born in 1957 in the village of Karz in the Kandahar province. His father, Abdul Ahad Karzai, was a leader of the Popalzai tribe until he was killed by the Taliban in 1999, and Hamid Karzai—one of eight children—took the position of his father, even though he was not the oldest son. The family was relatively well-off economically and had a close relationship with the king. When the young Hamid started school the family moved to Kabul, where his father became deputy speaker of the National Assembly. Like many young Afghans, Hamid Karzai traveled to India for his higher education. He spent much of the time at the University of Simla in the north, the city used by the British as their summer seat during the colonial time. He finished his education in 1983. Instead of returning to Kabul—which was occupied by the Soviets—he settled in Quetta in Pakistan near the border of Afghanistan. Many of the Afghan refugees had come here after the Soviet invasion in December 1979, and the mujahideen organizations had established their headquarters and waged their jihad against the Soviet occupation force in Afghanistan from Quetta.

Karzai became a prominent member of the Afghan National Liberation Front (ANFL), one of the smaller and more moderate of the seven mujahideen groups allowed by the Pakistanis to operate from their territory. The ANLF was led by the highly respected Professor Sibghatullah Mojaddedi, who was the president of the upper house of the National Assembly during my time in Kabul. Neither Karzai nor Mojaddedi had a talent for organizing armed struggles. Karzai's functions were those of a political officer and spokesman of the ANLF. Karzai's English—one of his six languages—was excellent, he moved with great ease in international circles, and he became a well-known person among foreign diplomats, journalists, and aid organizations operating inside Afghanistan.

In 1992 Karzai returned to Kabul. The Soviets had been defeated and the Communist regime finally thrown out of power. His old mentor, Mojaddedi, had become president for a brief period of two months before handing the office over to Professor Rabbani. For a short period Karzai was deputy foreign minister and could make use of his international contacts and qualifications. However, life in the capital became unbearable as a result of the civil war, and Karzai decided to move back to Pakistan. In Peshawar he worked to mobilize against the Taliban as the movement gradually took control of the country. He traveled abroad to Washington and Europe, without receiving the support he had hoped for, and to Rome, where the king had settled.

Following the attack on the World Trade Center on September 11, 2001, Karzai returned to Afghanistan. He traveled to Uruzgan province in the south with a group of his fighters. The Taliban was abandoning control over its last strongholds in the south. Karzai tried to convince Mullah Omar to surrender to him without success. On the contrary, before he was forced to leave the country, Mullah Omar had sent fighters to kill Karzai, one of very few Pashtun leaders in the south who had dared to stand up to him. The UN had then called the conference in Bonn to agree on the establishment of an interim administration. Karzai addressed the opening of the meeting by phone from Uruzgan. When the Bonn Conference was coming to a close on December 5, Karzai received the most important phone call of his life: BBC reporter Lyse Doucet phoned him from Kabul to inform him that he had just been elected leader of the new interim administration of Afghanistan. She managed to break the news to Karzai before the chairman of the conference, Lakhdar Brahimi, could reach him. "That's nice," Karzai replied. It probably came as no surprise to him as he must have been kept informed about the deliberations in the former German capital. His comment was hardly the kind of political statement Lyse Doucet had hoped for as she prepared her broadcasts.

With a U.S. military plane Karzai was brought to the former Soviet military base at Bagram, a short helicopter ride to the northeast of the capital, and from there to the king's palace in Kabul. On June 7, 2002, a Loya Jirga—a traditional Afghan grand council— elected him interim president of Afghanistan, and two years later, in October 2004, he won the first presidential election ever held in Afghanistan.

Karzai had not been among the most prominent leaders during the jihad against the Soviets in the 1980s or in the fight against the Taliban. However, it was generally accepted that the new leader of Afghanistan would have to be a Pashtun, a representative of the largest ethnic group. And Karzai was, as I mentioned, among the few leading Pashtuns who had fought against the Taliban. The fact that he did not have a strong organization behind him was seen more as an asset than as a handicap. He was not a threat to the leaders of the Northern Alliance who had fought against the Taliban but was considered by many as a person who could bring the country and its ethnic groups together. In addition, he was liked and respected in the international community.

The new president quickly became one of the world's most well-known politicians. He was charismatic and a good speaker. He traveled to the world's leading capitals in his traditional Afghan green chappan and was proclaimed by the media as the world's most well-dressed man. Karzai was treated like a movie star wherever he visited.

By the time I first met Karzai, the Taliban had again become stronger. The struggle of everyday political life in a country in the midst of an ever-increasing conflict had started to take its toll. His relationship with the international community was no longer so harmonious, with disappointments and setbacks on both sides. And inside Afghanistan the voices of criticism had become more vigorous.

Nevertheless, Karzai was still a charismatic politician, who could captivate his audience. During the opening of a new institute for training of future managers in 2008, he created enormous enthusiasm and motivation among the 700 young students present in the hall. He interacted with the young audience in a way I cannot remember to have seen a contemporary Western politician do and gave the impression that he was speaking directly to each and every student present. Karzai can—as can so many—be a boring speaker when he reads manuscripts that have been prepared for him, but when he puts his manuscript aside and speaks to—or even with—the audience, he becomes an unusually engaging politician.

Often, in discussions with foreigners, I thought it was important to recall some of the basics about Karzai's background. He was the son of an Afghan tribal leader, and he was rightly proud of his background. From a very early age he had traveled with his father and been brought up in an environment of Afghan culture and traditions. He was familiar with the Afghan way of solving conflicts through a process of consultations and inclusiveness, sometimes a laborious process and different from the rules of the game in Western politics. This was how his father played his role in Kandahar and later in Kabul. These were the traditions his son inherited.

Hamid Karzai did not have any education from the West as did so many other Afghan politicians we worked with in Kabul. He had not spent years in Germany, the U.K., Canada, or the United States as many members of his government had done. He did not have one foot in the West and one in Afghanistan. Karzai was and remains an Afghan politician to the core. When foreign visitors met him in his traditional Afghan clothes, it was easy to believe that what they saw was an Afghan on the surface and a Western politician underneath. His excellent English and contacts with Western diplomats, journalists, and NGO representatives over many years had made him familiar with Western thinking and politics and encouraged this misreading of his personality. His daily reading of U.K. and U.S. media kept him remarkably well informed about what was written and said about him and his country. He was influenced by Western political thinking. But none of this made him less Afghan in his political instincts. When he was confronted with a difficult political challenge, his reflexes were those of an Afghan and not a Western politician.

Karzai is certainly a moderate politician. His Muslim faith is important to him, and he strictly observes the daily rituals of prayer. But in his religion he is also a moderate man. Most of the other political leaders, certainly those who also played dominant roles in the mujahideen movement, are more conservative than Karzai in their political outlook as well as their interpretations of Islam. Karzai had become president in a tribal, conservative, desperately poor, and conflict-ridden country, embarking on a process of transformation into a Western-style democracy with 80 percent of its population being illiterate. Nobody could possibly be prepared for such a role. Karzai was not an institution builder in the Western sense and lacked experience in the functioning of a democratic political system. The old power structures of tribal and religious elders as well as more recent warlords and powerbrokers still dominated Afghan politics as fragile democratic institutions started to emerge. It would take time for them to take root in the Afghan society. Karzai was expected to operate in both these very different worlds at the same time.

Karzai was totally dedicated to his work and the immense challenge he had been given. When I met him, I think he had never taken a holiday or a day of real rest if not forced to stay in his relatively modest residence by a bad cold. Fridays would have a somewhat lighter program, and he would be reluctant to receive foreign visitors on this Muslim weekly holiday, but he would almost always share lunch with visiting religious leaders or local elders and selected members of his own staff or government. There would be informal chats around the meal, with the president leading the conversation in a light and sometimes humorous way. Most often no decisions were made, but these gatherings were part of the consensus-building process. His only distraction as far as I am aware is his son. When I saw little Mirwais playing around him it was wise to stay far away from politics. Karzai's son makes him happy and proud, but also concerned about the future of the country where he wanted to see his son grow up. I know of no other interests or hobbies that could catch the president's interest. He would ask about visits that I made to various parts of the country and what I had experienced. It could trigger interesting stories about his own excursions to the same places as a young man, but these were stories about the past. During the many visits he made abroad I never saw him seek distractions or entertainment that could take his mind away from his work, even for a little while.

There is a dramatic difference between Karzai and any other leader in the region surrounding Afghanistan. Karzai is not a self-important person. He is accessible and his tone is mostly mild and friendly. He does not speak at length as some of his counterparts in neighboring countries but is curious about others. Karzai does not surround himself with protocol or formalities. His lifestyle is modest compared to any other head of state and government I have ever met. There is no luxury in his life. However, he rightly expects respect for the position he holds.

The new Afghan president was welcomed with great expectations. A new and modern democratic Constitution was adopted and the international community expected Karzai to turn a desperately poor country without democratic institutions into a functioning democracy faster than any of us had developed our own democracies. Afghans expected the new president to bring development and economic progress to a country without institutions, infrastructure, and an educated population. Karzai had seen how the United States turned its attention away from Afghanistan as soon as the Soviets were defeated. Now he saw the reluctance of the United States and other international partners to assist him with financial support to build his country and the new institutions. Soon, he was criticized for being unable to extend the influence of the government and for being the "mayor of Kabul" rather than the president of Afghanistan. But after the fall of the Taliban, he had been left as a president without the means to exercise his authority and surrounded by strong warlords who had come back as the victors, with their own militias and their pockets filled with U.S. dollars. He was criticized for not bringing social and economic progress to the countryside while donors spent their development money on projects that had little impact and no strategy. Karzai is genuinely skeptical about the international community's commitment and ability to "stay the course." His experience gives him good reasons to be skeptical.

Is Karzai then a strategic partner to the international community? Eikenberry asked the question in his cable to Secretary Clinton in fall 2009. His answer was negative; Karzai was not a strategic partner. And I may well have agreed with Eikenberry in moments of despair after tense discussions the two of us had with Karzai. He is certainly not a strategic partner in the sense many Western representatives would have hoped for. But there are obvious reasons; his perspectives and priorities as leader of one of the poorest and technologically least advanced countries in the world are not the same as those of the president of the world's superpower. Furthermore, there has been a constant debate over strategy in the international community, a debate that has sometimes revealed a frightening level of confusion. One strategy has been succeeded by another without proper consultations with the Afghans. How could one be a strategic partner when there is no strategy or the strategy is constantly changing?

During my first months in Kabul in 2008 Karzai did not come across as confrontational, even if he had outbursts of irritation. He had been described as being calm and persuasive and that is how I experienced him. When there was disagreement, he would explain his positions with firmness and conviction, but rarely with anger. Gradually I had seen him becoming more aggressive and more confrontational. Sudden and explosive outbursts became more frequent. The controversies over civilian casualties during the summer of 2008 had been a turning point. Karzai was aware of his dependence on the United States and its main allies. However, his instincts made him less prepared than most of his advisors and many other international politicians to live with what he saw as a lack of respect from his most powerful international partners.

As a result of his suspicion toward members of the international community he could sometimes develop remarkable conspiracy theories. When I first heard such theories, I was astonished. But I quickly learned that Karzai was not the only Afghan to suffer from conspiracy theories. It rather seemed to be a phenomenon that affected much of the Afghan political elite and many of my other interlocutors in Afghanistan.

There were certainly areas where Karzai could have been more vigorous. He could have articulated more clearly a strategy for Afghanistan. Angela Merkel prompted him to do so at the Bucharest summit in 2008: "President Karzai, Afghanistan is foreign to us. You must tell us what you expect us to do!" Karzai has never given a convincing answer to Merkel's question. He has not provided the sense of direction to his government that was required or communicated his vision for the country to his public. However, when Karzai is criticized for lacking a strategy and for not being visionary enough, we should ask ourselves how many strategic and visionary politicians we find in our own Western societies.

Often members of his government would complain to me about his lack of attention to economic issues and his reluctance to make difficult decisions. His support for dedicated and reform-oriented politicians who could help him has often been lukewarm. He has been ready to sacrifice some of those that he needed the most, especially if he believed that they had close contact to the United States or to the British. Karzai could also have shown greater readiness to fight the endemic corruption. Certainly there were limits as to how far he could go in challenging powerful people among his allies as well as in the opposition. But he could at the very least have set examples when even his own closest advisers misused their positions for illicit economic purposes. Unfortunately, he has failed to take his share of responsibility for addressing a phenomenon that is crippling Afghanistan's economy, demoralizing its youth, and fueling the insurgency.

Karzai does not have a broad power base of his own. He does not control the Pashtun provinces in the south and east because of the conflict with the Taliban. And he depends on warlords and power-brokers to secure the support he needs in the north of the country. Therefore, he seems more concerned about buying legitimacy and support through shifting and sometimes shaky alliances than about exercising his authority. This is a part of the Afghan traditions he has inherited. In his attempts to build broad coalitions his ability to shape a convincing strategy has diminished. By trying to co-opt so many he risks being co-opted himself by people who have no interest in reforms, but rather draw their strength from the status quo. His constant balancing act between different Afghan constituencies is made even more difficult by the fact that he is still considered as a president installed by the West—and in particular, the United States. With increasing public opposition to the foreign military presence, he has to avoid the impression of being a puppet of the West.

The pressure against him from so many sides has increased. He is under pressure from the reformers for not moving toward a more reform-oriented policy. He is under pressure from leaders of the former Northern Alliance for his efforts to launch a dialogue with the Taliban. And he is under pressure from other prominent members of the opposition who, sadly, simply want to bring him down. There is—understandably—an increasing discussion in Kabul on who will be the Afghan president after the next elections. Beginning in summer of 2013 most of the political energy will be focused on the elections the following year. The discussion of possible successors will start even sooner. However, a solution to Afghanistan's conflict will, as I have mentioned, have to be found before the end of Karzai's second term. He knows Afghanistan better than any other Afghan politician I have met. And he has a profound sense of duty toward his country. A successful exit strategy will depend on our ability to see him as a partner, to work with him and not against him.

CHAPTER FORTY-ONE

REFLECTIONS

I have repeatedly mentioned our failure to understand Afghanistan. It is a failure to understand how Afghans live and how they think. Certainly I do not claim to understand this complex country. My ability to travel and meet ordinary Afghans was severely limited. I often wished I could have stepped out of the car and walked around in markets or villages we passed on our visits, places where Afghans went about their everyday business. Fortunately we had people in UNAMA with profound understanding of the society, people who had spent many years in the country, understood its languages, and shared its religion. And the majority of our staff was Afghans. Many of them could give us a glimpse of the Afghan reality that few internationals had access to. But it was only a glimpse.

International visitors are most often confined to the most secure parts of Kabul, where they meet other international representatives and discuss with the most Western-oriented among the Afghan leaders. They visit their own troops, see their own bases, and eat their own imported food. They meet local Afghan leaders at the base or during a brief excursion in heavily armored vehicles to the local governor's office. But they do not experience villages, where donkeys are still the main means of transportation, where illiteracy is almost total, and where farmers cultivate their land the way their forefathers did centuries back. Even the Afghan politicians we relate to on a daily basis are sometimes surprised. Following a visit with the president to one of the southern provinces, a prominent minister wrote to me, "Today, I have been to the real Afghanistan!"

Often Europeans and North Americans also fail to understand how much religion and traditions mean in the Afghan society. During a celebration of the "Education for All" campaign in 2008, I met a group of young girls who were sitting in the first row, dressed in their finest costumes. I asked them about their favorite subject at school—was it mathematics, geography, history? They all gave the same answer: their favorite was history. I asked them why. Their answer surprised me: "Because then we learn about the life of the prophet."

It was about the same time that I met another young Afghan girl in her early teens. She had performed on television and had ambitions to go abroad for her education. I encouraged her to improve her English and did my best to help her. We discussed Western pop stars and movie actors, places she wanted to see, interesting articles she had discovered on the Internet and, above all, her ambition to have a Western education and become a lawyer. One day she proudly gave me a dissertation she had written in English for me—her very first, I think. I had expected her to write about her hopes for the future and her plans to be educated in the West. But there was nothing of that. Her entire story was about the prophet.

These girls all came from the center of Kabul, the capital itself, where young people are more exposed to impulses from abroad than in any other part of the country. If this was their relationship to their religion, then how would it be out there on the countryside? There is little that can cause such a sense of humiliation and disrespect as caricatures of the prophet. And there is little that can cause such indignation and anger as a rumor or—even worse, the sight—of the Koran being burnt. Nobody should accept and nothing can justify the reaction of violent extremists. But the indignation and sense of humiliation so profoundly affect the vast majority of the population, their image of themselves, their lives, and their societies.

To me these examples illustrate how different the Afghan society is from ours and how easily we can go wrong. They illustrate how cautious we should be in prescribing solutions that do not correspond to the realities of the Afghan society. If we are to succeed, we have to understand.

We have made many mistakes in the past and must be careful not to make even greater mistakes in an effort to find a quick way out of Afghanistan and declare "mission accomplished." It scares me when foreigners irresponsibly talk about decentralization or—even worse—a division of Afghanistan as a way out of the conflict. A division of Afghanistan is probably the most dangerous scenario that can be envisaged. If this idea gained momentum it would inevitably lead to civil war and have serious repercussions on stability in Pakistan. It is an idea that is dangerous to Afghanistan and dangerous to the region. But even decentralization is a process that should be left to the Afghans without being pushed by an ignorant international community. The Afghans need our assistance to come together, not to drift apart.

It is easy to despair and believe that the conflict in Afghanistan is a lost war and that Afghanistan itself is a failed state that cannot be repaired. I do not agree. Afghanistan's long-term economic prospects could be promising. In July 2011 the Afghan minister of mines, Wahidullah Shahrani, told the upper house of the Afghan National Assembly that his ministry's income could reach $1.5 billion in five years. If this income is invested in infrastructure employing thousands of Afghans, then the economy could receive a significant boost. The United States has publicly estimated the value of Afghan mineral resources at $1 trillion. Probably the value is many times higher. Hopefully, these resources will not be plundered by corrupt officials and international companies hungry for big profits. The most immediate challenge is to spend donor assistance wisely and invest in sustainable, Afghan-owned projects that can soften the impact of an almost inevitable economic recession following the international withdrawal and provide a bridge until such resources can be exploited.

Soon millions of better-educated young people will graduate from schools and universities and gradually strengthen the forces of reform. In particular in the big cities, this young and educated generation will dominate the economy as well as the institutions of Afghanistan. They will want a democratic political system that can give them influence over the development of their own society. These modern forces are supported and stimulated by the ongoing media revolution, although many of the new media cannot be called independent. Today Afghanistan has around 140 radio stations and 65 TV stations. In Kabul alone there are more than 20 TV stations, and TV is gradually replacing radio as the dominant media in the big cities with the increasing availability of electricity. Access to Internet, websites, and social media is modest but expanding fast as fiber optic cables link Afghanistan to the outside world. Soon, 20 percent of the population may have access to Internet.

The technological revolution cannot be stopped, and Afghanistan is no exception. It has already opened up space for debates about difficult political issues, such as violations of human rights and corruption, and it will increasingly bring impulses from outside, not only from Western societies but also from other, modern Muslim countries. This is the real battle for the hearts and minds of the Afghan people, and it is fought by the Afghans themselves. If we, the international community, can demonstrate patience and not rush to the exit door, I believe that Afghanistan's natural resources, human capital, and media revolution will gradually create a more modern and stable Afghanistan. But if the international community leaves prematurely, then many of those who can modernize Afghanistan will decide to leave as well.

CHAPTER FORTY-TWO

DEPARTURE

My two years as UN envoy came to an end in March 2010. The following year was full of reflections about successes and failures, in particular my own and those of the wider UN family. In some areas, we had managed to play an important role. I was proud of our constant attention to the civilian casualties. It had been initiated by my predecessor, Tom Koenigs, who was deeply dedicated to the protection of human rights. The political coordination among international representatives had improved, and the international community was, more than before, speaking with one voice. We had been the government's closest ally in formulating a real development strategy and trying to force donors to concentrate their assistance but had not managed to bring about sufficient change. We had constantly argued for a political solution to the conflict, a position that was controversial in 2008 but shared by most two years later. And we had—in spite of all the tension and conflicts—managed to get through the presidential elections without serious unrest in the streets of Kabul and other cities.

Nevertheless, I left Kabul with disappointment over not having been able to fulfill the mandate the UN had been given. In reality, we struggled with a mandate that did not reflect realities: the complicated relationship with the military and the stubbornness of the donor community. And we struggled in a regional environment we were not able to influence.

My relationship with President Karzai became more complicated during the last weeks of my term in Afghanistan. I was not surprised; the political storms we had experienced together had to affect our relationship. The day before my departure, I visited his office for the last time as UN envoy. Karzai generously gave me an Afghan decoration—named after an Afghan, who fought the British during the Anglo-Afghan wars. I expressed my gratitude to him, but added that I would have been even more grateful if we could have sorted out the remaining election problems before my departure. He looked at me and said, "It would have been easier if you and I could have solved the problems without any interference, but life is not like that." Obviously the presidential elections had made him bitter and the bitterness was not going away.

The last few days and evenings were spent with international and Afghan colleagues and my closest staff. Repeatedly I had to change my plans due to threats of suicide bombers. Visits to people I had wanted to see for the last time were canceled. Finally only the last evening remained—with my very closest staff, the Romanian close-protection team, and those who had made life in Palace 7 as good as it could possibly be. Saying good-bye to Ka ka Sher was particularly difficult. For two years he had seen and heard everything, and he understood that I was filled with respect and gratitude.

Scott Smith and Tom Lynch, one of our best election experts, had offered to accompany me to Dubai to spend one last evening together. There was silence in the plane as we took off. There was nothing more to say. Two years had come to an end.

I had been warned by many that the next months would be difficult. I was surprised to see how easily I tackled the change from the intensity of my life in Kabul to the relaxed atmosphere at home—at least for two weeks. Suddenly, all my energy was gone. For months I spent every moment rewinding difficult conversations from Kabul and reliving conflicts and confrontations with Afghans and internationals.

One Sunday morning I received the message that Ka ka Sher had been hit by a car and killed on his bicycle on his way home from work. I could see him standing there in front of me saying, as he did every day, "See you tomorrow, *Insha'Allah.*" *If it is God's will.* That day it was not God's will anymore. It was as if that message marked the end of my own direct involvement in Afghanistan. I felt a mixture of profound attraction to the country and a need to establish a distance to so much of all I had experienced.

ACKNOWLEDGMENTS

I am grateful to the UN secretary-general, Ban Ki-moon, for having given me two unforgettable years in Afghanistan. They were the most difficult years of my life, but I nevertheless am grateful for the opportunity he gave me. Ban Ki-moon was always ready to listen and gave me the support I needed. The profound sense of loyalty he always demonstrated toward me and my staff was of great value to us all.

My profound gratitude also goes to Hanne Melfald, Scott Smith, Tom Gregg, and Radha Day. I could not have found more loyal and dedicated people. They formed my closest team, together with Penelope Faschingeder, my personal assistant. In addition to being efficient, she had a sense of humor that was of great help during difficult days. Penelope was respected and liked by ambassadors, ministers, and presidential candidates who frequently called her to have her solve a problem for them. Our office assistant, Rahimi Zaman, was of great value in trying to teach us about Afghan society.

My Romanian close-protection team could not have been more professional. They were an important part of my "family." The fact that they were prepared to risk their own lives to protect me creates a special kind of respect and loyalty.

There were extraordinarily competent people in UNAMA and the UN special agencies. Talatbek Masadykov knew the country better than any other international I have met—and better than many prominent Afghans. Mark Ward became a source of inspiration for me as well as for Afghan ministers. Norah Niland was a strong and dedicated head of our human rights office. Dan McNorton became my most trusted media adviser and went through difficult times with me.

Wolfgang Weisbrod-Weber came to Kabul from DPKO at the UN Headquarters as my political deputy in October 2009 and became a pillar of stability in a period of great turbulence.

In the UN special agencies, Stefano Porretti from the World Food Program, Peter Graaf from the World Health Organization, and Catherine Mbengue from UNICEF were all profoundly dedicated to the most vulnerable of Afghans and represented the best the UN can provide.

Among my international colleagues, many deserve to be thanked. Some were particularly close: the U.S. Ambassadors Karl Eikenberry and Frank Ricciardone, the British Sherard Cowper-Coles and Mark Sedwill, the EU Envoy Francesc Vendrell, and the Russian ambassador, Zamir Kabulov. The two latter had been involved with Afghanistan for more than a decade and could—better than anybody else—maintain calm even in the most critical periods. Richard Boucher in the U.S. State Department became one of my most valuable interlocutors. He was always generous in sharing his rich experience and insight.

Members of the Afghan government as well as so many other Afghan politicians gave me all the access I needed. Sima Samar was always a source of inspiration and I have profound admiration for her.

I would probably never have been in Kabul without the inspiration and support of my colleague in the Norwegian Ministry of Foreign Affairs, Stig Traavik. We traveled together to Kabul on numerous occasions in the years before my appointment. Stig had been a diplomat and aid worker in Kabul, he had worked for the Afghan Olympic Committee, and he had given young Afghan girls judo courses. His knowledge and dedication to the Afghan people was exceptional.

My wife, Gro, has been more patient that I deserved, but also my most valuable interlocutor. As a foreign affairs journalist, she provided a good deal of input on my work in Kabul and on this book. At times, she has been more critical than I appreciated, but always frank and supportive. I am deeply grateful to her.